A SHORT HISTORY OF NIGERIA

A SHORT HISTORY OF
NIGERIA

by
MICHAEL CROWDER

FREDERICK A. PRAEGER, *Publisher*
NEW YORK

BOOKS THAT MATTER

Published in the United States of America in 1962
by Frederick A. Praeger, Inc., Publisher
64 University Place, New York 3, N.Y.

Library of Congress Catalog Card Number: 62–11595

© *Michael Crowder*
1962

Printed in Great Britain by
Latimer Trend & Co Ltd Plymouth

For
Laz Ukeje
and
Onuora Nzekwu

Contents

		page	13
PREFACE *page* 13

I. THE BIRTH OF NIGERIA 19

II. SUDANESE STATES 31

III. KINGDOMS OF THE FOREST 46

IV. THE ATLANTIC SLAVE TRADE 57

V. THE HOLY WAR OF USMAN DAN FODIO 78

VI. YORUBA CIVIL WARS 96

VII. THE SUPPRESSION OF THE SLAVE TRADE 108

VIII. EXPLORERS AND MISSIONARIES 118

IX. THE GROWTH OF LEGITIMATE TRADE 134

X. THE CONSOLIDATION OF BRITISH INTERESTS 155

XI. COMPANY AND CONSULS 169

XII. EMIRS AND MAXIMS 191

XIII. THE UNIFICATION OF NIGERIA 204

XIV. THE RISE OF NIGERIAN NATIONALISM 225

XV. THREE CONSTITUTIONS 242

XVI. INDEPENDENCE ACHIEVED 258

SELECT BIBLIOGRAPHY 274

INDEX 281

LIST OF MAPS

General Map of Nigeria *page* 16–17

1. Nigeria's major ethnic and linguistic divisions 22

Contents

2. Nigeria's states in the sixteenth century   *page* 32
3. Nigeria's slave-trading ports, sixteenth to eighteenth centuries   58
4. The Fulani Empire and Bornu, *circa* 1850   79
5. Metropolitan Oyo and Yorubaland in the nineteenth century   97
6. Niger Delta oil markets in the eighteenth century   135
7. The growth of British influence in Nigeria   170
8. Proposed administrative reorganizations of Nigeria, 1914   214
9. The various proposed political reorganizations of Nigeria, 1945–60   266
10. Nigeria's economy today   269

Illustrations

1. Nok terracotta: 'The Jemaa Head'   *facing page* 64
2. Ife bronze: head of an Oni of Ife   64
3. Benin bronze: a Portuguese soldier   64
4. Igbo bronze: detail of drinking vessel   64
5. Captain Hugh Crow: a Liverpool slaver   65
6. Survival of the Slave Trade   65
7. Reception of the Denham-Clapperton Mission   80
8. Habe Tower in Katsina   80
9. Nigerian warriors in chain mail   80
10 (*a*), (*b*). Nigerian Explorers: Clapperton and Crowther   81
11. Richard and John Lander proceeding down the Niger   81
12. James White preaching before King Akitoye of Lagos   176
13. King Jaja of Opobo   177
14. King Pepple of Bonny   177
15. King Obie of Aboh visiting the steam vessels *Alburkah* and *Quorra*   177
16. Makers of modern Nigeria   192
17. Onitsha: a large trading port on the Niger   193
18. Modern Ibadan, capital of the Western Region   193

The author and publishers are grateful to *Nigeria Magazine* for plates 2, 3, 4, 8, 9, 14, 17 and 18; to the Federal Information Services of Nigeria for the various portraits on plate 16; to Mr. Bernard Fagg for plate 1; and to Monsieur Pierre Verger for plate 6.

Preface

The Story of Nigeria is an attempt to bring together in one short volume the history of the various groups that go to make up modern Nigeria, to trace their connexions with each other and to dispel the assumption of which I was once guilty and which is still often made that before the colonial period Africans had very little history. It is essentially a political history of Nigeria, largely owing to the scarcity of source material on the social structure of Nigerian societies before the colonial period. I am also conscious that I have devoted more space to the history of certain groups than others, but once again this is because of lack of material. When the results of present research by African and European scholars are published it may be possible to draw a more detailed picture of these communities as well as the ones about which we know something already. I have also devoted comparatively little space to the history of the Southern Cameroons, since it is now no longer part of Nigeria, and has a rather special history of its own.

A history such as this must necessarily rely heavily on the original research of others, especially since investigation into all but the most recent history of Nigeria is hampered by the sparsity and dispersion of documents as well as language difficulties. For certain periods of Nigerian history there is often only one source or one authority, and I wish here to acknowledge the debt this general history owes to the original research of others, especially since it is the policy of the publishers of this series to keep footnotes to a minimum. For the history of Hausaland and Bornu I am particularly indebted to the works of Sir Richmond Palmer, Yves Urvoy and S. J. Hogben; for the history of Yorubaland to the research of Peter Morton-Williams and Dr. Peter Lloyd, as well as to Samuel Johnson's compen-

Preface

dious *History of the Yorubas*; for the history of Benin, the work of Chief Jacob Egharevba and Dr. R. E. Bradbury has been indispensable. I have drawn heavily on research of Pierre Verger into contact between Nigeria and the New World for my chapter on the Atlantic slave-trade. The whole history of nineteenth-century Yorubaland has been made much simpler to follow by Dr. S. O. Biobaku's *The Egba and their Neighbours 1830–72*. My understanding of missionary factors in Nigeria has been much increased by Dr. J. F. Ade Ajayi's thesis on this subject. Invaluable to an understanding of nineteenth-century trade on the Niger has been Dr. Kenneth Dike's admirable work, *Trade and Politics in the Niger Delta 1830–85*. For more recent history I have relied heavily on Margery Perham's biography of Lugard, on James Coleman's *Nigeria: Background to Nationalism*, and Dr. Kalu Ezera's *Constitutional Developments in Nigeria*. I owe Miss Perham a particular debt of gratitude, for she very generously allowed me to see page proofs of the second volume of her biography of Lugard several months before its publication. This enabled me to complete the last few chapters of this book much earlier than would otherwise have been possible, since her work was indispensable to any serious study of the years 1900–18. There is a full list of books that I have considered essential to an understanding of Nigerian history at the end of this book.

It is impossible to acknowledge all the help I have received in writing this history, but I should especially like to thank Mr. Robin Horton for his valuable advice on the history of the Niger Delta and his more general criticisms of the rest of the book, as well as Dr. David Bivar who has provided me with much material for my chapters on the history of Hausaland and Bornu, and has offered many valuable criticisms. Mr. Kenneth Post has made many valuable suggestions about the period 1900–60 and saved me from a number of factual errors. Individual chapters have been read by several people and I should like to thank the following for their help: Mr. Peter Morton-Williams; Dr. R. E. Bradbury; Mr. Akin Mabogunje; Dr. Peter Lloyd; Mr. Y. Ajumogobia; M. Pierre Verger; Mr. Thomas Hodgkin; Mr. George Vellacott; and Mr. Bernard Fagg. Of course none of them is in any way responsible for any of the opinions I have expressed.

14

Preface

I must also thank the staff of the following libraries in which most of my reading was carried out for their considerable help: the Africana section of the Library of University College, Ibadan, the Library of the Nigerian Museum, Lagos, the Library of the School of Oriental and African Studies, and the Library of the International African Institute.

Finally, I should like to thank Mr. Roland Brown who has read the manuscript for textual inconsistencies and stylistic infelicities; Mr. Alan Pringle of Fabers, who has had the hard task of preparing a slipshod manuscript for the printers; Dr. J. F. Ade Ajayi, of University College, Ibadan, for reading the final page proofs and eliminating hitherto undiscovered errors of fact and opinion, and Mr. Solomon Awosile who typed most of the manuscript.

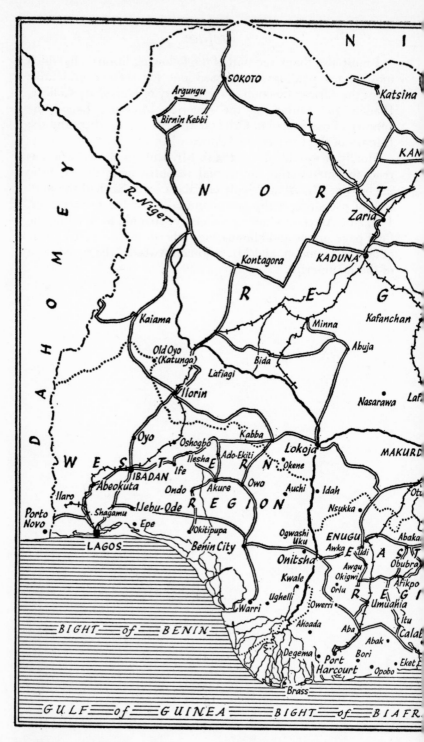

General map of Nigeria

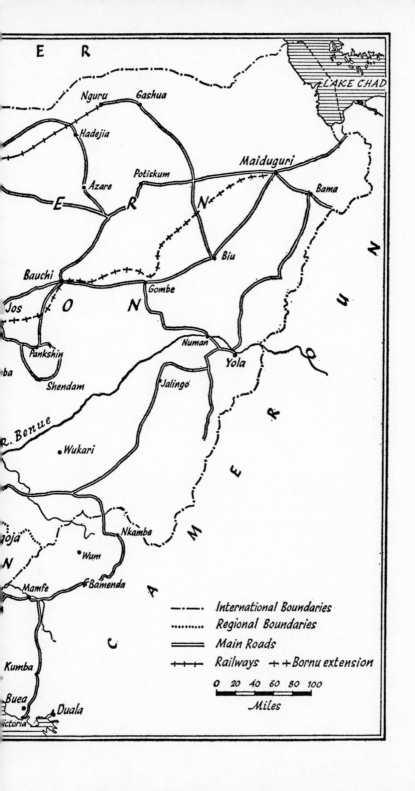

E   R

Nguru   Gashua

Hadejia

Azare   Potiskum

E   R

Bauchi

Gombe

Jos   O   N

Pankshin

Shendam

R. Benue

Wukari

Nkambe

Wum

Mamfe Bamenda

N

Kumba

Buea

Duala

Victoria

LAKE CHAD

Maiduguri

Bama

N

Biu

N

Numan

Yola

Jalingo

R

E

M

E

R

O

U

N

C   A   M   E   R

. . _ . . _   International Boundaries
. . . .   Regional Boundaries
————   Main Roads
+++++   Railways   + + Bornu extension

0   20 40 60 80 100

Miles

CHAPTER I

The Birth of Nigeria

T he independent federation of Nigeria, the most populous
country on the African continent, only came into being
in 1914 when the two protectorates of Northern and
Southern Nigeria were amalgamated by Sir Frederick Lugard.
Sixteen years earlier, Flora Shaw, who later married Lugard,
first suggested in an article for *The Times* that the several
British Protectorates on the Niger be known collectively as
Nigeria.

Although Nigeria was the creation of European ambitions
and rivalries in West Africa, it would be an error to assume that
its peoples had little history before the final boundaries were
negotiated by Britain, France and Germany at the turn of the
twentieth century. For this newly created country contained not
just a multiplicity of pagan tribes, but a number of great kingdoms that had evolved complex systems of government independent of contact with Europe. Within its frontiers were the
great kingdom of Bornu, with a known history of more than a
thousand years; the Fulani Empire which for the hundred
years before its conquest by Britain had ruled most of the
savannah of Northern Nigeria; the kingdoms of Ife and Benin,
which had produced art recognized amongst the most accom-
plished in the world; the Yoruba Empire of Oyo, which had
once been the most powerful of the states of the Guinea Coast;
the city states of the Niger Delta, which had grown in response
to European demands for slaves and later palm oil; as well as
the loosely organized Ibo peoples of the Eastern region and the
small tribes of the plateau. Between these very diverse groups
there was much more commercial and cultural contact than has
often been appreciated, and only recent research has begun to

The Birth of Nigeria

reveal how much the superficially disparate peoples of Nigeria have in common.

In a sense any country can be called an artificial creation; it is only that in the case of Nigeria union has been so sudden and has covered such widely differing groups of peoples that not only the British who created it, but the inhabitants themselves have often doubted whether it could survive as a political entity. Fortunately, on 1st October 1960, despite many difficulties, mainly focused on the differences between its various component groups, Nigeria became a sovereign federation. The pages that follow, starting with the earliest known history of its various inhabitants, tell the story of the young country of Nigeria. They may serve to illustrate some of the difficulties that impeded progress towards independence, as well as the common factors in the past of its peoples, which are so vital to its success. And if the term Nigeria may appear anachronistic in references to ancient Kanem and Ife, one must remember that the history of Mercia and Wessex are considered just as much a part of the history of the British Isles.

The federation of Nigeria covers an area of 355,174 square miles and according to the 1953 census has a population of 31,168,000 people. This is probably approaching 36 million today. The coastline stretches for 500 miles from Dahomey in the west to the Southern Cameroons in the east, and includes the Bights of Benin and Biafra. Its borders are contiguous with the Cameroon Republic in the north-east, the Southern Cameroons in the south-east, Dahomey in the west and Niger in the north. Today it is divided into four political units, the Northern, Eastern and Western regions, and the Federal Territory of Lagos. It falls more naturally into four geographical regions: a dense belt of mangrove forests and swamps stretching along the coast, often as much as sixty miles wide; the forests of the Eastern and Western regions; the northern savannah; and the great Jos and Bauchi plateaux. The northern savannah, which lies on the marches of the Sahara, stretches from Sokoto to Lake Chad, and in parts reaches as far south as Ilorin. This great plain, punctuated by occasional outcrops of granite rock, forms the basis of the wealth of Northern Nigeria, producing groundnuts and cotton. In pre-colonial days it was ideal for easy movement, especially of large armies. It is densely populated and, in parts, as heavily cultivated as Holland. In Kano province certain areas support as many as 1,300 inhabitants per square mile. From the air the land is a jigsaw of fields and irrigating rivers. The main subsistence crops of the North are guinea corn, bulrush millet, peas, beans, and, of late, cassava, introduced from the South. Specialized crops include tomatoes, onions, maize, sweet potatoes, sugar-cane, rice, wheat and tobacco. Groundnuts and cotton are the main crops grown for export. Goats are reared to provide the superb leather known to the outside world as Morocco leather, because traditionally the North exported its goods by caravan across the Sahara to the countries of the Mediterranean littoral.

The southern edge of this great plain is bounded by the Jos and Bauchi plateaux. In the days of slave raiding by cavalry of the northern states, pagan tribes sought refuge there, protected by the rocky terrain, and aided by the tsetse fly which has otherwise contributed to the poverty of the region, which apart from tin produces only subsistence crops.

South of the confluence of the great Niger and Benue rivers lies the forest belt of the Western and Eastern regions. The subsistence crops of this area are yams, coco yams, cassava, maize, plantains, palm produce and rice, as well as secondary crops of tomatoes, fruits and other vegetables. The West is the richer region of the two, producing for export cocoa, kola-nut, palm oil, rubber and timber. The East produces timber, palm oil, rubber and coal, whilst petroleum is now being exploited. Poor land, and in parts chronic overpopulation, have forced many of the inhabitants of the Eastern region to seek work in other parts of the federation.

Nigeria today is inhabited by a large number of tribal groups ranging in size from a few thousand to many million, speaking between them several hundred languages or dialects. Though at first their variety of customs, language and social organization is bewildering they can be classified into a number of linguistic groups which give a fairly good index of their wider cultural affiliations. Of course linguistic affiliation does not necessarily imply common descent, since contact between two very different groups can result in the assimilation of the linguistic system of one by the other. For example, the Fulani, who are of Caucasoid stock, speak a Niger-Congo language. By contrast, the

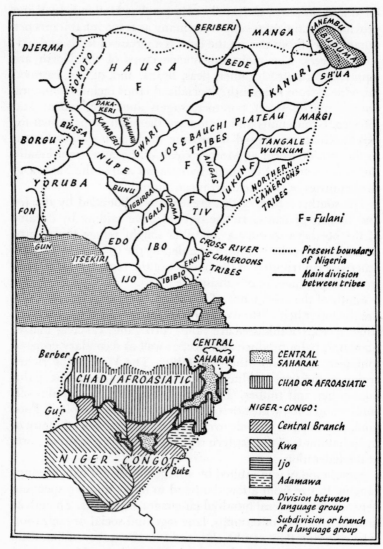

1. Nigeria's major ethnic and linguistic divisions

Hausa of Northern Nigeria are of negroid physical, stock yet speak a Hamitic language. However, the majority of Nigeria's inhabitants speak one of the large group of languages which Joseph H. Greenberg, in his *Studies in African Linguistic Classifica-*

tion, has defined as the Niger-Congo family. This family is broken down into a number of sub-families, one of the most important of which as far as Nigeria is concerned is the Kwa sub-family. The Yoruba- and Edo-speaking peoples of the Western region, the Nupe of the Northern region, and the Ibo of both Eastern and Western regions, speak languages classified as Kwa, which also includes the Twi- and Kru-speaking peoples of modern Ghana. The Ijo, a fishing population of the Niger Delta, speak a language that bears no immediate relationship to any other language in the Niger-Congo group, but which is nevertheless a member of this family. The Ijo include about twenty groups, amongst them the Kalabari, Okrika and Nembe peoples. All the other inhabitants of the Eastern region, the best known of whom are the Ibibio and Efik, speak languages generally classified in the Cross River group, which in turn falls into the huge sub-family defined by Greenberg as the Central Branch. This also includes many of the major tribes of the Middle Belt, such as the Tiv, who number nearly a million, as well as many of the small tribes like the Batu who are but two thousand strong. These tribes have in common that until the arrival of the British their political organization was rarely more complex than that of the village. The Central Branch sub-family is often described as semi-Bantu and is certainly closely related to the Eastern, or Bantu branch, which predominates in Equatorial Africa. The Cameroons foothills in Benue and Adamawa provinces are inhabited by small tribes, most of whom speak languages of the Adamawa sub-family. The light-skinned, nomadic Fulani who graze their cattle throughout the Northern region speak a language of the Niger-Congo family, though it corresponds more closely to the Western Atlantic languages spoken in Guinea and Senegal where the Fulani first made their home in West Africa. The neighbouring Hausa speak a language which is connected with the Hamitic languages spoken in North and East Africa, whilst the Kanuri, who inhabit north-eastern Nigeria, speak a language classified by Greenberg as Central Saharan, linking them with Fezzan and Darfur. With certain qualifications, which will soon become apparent, the ethnographic pattern of Nigeria has remained roughly constant for the past 800–1,000 years.

The story of Nigeria as it is known today goes back more than two thousand years. Much of the earlier history of Nigeria is contained in myths and legend, for only in the north, where the Kanuri and Hausa came into contact with the Arabs, are there any extensive written records before the nineteenth century. We can, of course, reconstruct something of the history of Africa and its contemporary political divisions from botanical evidence and the distribution of cultivated plants; from archaeological research which is still in its infancy in Nigeria; from linguistic relationships and ethnographic distribution. But for the most part we must still rely on oral tradition and on a few written records whose veracity we have few means of checking. A proper appreciation of the difficulties of interpreting oral tradition of African societies is essential to a realization of the approximation which colours most dates and most statements of fact until the beginning of the nineteenth century. In a number of societies which had no written languages, there were certain members of the community whose duty it was to remember the history of the tribe, or of the rulers of the tribe. Thus in a Yoruba court a professional oral historian was retained by the Oba, and he was usually responsible for reciting dynastic lists. In an illuminating article on the problems of recording oral history amongst the Bakuba, Dr. J. Vansina has listed the six sources of oral tradition available amongst these people. In Nigerian tribes, too, these are the commonly available sources: formulas including titles and names; poetry; lists including genealogies; tales; commentaries; and precedents in law. It can be readily appreciated that for a proper interpretation of oral traditions a thorough knowledge of the indigenous language is necessary. But there are greater difficulties in interpretation itself. Since so much of oral tradition is intimately bound up with the socio-political relationships of the tribal group, it is often in the interests of factions to distort it. The most common motive for distortion is occasioned by dynastic disputes, and if the party with the weakest claim to the throne succeeds, it is certain that it or its court historian will immediately modify history to create an air of legitimacy around the new régime. There is also the basic distortion of memory, even though the memories of non-literate people are often less fallible than those of a literate people. The dynastic list of the Yoruba kingdom of Kétu in Dahomey, where an individual was responsible for reciting the full rote, and suffered death if he made a mistake, is obviously more reliable than one where no such penalty was imposed. There is also a tendency to telescope early history. Kings drop out of the list if they achieved nothing of significance in their reigns, or else a single heroic act by one may be attributed to another with a fuller list of memorable deeds. There is thus an immense task before the historian who has to compare different versions of the same tradition, and take into account all these possible sources of distortion wilful or otherwise. It will need many years of patient work before more definite statements on early Nigerian history can be made. Fortunately there are already two major research schemes investigating the history of the Yoruba and Benin. Their findings may radically change the present picture we have of the past of these two groups. It is also very important in talking of the history of Nigeria to appreciate Dr. Vansina's warning: ' "Written sources are better than oral ones," is the maxim of a non-historian. For the practitioner sources are sources. They can be good or bad, but there is nothing intrinsically less valuable in an oral source than in a written one.'

In Northern Nigeria we are fortunate in the number of documents available to us on the history of Bornu and Hausaland. But these, too, are subject to many limitations. Some have been copied and may have been changed. For instance, in one copy of a treatise by the Moslem reformist Usman dan Fodio, his attack on the use of titles is tactfully left out by the copyist in deference to his titled master. Naturally there were often the same political motives for distorting history as there were in non-literate societies. The Kisra legend which traces the origin of the peoples of Hausaland and Bornu to the Near East is supported by local as well as Arabic documents, which may seem to lend it greater credibility. However this may well be an attempt by Moslem Arabs to rationalize the origin of the peoples they encountered in Northern Nigeria, for the North African Arabs lived in societies in which all relationships with other people were conceptualized in lineage terms. The Kisra legend might therefore be an attempt to place the negro peoples in relationship to themselves. A more recent example of this can be found amongst the Tiv, who also place great emphasis on their genealogical relationship with each other. Theoretically all Tiv can trace their ancestry back to Adam, who it is said had one son, Tiv, the ancestor of the tribe, and another from whom all foreigners including white men are descended.

Finally, we find that the early records of traditional history made by European District Officers and published in book form have come to be the 'official history' of a particular people. Thus an investigator is likely to have Meek's, Talbot's or Palmer's version of tribal history given to him as the authoritative version.

All these factors necessarily mean that for the present we must treat Nigeria's early periods of history with considerable circumspection. The broad outlines may be there, but they may yet be subject to radical changes in the light of research being carried on at the present time.

In Nigeria, as in the rest of Africa, there is evidence of social change and cultural development during the Palaeolithic period which lasted from about a million to 10,000 years B.C. It is probable that the African continent played a significant role in man's early social and physical development, especially in the neolithic revolution. One authority, G. P. Murdock, in *Africa: Its Peoples and their Culture History*, has suggested that there was a spontaneous development of agriculture in the region of the Upper Niger between 5000 B.C. and 4000 B.C. He believes that among other things these early West Africans were the first to cultivate cotton. He bases his theory on botanical evidence, but it must be stressed that at the moment there are few botanists who support his hypothesis. Whatever the origin, there is no doubt that during the years from 5000 B.C. to A.D. 1 African tribes, including many of those inhabiting modern Nigeria, started to practise settled agriculture. In the north-east of the continent Egypt developed a powerful monarchy and an impressive civilization. Trade was carried on across the Sahara desert by the Berbers who introduced domesticated animals and plants of the South-West Asian agricultural complex to the negroes of the Sahara fringe. In the millennium of 2000–1000 B.C. the influence of Egypt extended to Nubia and Ethiopia where monarchical states developed. Indeed Egypt was to influence for many centuries to come the whole of East and Central Africa, and there are reasons to believe that this influence may have extended as far as the western Sudan. For striking

The Birth of Nigeria

similarities in the role of monarchy in West African kingdoms and the monarchy of ancient Egypt have been observed, particularly with regard to the Jukun and Yoruba of Nigeria, and the Akan of modern Ghana.

Unfortunately, research has not yet gone far enough for us to determine whether these similarities are purely fortuitous, the result of long-term culture contacts right across the Sudan, or the outcome of migrations from north-east Africa to the western Sudan which certain authors believe took place during the first millennium A.D.

The thousand years before the birth of Christ witnessed some of the major changes of the African continent. The North African coast was colonized by the Phoenicians and the Greeks. At the same time the decline of Pharaonic Egypt was paralleled by the rise of the Meroïtic civilization of Nubia in the eastern Sudan. Here, many believe, may lie the solution to the problem of Egyptian influence in the western Sudan. Meroë may well have been one of the crossroads of African culture. Further down the east coast trade was carried on with Indonesia and crops of the Malaysian complex were introduced. Some, like yams, quickly spread across Central Africa to the Guinea Coast, showing the long distances over which agricultural, if not political, ideas could travel.

Against this general setting we can now take up the history of Nigeria. There appears to have been a general similarity between the Nigerian Stone Age and that of East Africa. Neolithic polished axes have been found all over Nigeria, and today these are frequently found in shrines where they have attained sacred status as thunderbolts. As a result many such axes that geologically could only have originated in Northern Nigeria have been found in Southern Nigeria, suggesting that early on there was probably contact between north and south. The wide distribution of stone-axes in Nigeria indicates that, as in East Africa, there was a wide distribution of population in Stone-Age times. Present evidence suggests that it dated back nearly a quarter of a million years. On the Jos and Bauchi plateaux there are ancient fortified villages and (possibly) Stone Age foot-bridges, still in use. At Birnin Kudu, rock paintings which appear to be about two thousand years old have been discovered.

The Birth of Nigeria

Over the past twenty years more and more evidence has been collected of what must have been an exceptionally vigorous late Stone Age culture in the plateau area of Northern Nigeria. In 1936 a small terra-cotta head of a monkey was found in a tin mine south-west of Jos, in the village of Nok. Eight years later a beautiful terra-cotta head was found at Jemaa, and was immediately linked with the monkey's head found at Nok. Subsequently the name of Nok was given to a widespread culture that seems to have flourished on the plateau from 500 B.C. to A.D. 200. It spread over an area 300 miles long by 100 miles wide, stretching diagonally from Katsina Ala in the south-east to Kagara in the north-west. These Nok terra-cottas are generally of a high technical standard, and some of them rank as considerable works of art.

There is one remarkable fragment showing half an eye of what must have been an enormous head, since the eye alone is three inches wide. Apart from their artistic and technical accomplishments, these figurines tell us much about the people who made them. They were evidently agriculturalists, and some of the more recently discovered fragments suggest that they kept cattle. They were certainly interested in the animal world around them, for elephants, monkeys and other animals form the subject of a number of their studies. They were fond of ornaments, for not only do many of the figurines wear necklaces and bracelets, but a number of tin and quartz beads have been found in the tin mines of the plateau. Other evidence suggests that they knew how to work iron, though the frequency of stone implements shows either that they were only in the early stages of this development or else iron ore was scarce. The sophistication of the sculpture of these people suggests that it was a long-established tradition. Nok does not appear to have been a cultural dead end, for recent comparisons of the Nok figurines with those of later West African art reveal striking similarities in style and technique. It is too early yet to establish any direct relationships, but Bernard Fagg, who has been responsible for the uncovering of the Nok culture, has suggested that it appears to show many of the cultural characteristics of later West African art. 'But by far the most striking similarities of style and subject matter', he has written, 'can be seen in a comparison of the Nok figurines with Yoruba art, which seems to indicate a profound influence on Yoruba art tradition.' Recent discoveries of Nok type terra-cottas at Abuja only two hundred miles from Ife, the seat of Yoruba art, add weight to this hypothesis.

For the first thousand years A.D. we have almost no knowledge of the history of Nigeria. It was this period that saw the spread of Malaysian food plants throughout the Guinea Coast, amongst them yams, rice, bananas, mangoes, coconut palms and sugar-cane. People from the Nigerian plateau, possibly as a result of population pressures from the north, moved south-eastwards through the Cameroons into Equatorial Africa where they displaced the local pygmy hunters. This theory would certainly account for the close linguistic relationship of the peoples of the plateau with those of Equatorial Africa. In connection with this a fertile, though as yet unproved hypothesis has been put forward that there are close similarities between the art of Nok and that of the Congo basin.

Though we know little that could be called specific about the period A.D. 1–1000 we can fill in a rough picture of what Nigeria might have been like in those days. The first major division between the peoples of Nigeria a thousand years ago was that dictated by geography. In the forest belt of the south the people were largely dependent on root crops, fruits and a few domestic animals for their food. Weaving was of a rudimentary kind. The only well-developed crafts were pottery and wood carving. Iron smelting tended to be restricted to particular centres, and iron was generally scarce. The social organization of the peoples of the forest belt was generally small in scale, based largely on local kinship ties, contained within small villages rarely exceeding a thousand in number. There was usually contact between neighbouring groups either through kinship, or for co-operation in times of need. 'Nowhere', as Professor Daryll Forde has written in *The Cultural Map of West Africa*, 'except where the extraneous influence of invading minorities is both traditionally asserted and intrinsically probable were politically centralized states with an administrative and territorial government established.' It seems fairly clear from an examination of the legends and myths of the various peoples of the Nigerian forest belt that the invading minorities, who were ultimately responsible for the growth of centralized states in this area, came originally from the north. This is not surprising when one considers the easier conditions offered by the open savannah of the north compared with the dense forests of the south where tsetse flies abounded. Grain grew easily in the northern savannah; there was always the possibility of irrigation; there was even enough food to provide sufficient surplus to allow for the specialization of other sections of the community in crafts like leather working, weaving, and smithing, and in the various tasks of large-scale government such as soldiering and policing. Cattle survived away from the tsetse belt; cotton flourished and stimulated the use of the loom. Conditions were altogether more favourable in the north, and the people early on developed a more complex economy than in the south. A comparison of the Hausa of the plains with the peoples of the less accommodating plateau shows how much influence environment has on development, for on the plateau people lived at bare subsistence level. Although the organization of the northern peoples, 1,500 years ago was probably on as small a scale as that of the southerners, the pattern in the north was changed by the growth of centralized states, ruled by powerful monarchs, and based on the agricultural and physical advantages of the northern savannah.

CHAPTER II

Sudanese States

The social organization of the peoples living on the southern fringes of the Sahara desert was radically altered by the arrival of groups of nomads during the seventh and eight centuries A.D. These nomads, known as the Zaghawa and thought to be of Berber origin, were probably being pushed southwards both by the shifting desert and the Arab invasion of North Africa. In A.D. 666–7 one of their leaders Okba ben Nafi actually conquered Fezzan, which lies just to the north-east of Lake Chad and was inhabited predominantly by negroes.

The Zaghawa established themselves as the ruling aristocracy throughout a large part of the western Sudan, though today they are identifiable only as a group of negroes in Wadai. At the time of the Zaghawa domination of the western Sudan the Arab historian Muhallabi described their kingdom as a great kingdom among the kingdoms of the negroes. It was bounded by Nubia to the east and from there to its western frontier was a twenty days' journey. The kingdom consisted of many tribes and was ruled by a divine king, worshipped by his people, who believed not only that he was the giver of life and death, but that he existed without food. He imposed taxes on the peasantry and was at liberty to take their goods or domestic animals for his own use. The subsistence crops of the people at that time were millet and beans.

The shadowy Zaghawa kingdom is usually thought to be the precursor of the Kanem Empire about which we have a little more information, though until the sixteenth century this is very sparse and inaccessible to those who do not read Arabic, except through the work of Sir Richmond Palmer, many of whose

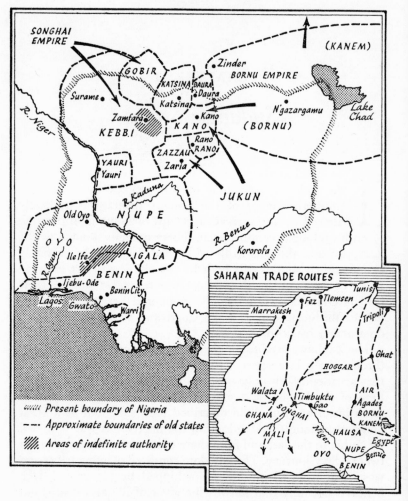

2. Nigeria's states in the sixteenth century

theories are open to doubt, and Y. Urvoy's *Histoire de l'Empire du Bornou* which represents the best summary of the history of Kanem and Bornu yet made.

Before outlining the early history of the Kanem Empire, it is important to consider in what way these desert nomads were able to take over control of the sedentary agriculturists of the western Sudan. Obviously in the lands of the Chad basin the desert nomads, used to wandering from oasis to oasis, found what was by comparison a fertile paradise where the local inhabitants, though organized only into small village groups, lived a life of considerable agricultural prosperity. At first they probably lived peacefully alongside the indigenous inhabitants, pasturing their goats and sheep. However, these nomads through the harsh force of circumstance were rigidly organized in their tribal groups, acknowledging a chief and a hierarchy of leaders, whilst the local inhabitants were loosely organized with no centralized government. Thus when some of the nomadic groups began to take control of the land they met with either no resistance at all or resistance of very little effect.

It is reasonable to suppose that in the early stages this pattern of conquest was not restricted to one or two tribes for it seems that during the seventh and eighth centuries many different nomadic groups from all parts of the Sahara moved southward or westward to the more fertile lands of the central and western Sudan. And it is possible that the later break-up of the Zaghawa kingdom into several states followed original tribal divisions. One of these nomadic groups, the Beni-Sef, under its leader Dougou, a figure with one foot in history and the other in legend, set up a small state east of Lake Chad some time in the eighth century. This state, later to become the Empire of Kanem, started from rudimentary beginnings but, whilst other states faded into obscurity, Dougou's dynasty was to last a thousand years, one of the longest known to history. At first these nomads brought about no cultural revolution, for the agricultural achievements of the indigenous inhabitants were far in advance of the rude, Spartan life they had enjoyed in the desert.

The first capital of Kanem was established at Njimi, whose location has not yet been settled satisfactorily. Palmer, in his *Sudanese Memoirs*, placed it within modern Bornu, whereas it is clear that early Kanem lay to the north-east of Bornu. Urvoy placed it at Tié, some twenty miles east of Mao in Kanem. Though ruins of some brick buildings remain there it seems far too small to have been the capital of any kingdom, and was more probably just a desert fort. Urvoy provided the ingenious theory that the nomadic rulers lived outside the settlement in tents, which is a possible answer, but based on no definite evidence. The Kanuri today say that the old capital of Njimi is in Niger not far from N'Guigmi. In fact, there is a large site with walls 800 yards by 1,600 yards, 10 miles south of N'Guigmi, but the likelihood of their story is reduced by the fact that in the reign of Mai Idris, about A.D. 1600, there were several large towns in that region. Other alternatives present themselves. On some contemporary maps there is an Njimi on the south-west end of Lake Fitri. There are three or four ruins of baked brick in fields round Mussoro in Chad. Possibly one of these marks the site of the ancient capital. Unfortunately Arab historians and geographers who refer to Njimi are not very helpful since their other reference points are unknown to us.[1]

Whatever the location of the capital, by the end of the first millennium, the kingdom of Kanem was beginning to take shape. There was considerable contact across the desert and during the eleventh and twelfth centuries we may be sure Islamic ideas filtered through to Kanem, followed by the slow introduction of Koranic Law and the Moslem administrative system. But the basic political system had been laid down by the non-Moslem rulers, known by the title of Mai. Indeed the first ruler to be converted to Islam according to tradition was Mai Humé, who is said by Urvoy to have ruled from 1085–97.

The Mai was the central authority in the state, probably having some degree of divine authority over his subjects. Control of outlying lands was in the hands of relatives. There was a court, with councillors to advise the king, buttressed by a petty aristocracy. There was probably rudimentary taxation levied on the products of the peasants. There was a class system, with slaves at the basis of society. Indeed the wealth of Kanem depended largely on the export of slaves from the south to the markets of the North African littoral. The ruling Sefawa dynasty obviously integrated with the local inhabitants from an early stage, for Mai Selma (*c.* 1193–1210) is recorded as being the first black ruler. El Edrissi, in his *History of Africa and Spain*, described his visit to the capital Njimi in the middle of the twelfth century, when he found it a miserable place. However within the next two centuries Kanem was to become one of the most important kingdoms in the Sudan.

[1] I am indebted to Dr. A. B. H. Bivar for this discussion of the location of Njimi.

Sudanese States

Under the Moslem kings succeeding Mai Humé—Dunama (*c.* 1097–1150) who made the pilgrimage to Mecca three times, Biri (*c.* 1150–76), Bikorom (*c.* 1176–93)—there was a gradual extension of the power of Kanem over the Chad basin. By the thirteenth century the influence of the new kingdom was being felt as far afield as Egypt, Tunis, Fezzan and the middle Niger, which had already seen the rise of the great negro empire of Ghana and its successor Mali. Under Mai Kashim Biri a rest-house for students and pilgrims from Bornu was built in Cairo, and at the same time religious leaders from Mali visited the court. Ibn Khaldun even records the receipt of a giraffe by the Hafside prince of Tunis, sent by 'the King of Kanem and Master of Bornu'.

As the kingly title implied, the empire was already expanding south of Lake Chad into modern Bornu, where the people of Kanem, particularly the Kanuri, were moving in search of new lands. Thus, with its influence stretching north to Fezzan, control of which was necessary to secure the Sahara trade route to the Mediterranean seaboard, and south into the largely untapped lands of the negroes, Kanem was an impressive political entity. The Mai ruled through a council of twelve, which had considerable control of his policy. This council was made up of free and slave-born members. The provinces were ruled by four provincial governors, the most important of whom were the Yerima, controlling the lands of Yeri against attacks from the Tuareg, and the Galadima who controlled the lands of the West. These governorships were always in the hands of members of the royal dynasty. That the political system was a compromise between Moslem requirements and the dictates of earlier practices is most obvious from the important role women played in the state. This was undoubtedly a legacy of the matriarchal system of the original nomadic rulers. The Magira or Queen Mother, for instance, had enormous influence and one Magira even imprisoned a Mai for not enforcing Moslem law correctly. This had parallels in many later African kingdoms, particularly those of Benin, Jukun and Ashanti. Again, the senior wife of the Mai was honoured with the title of Gumsu and apparently exercised great power. The Mai himself was treated as a divine monarch. The army which was reported by contemporary travellers to be very extensive was under the control of the Kaigama or Generalissimo. The break-up of the empire in the early fourteenth century can largely be attributed to the main defect of this system, which was the entrusting of the important post of provincial governor to members of the royal family, who constantly intrigued against the Mai.

To rule the expanding territories of Kanem-Bornu, which included Fezzan to the north and the young Hausa states to the west, necessitated the delegation of considerable powers to the provincial governors who, if minded to revolt, had remote and secure footholds from which to organize their rebellions. In the reign of Mai Dunama Dibbalemi (*c.* 1210–24), which marked the apogee of old Kanem, there were a number of revolts by members of the royal family. Though these were put down and three reigns of comparative peace followed, by the end of the century the royal house was divided in a bitter struggle for control of the empire. This weakened Kanem, and a neighbouring tribe of nomads (the Bulala) took advantage of the situation and expelled the Sefawa dynasty which was forced to move south to Bornu, into which for the past two centuries the Kanuri had been slowly infiltrating. Here with their followers they came up against the So people who are now no more heard of. Either they were annihilated or absorbed by the Kanuri; but archaeological evidence suggests they were economically well advanced, inhabiting an area south of Lake Chad extending into modern Bornu. They built numerous villages and possibly even erected stone buildings.

At the turn of the century the ruling king, probably Mai Umar, *c.* 1380–8, abandoned Kanem and withdrew to the west of Lake Chad. It took nearly a century for the Sefawa dynasty to re-establish its old power, since the new state was troubled not only by hostile tribes to the south but by continued civil war. Yet as early as 1391, Mai Abu Amr Uthman b. Idris was in correspondence with the Mamluk Sultan Barquq in a long diplomatic letter which still survives. By the middle of the fourteenth century the new state was powerful enough to exact tribute from the rising city state of Kano under its king Abdullahi Bongia (1438–52), with whom it carried on extensive trade. But it was only with the accession of Mai Ali Gazi (1473–1501), son of a preceding Mai, that an end was put to these civil wars and the occupation of Bornu completed. He built the new capital of Ngazargamu.

Sudanese States

While Kanem was being transformed into the new kingdom of Bornu, significant developments were taking place in the savannah lands west of the new homes of the Sefawa dynasty. A group of small related city states, usually known as the Hausa Bakwai (or seven Hausa states) were developing considerable commercial power. Their origin is more obscured by legend than that of Bornu. Most of the extant chronicles of the Hausa states place their foundation between A.D. 100 and 1200. It is probable that they were founded at different times, even if as the result of a related invasion. The tradition of their foundation is very coherent. A certain man, Bayajidda (Abuyazidu), son of Abdulahi, King of Bagdad, after quarrelling with his father journeyed to Bornu, and thence to Daura, where he killed the snake that had long prevented the people from drawing water from the well. The Queen of Daura then married Bayajidda, and they had a son called Bawo. When his father died, Bawo ruled in his place, and had six sons who became the kings of Daura, Kano, Zazzau (Zaria), Gobir, Katsina and Rano. These were known as the Hausa Bakwai, or Seven Hausa states, for to their number was added the state of Biram. In addition, there were the Banza Bakwai, or seven 'bastard' Hausa states, which probably represented states that came under Hausa influence, namely: Zamfara, Kebbi, Nupe, Gwari, Yauri, Yoruba and Kororofa. Several versions of this legend exist. For instance, Sultan Bello of Sokoto wrote that Bayajidda was a slave from Bornu. The versions that speak of Bayajidda coming from Mecca, or the Middle East, may well be later in origin, probably influenced by Moslem *mallams*. From the traditional histories of both Kano and Katsina it is clear that both were inhabited before the 'Bayajidda invasion'. Kano and Daura already had a large colony of ironworkers. It is probable that the 'Bayajidda invasions' took place over a fairly long period of time, and that this myth merely telescopes the events into a convenient explanation of the cultural unity of Hausaland. The origin of the invaders is also obscure. Tradition ascribes it to nomadic desert tribes, though Sultan Bello's explanation that Bayajidda was a slave from Bornu might connect it with political events in Kanem at that time. It is also not clear whether they arrived and settled in Hausaland, later taking over control of the various towns, or whether the legend of Bayajidda represents an act of simple conquest.

Fortunately chronicles of the history of the various states exist, the most notable of which is the Kano Chronicle. Both Kano and Katsina record events in their local histories dating back to 1100, although there is little of significance in their history until after 1300. Kano and Katsina seem to have assumed early pre-eminence among the seven Hausa states, which were said each to have a specific duty: Gobir on the fringes of the desert was the northern outpost of Hausaland, guarding it against the Tuaregs; Zaria to the south was the slave raider; Kano and Katsina were occupied with trade; Rano was an industrial centre; whilst Daura remained the spiritual home of the Hausa. In the fourteenth century the chronicles are much more detailed in their accounts of each reign. Islam appears to have trickled through to Hausaland at that time, undoubtedly from Mali which was at its apogee. Ahmed Baba, the Timbuktu historian (1556–1627), records that Borgu was a province of Mali at that time; and Mali probably held sway over the Hausa states. Two important kings are recorded as being converted to Islam in the fourteenth century, Mohammed Korau of Katsina, who is dated variously as acceding to the throne in 1320 and 1380, and King Yaji of Kano whose successor, King Kanajeji, is said to have reverted to paganism. In 1353, Ibn Battuta gave a brief description of Gobir, siting it roughly where it is now. A measure of the growth of these cities is the recording of wars between Katsina and Kano, and Katsina and Gobir, undoubtedly centred in the struggle to hold the position as terminus for the trans-Sahara caravan routes, a factor that was to dominate the politics of Hausaland, particularly those of Katsina and Kano, throughout the century.

During the fourteenth century, legend has it that Zaria achieved considerable influence in Hausaland under its queen, Amina, who is said to have taken lovers in every city, and executed them when she had done with them. She was also supposed to have built great fortified walls all over Hausaland like the great earthworks round Katsina. The new powers of Kororofa and Nupe, a shadowy but influential state to the south of Hausaland, as well as most of the Hausa states were said to be her tributaries.

Zaria, as the southernmost of the Hausa states, was the chief source of supply of slaves for the markets of Kano and Katsina, where they were bought up by Arab merchants. The present wide diffusion of negro peoples in the Maghreb and north-east Africa is largely the result of a trade that was fundamental to the Sudanese states and was encouraged and indeed legitimatized by the spread of Islam which stated that it was lawful to enslave the infidel. Ahmed Baba, himself a negro, has left us a long and scholarly treatise on slavery. He was a Moslem and had been unlawfully enslaved by the Moors. In his treatise he makes it clear that slavery is meet only for unbelievers, and that whatever a man's racial origin, he cannot be enslaved if he is a Moslem.

The fifteenth century saw the apogee of Kano; although tribute was paid to Bornu, trade was also opened between the two. During the reign of Yakubu (*c.* 1452–63) divines from Mali visited Kano, bringing with them books on divinity and etymology, and later under Kano's greatest king, Mohammed Rimfa, Islam reached its zenith in Kano. Mosques were built, learned men visited the court, Koranic law was established and the administration of the state improved. Though Islam gained a foothold in all the Hausa states, and though most of the rulers officially accepted it, it was constantly challenged by recrudescences of the traditional religions until the Holy War of Usman dan Fodio at the beginning of the nineteenth century.

The spread of Islam was accompanied by a rise of Arabic learning in Nigeria and the whole of the western Sudan: witness the works of Ahmed Baba; of El Maghili (Abu Abdullah Muhammed b. 'Abd al-Karim al Maghili) whose work *The Instruction on the Obligation of Princes* was read by Hausa monarchs and is still widely read in Northern Nigeria today; of the Hausa (?) historian Baba Goro b. al Haji Muhammed b. al-Hajj al-Aminu Kano; of Muhammed Ibn Masanih from Katsina and Ibn al-Sabbagh from the same city. As in Europe at that time, learning was restricted to the aristocracy, scholars (*mallams*) and the merchant classes. Yet there is no doubt that a substantial number of men and women in sixteenth-century Hausaland and Bornu were in touch with the ideas of the Islamic world.

The main prop of Kano, as of most of the Hausa states, was agriculture, though Kano itself became an important international mart and commercial centre for the trans-Saharan trade. Over the ordinary peasant farmers, some of the most diligent in the Sudan, was placed a hierarchy of village and district heads, collecting taxes for the support of the central authority of the king, which does not appear to have been absolute, but limited by the power of certain hereditary officials. It is significant that Mohammed Rimfa of Kano offered titles to eunuchs and slaves, undoubtedly to check the power of the hereditary aristocracy. Though the political system of the Hausa states approximated to that prescribed by the Koran, it still contained many pagan practices. Rimfa's successor, Abdullahi, was dominated by his mother who managed to extend her influence through to the reign of his grandson Kisoki. There were also numerous, rather bloodthirsty rituals, surrounding the enthronement of Hausa kings. In Katsina, for instance, the new king was covered with the blood of a newly slaughtered bull, in which the body of the old king, who had been ritually killed, was buried.

By the end of the fifteenth century the Hausa states were becoming known to the outside world, and increasingly influenced by the politics of the western and central Sudan. By the sixteenth and seventeenth centuries the history of Hausaland had become inextricably involved in that of the two leading powers of the Sudan, the Songhai Empire of Gao and the reconstituted empire of Bornu.

Sixteenth-century Bornu regained most of the power it had lost after the conquest of Kanem by the Bulala. In the reign of Mai Idris Katakarmabe (1507–29), the Bulala of Kanem were defeated at Garni Kujala north of Lake Chad. The strength of Mai Idris was borne out when, in an attempt to throw off the Bornu yoke, the Bulala were again defeated in the battle of Lada. Bornu now became quasi-overlord of Hausaland, which was subject also to the great power of Songhai in the western Sudan. Songhai had originally formed part of the Empire of Mali, but during the decline of the latter it had asserted its independence. Based on the river port of Gao on the Niger, it had developed into as powerful an empire as Mali under the leadership of Sonni Ali (1464–92). His successor, Askia Mohammed I, extended its boundaries as far west as the Senegal, north into the Sahara desert and east to Hausaland. In 1504, Askia Mohammed invaded Illo and Bussa in Borgu; and in 1513 his armies attacked Katsina. Leo Africanus, the famous Maghribi traveller, who later made reports on Africa for Pope Leo X, visited Kano, Katsina, Zamfara and Zaria in 1526 and recorded that all were desolate from recent Songhai invasions. Kano had sadly declined in power since the days of Mohammed Rimfa. 'The inhabitants are rich merchants and most civil people. Their king was in times past of great puissance, and he had mighty troops of horsemen at his command, but he has since been constrained to pay tribute to the kings of Zaria and Katsina.' But the Songhai did not go unresisted in Hausaland, for when in 1528 Askia Mohammed, by now blind and invalid, was overthrown by his sons, Kanta, the governor of Kebbi, led a successful revolt against Songhai which, according to Leo Africanus, 'had mightily oppressed and impoverished the people that were before rich'. Kanta defeated a punitive expedition by the Songhai army, and proceeded to subject much of Hausaland to his authority. Bornu feared the growing authority of Kebbi, probably preferring a divided Hausaland as a buffer state between itself and Songhai, and after conquering Aïr, marched on Kebbi, but was defeated. Twelve years later Bornu again tried to assert its authority over Hausaland when it came to the rescue of Aïr, its temporary fief, which was being attacked by Kanta. There followed a tremendous battle which ranged over the present borders of Northern Nigeria, ending with the defeat of the Bornu army at Nguru, their western provincial capital, and seat of the Galadima. Kanta, returning to Kebbi in triumph was killed by the people of Katsina Laka, which may have been the old state of Guangara, about which contemporary writers talk, but which has not survived today.

Despite the success of Kanta against Gao, the Songhai armies still made expeditions to Hausaland. In 1554 Askia Daud, who restored some order to the Songhai Empire, invaded Kano, and a year later sacked Bussa, taking away a female slave who became mother of the next Askia of Songhai. On the other hand, Bornu seems to have been weakened through its defeats by Kanta, for it maintained its authority over the Bulala of Kanem only with difficulty.

If they did nothing else these wars brought Hausaland into the forefront of Sudanese affairs. Katsina and Kano became recognized as important cities of the trans-Saharan trade route. Katsina had become a large town with many quarters, including those for people from Songhai, Mali and North Africa, as well as a special quarter for students. There were twelve gates to the city walls. In 1529 the distinguished Moslem divine, Muhammed ben Ahmed from the Sankoré university mosque of Timbuktu, passed his last years in Katsina as Cadi, indicating the high prestige of Islam in that city. Barbary merchants were settled in all the important towns of Hausaland.

In 1591 Songhai's influence was brought to an end when the Moroccans under Judar Pasha invaded Timbuktu, and with the advantage of firearms were able to drive Askia Nuh out of his kingdom. The Askia retreated to Borgu where in the marshes of that land he was able to keep the Moors at bay. While the power of Songhai declined, that of Bornu rose under a brilliant ruler Mai Idris Alooma, who was fortunate enough to have his own chronicler Imam Ahmed-ben-Fartua. Under Mai Idris, Bornu was completely reunified and Kanem brought to heel.

Idris Alooma had only attained the throne of Bornu with difficulty. On the death of his father the throne had gone to his cousin Mai Dunama, who ensured that his own son Dala succeeded him. Dala likewise tried to keep the kingship within his own section of the family, but died without issue. At that time Idris Alooma was in Kanem, and the throne was taken over by Dala's sister Ais Kili N'guirmamaramama, who held power for seven years before handing over the throne to Idris Alooma, showing how powerful women still were in the state.

Idris Alooma undertook the unification and pacification of Bornu in a series of extensive wars against the peoples of the south, conquering the Marghi, Gamergum and Mandara. He also established some sort of sovereignty over Wadai in the east.

Despite close relationship through his mother with the ruling family of Kanem, he was forced to undertake war against them when they refused to recognize his sovereignty over certain border villages. He defeated them in a number of great battles so that, by the end of his reign, Bornu had become as powerful as it ever had been. He died in 1617 in a battle against rebellious subjects in the south of his empire.

Idris Alooma was a devout Moslem, trying to extend Koranic law to all parts of his kingdom. He built mosques in brick, and established a hostel for pilgrims in Mecca.

The basis of Idris Alooma's power was his army, of which we

get a vivid picture from Ahmed-ben-Fartua's chronicles of his reign. It differed little from other Sudanese armies, except in its efficacy. The vanguard of the army was the cavalry of the nobility, superbly caparisoned, both horse and rider in armour, bearing decorated shields, feathered lances, a riot of colour in the fierce Sudanese sun as drummers urged them on and slaves sang their praises to a cacophony of brass trumpets. Behind them followed the infantry, the peasants, sparsely armed with bows and arrows or spears. The rear was brought up by women carrying loads, or possibly by some ferocious-looking group of naked pagan warriors, called in from the outskirts of the empire. Idris Alooma's army benefited by the presence of a band of musketeers, trained by Turkish instructors and selected from among his household slaves. The army was ill-disciplined and incoherent, relying as much on numbers as anything else. Its recompense was pillage or slaves, and it was more often deployed against defenceless villages than against formidable enemies like Kanem or Kano. Yves Urvoy, in a brilliant description of this Sudanese army in his *Histoire de l'Empire du Bornou*, sums it up thus: 'This braggart and anarchic cavalry, the despised and badly organized plebeian infantry, the surprise raids, the pillaging of hamlets, the rare and brilliant battles, the confused multiplication of individual combats, is our own feudal army of Crécy and Agincourt.'

There were few significant changes in the organization of the empire: the central administration still subsisted on tribute from outlying states, the income from slave raids, and the taxes collected by the local administration in Bornu itself. Slaves or members of humble families, who owed their all to the ruling Mai, were made governors of the provinces instead of members of the Mai's family who were given honorific titles and kept safely at home, no Mai caring for a repetition of the events that led to the break-up of the old Kanem Empire.

Mai Idris left a secure state for his successors, but after forty years, on the accession of Mai Ali (1657–94), the state began to weaken under attacks from the Tuareg in the north and Jukun in the south. The Jukun kingdom of Kororofa was based on the Benue near Ibi. The Jukun themselves claim affinity with the Kanuri, stating that they came from Yemen with them, and parted ways in Bornu. It is possible that the founders of the

Jukun kingdom were either another group of nomads, settling in Nigeria about the same time as the Beni-Sef, or else a dissident branch of the Bornu Empire. Alternatively they might represent one of the large tribes who were driven south by the Kanuri when they moved into Bornu. Not much is known about their early kingdom. The Kano Chronicle states that Yaji, King of Kano (*c.* 1349–85), attacked Kororofa for refusing to pay tribute to him; Amina, Queen of Zaria, is said to have conquered Kororofa in the fifteenth century. In the reign of Mohammed Zaki of Kano (1582–1618) they forced the people to flee to nearby Daura. A further attack on Kano was made in the reign of Mohammed Kukuna (1652–60). It is evident that by the end of the sixteenth century the Jukun were becoming a power of great influence.

Their main strength lay in their cavalry, and one suspects they made highly mobile and lightning raids on the northern cities, terrorizing the country-side but rarely occupying it effectively. They were ruled over by a divine king, who was surrounded by an elaborate and complex rota of ceremonial. Much in this ceremonial has led early anthropologists to seek connections with Egypt. It is possible that the Aku, as the king was known, held authority over local tribes largely through his divinity and magical powers; for though the Jukun had such staggering success in their expeditions to the north, they do not seem ever to have been many in number. Today they are not even classified individually as a Nigerian tribe.

The Jukun first started to be a serious factor in Northern Nigerian politics in the reign of Mai Idris Alooma of Bornu. Zaria was made tributary to them at the end of the sixteenth century, and throughout the seventeenth century raids were made on the walled cities of the north. In 1653 they invaded Kano, and in 1671 they attacked both Kano and Katsina. They even besieged Mai Umarmi of Bornu in 1680. Later, however, in a great battle the Bornuese king drove off the Jukun, and a peace treaty was signed between the two powers, whereby a permanent Jukun representative was sent to Ngazargamu, whilst Bornu sent a Zanna to Kororofa. This title is significant; it was usually given to a representative sent to a tributary state and may indicate the beginning of Jukun decline.

In Hausaland the city of Kano, worn out by a century of

wars with Katsina and Kororofa, declined in importance. It was Katsina that profited from the break-up of the Songhai Empire, quickly establishing itself as the leading city of the western Sudan, both in commerce and culture, even though it still paid tribute to Bornu.

At the end of the seventeenth century Northern Nigeria was still dominated by Bornu, Katsina had replaced Kano as the leading city of Hausaland, and all were subjected to the occasional incursions of the Jukun. The next century was to see the rise of two other Hausa states, Zamfara and Gobir, and the conflict between them was to have monumental consequences for the future of Northern Nigeria.

CHAPTER III

Kingdoms of the Forest

Legends in Yorubaland frequently talk of migrations from the north or north-east, and it is possible that the growth of the highly centralized kingdoms of Oyo and Benin in the forests of the south was associated with those of the north. The establishment of Oyo and Benin was certainly not the result of mass migrations from the north, since the Yoruba and Edo (Benin) languages bear no relation to Hausa or Kanuri. It could only have been the result of incursions by small groups who imposed their ways on the indigenous population but were linguistically if not culturally assimilated by them. It appears that some time during the first millennium strangers from the north-east either invaded or settled at Ile Ife, establishing a small kingdom there. The Yoruba creation myth that probably parallels this event talks of Ile Ife as the origin of life. In the beginning the earth was covered with water. Olorun, the supreme god, let his son Oduduwa down a chain carrying a handful of earth, a cockerel and a palm nut. Oduduwa scattered the earth over the water and the cockerel scratched it so that it became the land on which the palm tree grew. Its sixteen branches represented the sixteen crowned heads of Yorubaland, probably the heads of the main settlements established by the new-comers. Unfortunately we know very little about ancient Ife, which is revered today as the original home of the Yoruba.

A second version of the myth of origin recorded by Samuel Johnson in his *History of the Yorubas*, tells that Oduduwa was an easternp rince driven out of his kingdom. After long wanderings he conquered the local inhabitants of Ife where he settled. He had seven children who were the ancestors of the seven crowned rulers of Yorubaland, namely the Olowu of Owu, the Onisabe of Sabe, the Olupopo of Popo, the Oba of Benin, the chief of Ila,

46

the Alaketu of Ketu and the Alafin of Oyo. In this story the kingdom of Benin is included and both Benin and Yoruba traditions agree on the circumstances. Oduduwa sent his son or grandson Oranmiyan to rule over Benin, a task which the latter found impossible, deciding that only a prince of Benin blood could rule that kingdom. He therefore fathered a child by a Benin woman and left him as ruler. He then founded a new kingdom at Oyo, which he made his capital. Adimu, who was either a slave or the original ruler of Ife, was left there to guard its national treasures.

This myth and its variants seem to describe a second invasion of Yorubaland, and suggest that at the time Ife and probably Benin were well-established states. The date of this invasion is usually placed at the beginning of the present millennium.

There are at present no means by which the history of this very early period can be checked, but as Chief Jacob Egharevba shows in his *Short History of Benin*, there are many traditions and sayings associated with the first period of the Benin 'empire'. The rule of the Ogiso or early kings was apparently so unsatisfactory that the Bini tried to set up an alternative, non-hereditary 'republican' type of government, but the first of their leaders, Evian, immediately nominated his own son Ogiamwe as his successor. It was at this stage that the Bini sent to Ile Ife for a prince to rule over them. The coincidence of the decline of the first Benin state and the arrival of Oduduwa is significant, as indeed is the request of the Bini to a foreign people to come and rule over them. This could either be a convenient legend to disguise what in fact was a conquest by Oduduwa's party or alternatively it may represent a not uncommon occurrence in Africa. There are several examples of centralized states ruled over by a chief invested with supernatural powers and surrounded by a large number of small, headless, communities, constantly feuding and in daily terror of death and disorder, beset by droughts and other misfortunes. For these people the sacred kingship of their neighbours often seemed the source of good order, regular rainfall and other benefits. So they grouped together and demanded a prince of the royal blood to rule over them or sent a leader to be initiated into the mysteries of sacred kingship.

Kingdoms of the Forest

Though very little is known for certain about the early history of Oyo and Benin, there have fortunately survived from the ancient kingdom of Ife some remarkable and very beautiful bronzes and terra-cottas, some of which rank among the masterpieces of world sculpture. They give evidence of great technical accomplishments and the elaborate regalia of the Oni or Kings of Ife, whom many of the bronzes portray, indicate a complex society. Their naturalism still remains a puzzle for historians of West African art, most of which has been more formalized, more abstract and more symbolic than Ife art.

The bronzes were probably cast some time between the twelfth and thirteenth centuries, though it is not clear whether they preceded or followed the founding of Oyo. Mr. Peter Morton-Williams in a paper read to the Historical Society of Nigeria suggests that Oyo was founded at the earliest in 1388 and at the latest in 1438. References in legends to Adimu who was left to guard the national treasures suggest that sacred cult objects already existed, and these were very probably the bronzes and terra-cottas dug up at Ife. The fact that Benin history records the introduction of bronze casting in the reign of Oguola, who probably reigned in the early fifteenth century, would tally roughly with Professor A. W. Lawrence's opinion that if Benin style is derivative of Ife naturalism then the latter must have flourished some three centuries earlier. The conquest of Ife by Oduduwa's party might explain the apparent discontinuance of the Ife naturalistic style. The odds then seem to be in favour of Ife art's preceding the second invasion.

Even though the supposed invasions of Ife and Benin were associated, they would obviously have been invasions of a small group of people, for the languages of Benin and Yorubaland though related are very different. The languages of the indigenous people obviously survived that of the invaders.

Oranmiyan must have chosen Oyo as his capital because it was in the savannah belt and suitable for the horse on which his strength probably depended. It was also strategically placed to defend the new kingdom against the neighbouring powers of Borgu and Nupe, and probably was one of the terminations of the caravan trail from the north. This invasion, then, led to the establishment of two twin kingdoms, Oyo and Benin, which up until the establishment of the British Protectorate at the end

of the nineteenth century were to remain two of the most powerful kingdoms on the west coast.

Unfortunately little is known about the early history of Oyo,
for there was no written language, and unlike Benin which was
first visited by Europeans at the end of the fifteenth century, it
appears in European descriptions of the coast only as the vague
but powerful kingdom of 'Katunga' in the interior. For our
information we have to rely on tradition and the compendious
History of the Yorubas by the Rev. Samuel Johnson. Not until the
end of the seventeenth century are there any definite dates for
the history of Oyo.

At its height the new empire of Oyo covered a huge area,
bounded to the north by the Niger, to the east by Benin, to the
west by the frontier of modern Togo and to the south by the
mangrove swamps and lagoons that form a barrier between the
sea and the interior. The empire founded by Oranmiyan was
based on Oyo, commonly referred to as Old Oyo as a result of
its abandonment and transfer to a new site, which lies about
sixty-five miles to the south of Ilorin, in 1837. The King of Oyo,
known as the Alafin, became the supreme ruler of much of
what is now called Yorubaland.[1] Under him ruled a number of
provincial kings, the most powerful of whom was the Onikoyi
of Ikoyi. The system was a feudal one, with a supreme monarch,
ruling over other monarchs whose powers and independence
varied according to the calibre of the Alafin and their own
proximity to his capital. The Oyo kingdom was divided into a
number of provinces, comprising Yoruba proper, and possibly
even including the important town of Ife, the traditional birth-
place of the tribe. To the south-west lay the Egbado, closely
controlled by Oyo, and the semi-independent Egba; to the east
were the Ekiti and to the south the Ijebu, who were practically
independent, and may have been subject to Benin at various
times. In this feudal system only Oyo proper can be said to have
been completely under the rule of the Alafin. The remoter provinces were almost completely independent and, despite its
early connections with Ife, Benin soon achieved its independence.

It is not clear at what stage the political organization of Oyo

[1] Before the nineteenth century there was no one common term for the
Yoruba-speaking peoples.

D　　　49

Kingdoms of the Forest

developed into that described by Johnson, but from early times both Oyo and Benin developed a complex political structure of title grades and palace societies through which government was exercised. This differed considerably from the system generally obtaining in other Yoruba kingdoms.

The Alafin of Oyo was elected from among the members of the royal family by the *Oyo Mesi*, who were the seven principal councillors of state, though the number and composition of their group has varied over the centuries. His eldest son was appointed Aremo, and was not allowed to succeed him, being indeed forced to commit suicide on the death of his father, an arrangement which safeguarded the Alafin against plots by an over-ambitious crown prince.

Though the Alafin was considered as *Ekeji Orisa*, Companion of the Gods, he was also understood by the people to be in fact a man, and while he had absolute power in his lifetime, if he made excessive use of it, the people could through their chiefs resort to the ultimate check on the tyranny of an Alafin by forcing him to commit suicide. It was understood that if an Alafin was presented with an empty calabash or parrots' eggs, the people had rejected him. He then had to commit suicide.

The Alafin ruled Yorubaland[1] with the aid of a complex administration. He was also surrounded by a number of important palace officials including titled officers, eunuchs and Ilari, but their functions were largely restricted to the palace. Controlling the policy of state, were the Oyo Mesi, amongst whom the most important was the Basorun who functioned as 'Prime Minister' of the state. He it was who could inform the King of the people's decision that he should die. Beneath the Oyo Mesi came the non-hereditary class of Eso, or those with military titles. Their leader was the Kakanfo, who was the army commander. There was only one Kakanfo at any one time, and if he were to suffer defeat as leader of the Oyo army, then he had to commit suicide, which is certainly one explanation for the success of the Yoruba army.

Ife retained its spiritual importance in Yorubaland, but its power as a state obviously declined for two other great towns, Ilesha and Owu, which was destroyed in the civil wars of the

[1]See map of Yorubaland on page 97.

nineteenth century, were established within thirty miles of the city walls and owed no allegiance to the Oni.

The provincial kingdoms and towns differed somewhat in their organization from that of Oyo. Each town was an entity in itself, ruled over by an Oba who was supplied by one of the sections of the ruling lineages. In smaller towns, all the non-ruling lineages supplied chiefs, who together with heads of various cults and societies formed a council which exercised considerable control over the acts of the Oba. Since most lineages as well as associations, whether political or religious, were represented on the council the people of the town had a fair voice in their government.

The history of the Yoruba before the eighteenth century is extremely vague, the only available source for it at present being Johnson's *History of the Yorubas* written at the end of the nineteenth century. It is said that there is a Hausa history of the Yoruba extant in Katsina, but as yet this is not available. It would provide interesting material for checking the validity of Johnson's statements about the period before the eighteenth century, since it was written at that time. What follows is necessarily a paraphrase of Johnson's record of the Alafins of Oyo.

The first period of the Oyo Empire deals with what must be termed the legendary kings. Its history is further obscrued by the fact that several of the early Alafins were deified, and new, more dramatic legends woven around them.

Oranmiyan, founder of Oyo, son or grandson of Oduduwa, and direct ancestor of the present Alafin who is forty-third in line of succession, was succeeded by his son, Ajaka, who was so mild a ruler that the provincial kings encroached on his lands, and the people dethroned him. His successor Sango is one of the most glamorous figures in Yoruba tradition. He brought ruin on himself and his family by playing with magic. At the time of Sango's reign the supremacy of Oyo was by no means recognized by the other Yoruba kings, particularly the Olowu of Owu, and it was Sango who apparently subjugated this important monarch. Sango's downfall came through his fascination with magic. One day, so the story goes, he used a preparation to summon lightning, and thereby destroyed his own house and most of his wives and children. Either because of discontent among the people about his dangerous interferences with the forces of magic, or because of his desolation at the loss of his family, he hanged himself. He was then deified as the God of Thunder and Lightning, and today is recognized as one of the most important gods with followers all over Yorubaland.

Ajaka came out of retirement to rule once more. He is said to have waged war against the Nupe, as well as against many of his provincial kings. It is interesting that Yoruba tradition tells of contact between these early kings and both Nupe and Hausa. Indeed there is strong reason to suppose that from an early stage Hausa and Yoruba traded with each other. Johnson himself writes that 'Light and civilization with the Yorubas came from the North; the centres of life and activity of large populations and industry were in the interior'.

Johnson writes that the Alafins who succeeded Ajaka can be described as 'historical' Alafins. However, we are still very much in the realm of legend. An important successor of Ajaka was Kori who was responsible for the founding of the large town of Ede. The Ijesha were interfering with his subjects, on the borders of their own territory, so Timi, a famous hunter, was sent almost as a marcher lord to defend the Alafin's interests, which suggests that the outlying Yoruba provinces were far from being subject to the Alafin at that time. Timi established himself successfully at Ede, but refused to send Kori his rightful dues on the caravans trading with Benin. He therefore sent the Gbonka, one of his nobles of great influence, to deal with Timi, in the secret hope that Timi would kill him. However, it was the Gbonka who killed Timi and on his triumphal return he forced Alafin Kori to commit suicide.

The first king whose reign can be placed with any degree of probability in relation to other known events in the history of Nigeria is Onigbogi. It was during his reign that Nupe invaded Yorubaland and actually destroyed Old Oyo. Dr. S. F. Nadel in his study of the Nupe people, *A Black Byzantium*, says that the reign of Tsoede, who conquered and refounded Nupe, can be placed about 1531, though this date has no definite accuracy, especially since he is said to have reigned for 128 years. Mr. Morton-Williams has suggested *c.* 1516 on the long scale and *c.* 1549 on the short scale for the destruction of Old Oyo by Nupe, which is usually credited to Tsoede. So with some certainty the reign of Onigbogi can be placed in the first half of the sixteenth century. Even before Tsoede's reign Nupe appears to have been a powerful state. Tsoede was supposed to have been a son of the Ata of Igala whose capital was on the River Niger. Bronze casting is said to have been introduced by him from Idah, where the art had been learnt from Benin. However, the famous Tada (Nupe) bronzes which Tsoede is said to have brought with him from Idah, are stylistically closer to those of Ife, and the seated figure is probably the finest work of art to have been found in Nigeria.

It was left to Onigbogi's successor, Ofonran, to drive the Nupe away from his base in Borgu and eventually lead his people back to Oyo. His son Egugoujo continued the return from exile, for Ofonran died *en route*. It seems fairly evident that Oyo was destroyed by the Nupe for Egugoujo founded a new town called Oyo Igboho, where he buried his father. Four kings reigned at the new capital. Evidently life was not very secure there, for these kings were all engaged in continuous wars with the Nupe and Bussa people. However, Ajiboyede, Egugoujo's successor, not only drove back the Nupe but captured their king. During his reign there was celebrated the first recorded 'Bere' or festival to mark a long and successful reign after which peace should be maintained for a period of three years in Yorubaland. Unfortunately the king's favourite son died shortly after the end of this festival. Stricken with grief the king received the sympathies of his courtiers and nobles only to find them with hands fresh from eating. He accused them of feigning their condolences, since he, the king, had not eaten for days, and ordered their execution. The people were extremely annoyed by this tyrannical act and only the intervention of a Moslem priest from Nupe saved him from insurrection. The impact of the remonstrances of the Moslem priest were apparently so effective that the king apologized to the people publicly for his wickedness. The recorded presence of a Moslem priest from Nupe is significant, for Islam had first penetrated Hausaland on a large scale in the fifteenth century and was probably spreading southward by the end of the sixteenth century.

Abipa succeeded his father and moved the capital to Oyo against opposition from those who had by now established themselves firmly on the farms of the new land. But Abipa was adamant, and the capital was transferred to its original site, where it remained until its abandonment in 1837.

Little of interest is recorded about the Alafins who ruled at Oyo until the reign of Ojigi, twelfth Alafin to rule there after the return from exile. It was probably he who made war on Dahomey and attacked Porto Novo in 1698. With him we enter a phase of Oyo history about which it is possible to write with more certainty (see Chapter VI).

Like Oyo, the new Benin kingdom developed its own complex administration of title-holders and palace officials. There was undoubtedly contact between Oyo and Benin, if not through their marcher towns, certainly through Ife, which they both treated as their spiritual home. Caravans probably moved from Benin up to Oyo and the north.

The first king of the Ife dynasty in Benin was Oranmiyan's son, Eweka I, whose reign probably commenced in about 1300. At that time Benin was administered by a group of chiefs or Enogie, with direct responsibility to the Oba. This was obviously part of the indigenous system of administration, for the father of Eweka's mother was a powerful Onogie. Eweka consolidated his hold on the land by appointing his children Enogie in the various villages of the Benin kingdom. He also set up a state council of six hereditary members who became, in effect, kingmakers. At first, the principle of succession by primogeniture was not established in Benin as it is today, and Eweka I was succeeded by one of his elder sons, who was in turn succeeded by his brother. It was his son Ewedo who decided to transfer the capital from Usama to its present site, so as to be rid of the councillors of state, whose powers were becoming almost as great as his own. When he reached the city of Benin he was attacked and prevented from entering it by Ogiamwe, a successor of the administrator of Benin who had reluctantly allowed Oranmiyan to rule over Benin. A battle ensued in which the new Oba overcame Ogiamwe. This victory is celebrated in a Benin coronation ritual, where the Oba and the representatives of Ogiamwe do mock battle. This evidence could bear out the theory that the tradition which portrays the people of Benin inviting the Oni of Ife to send over a ruler was mere convenience to disguise conquest as more dramatically represented by the Oba's defeat of Ogiamwe, possibly a later leader of resistance to the new dynasty. Installed in his new palace, the Oba gradually but effectively reduced the power of the kingmakers. It is said that he changed the name of the country from Ile-Ibinnu to Ubini (Benin). Ewedo was succeeded by his second son Oguola. To him is attributed the introduction of the practice of making brass castings for the preservation of the record of events. Little is known of the reigns of his two eldest sons Edoni and Udagbedo. Ohen, his third son, succeeded him. It is said that he was paralysed, and to conceal this from his councillors, he was carried into the council chamber before meetings, and always left last. However, the Iyase, through whom he made all communications to his councillors and subjects, discovered this, and since a crippled Oba could not reign the Iyase was murdered lest he divulge the secret. This angered the people, who rebelled and eventually stoned the Oba to death.

Benin reached its apogee in the fifteenth and sixteenth centuries. In A.D. *c.* 1440 Uwaifiokun usurped the throne from Ogun, the rightful heir. Ogun murdered him shortly after, and took the title of Ewuare. He extended the empire to the west banks of the Niger and became known as Ewuare the Great. He also enlarged the city of Benin. His rule was unpopular and many citizens are said to have migrated to other lands beyond his jurisdiction. This is possibly the origin of some of the traditions of neighbouring tribes like the Urhobo, Western Ijaw, Western Ibo and Onitsha Ibo. An examination of the form of monarchy of these states suggests close relationship with Benin which could have come about through migration, culture contact or through the installation of a ruling class from Benin. Ewuare it was who changed Benin's name to Edo in memory of a faithful slave who had saved him from being murdered when Uwaifiokun usurped the throne. Under Ewuare, carving in both ivory and wood was greatly encouraged. Indeed his reign, the last before the arrival of the Europeans, is remembered in Benin as one of the greatest in its long history. The kingdom was highly organized, backed by a large and efficient army, which gave it control of a large area of the coast. Its influence extended as far as Idah and Lagos, which was a Benin colony. Its economy was such as to allow not only for sacred carvings such as one finds in the small headless societies of Nigeria, but for a great deal of secular art, such as superbly carved ornaments, bells, lamp-holders, doors and pillars, many of which are now scattered throughout the museums of the world. It seems then that Benin city, with its defensive walls, its large army, its hierarchy of chiefs, its elaborate court ceremonial, must have been based on something more than subsistence agriculture. It probably carried on considerable trade with its immediate neighbours, as well as Oyo and the northern states. Possibly it supplied slaves for the Hausa markets, though we have no definite evidence of this. What is remarkable about Benin, and indeed Oyo, is that both of them were purely African states, whose growth was stimulated neither by contact with Islam nor Europe.

CHAPTER IV

The Atlantic Slave Trade

Ewuare the Great may have been the first Oba of Benin to meet a European. According to Antonio Galvão, Ruy de Sequiera reached Benin in 1472 during his reign. However, it is more likely that the first European to visit Benin was João Affonso d'Aveiro who reached Benin in 1486. Whichever was the first, the encounter marked a turning-point in Nigerian history. Until the arrival of the Europeans the coast had been of little significance in the politics of West Africa. Benin and Oyo both looked to the interior for their trade. The creeks of the Atlantic littoral had been inhabited only by a few small fishing communities. Contact with the outside world was across the great Sahara desert. Benin and Oyo were probably the ultimate destinations of the trans-Sahara caravans. The arrival of the Portuguese in Benin marked the first stage in the complete reorientation of the economy of Nigeria, culminating in the establishment of the British Protectorate over Northern Nigeria in 1900–6 when trans-Saharan trade gave way to the speedier export of goods by road and rail through the ports of the Atlantic coast.

Until the fifteenth century Africa, south of the Sahara, had remained unknown to Europe largely because of contemporary theories as to the nature of the world. Believing that the world was flat, ships never dared to venture beyond Cape Bojador for fear of falling over the edge. Nevertheless, in classical times there are references to voyages beyond Cape Bojador, Herodotus recorded that Phoenician mariners successfully circumnavigated the continent, returning through the Pillars of Hercules c. 612 B.C. He also mentions Carthaginian trade in gold with West Africa. There are references made to a visit of Hanno the Carthaginian to West Africa in c. 500 B.C.

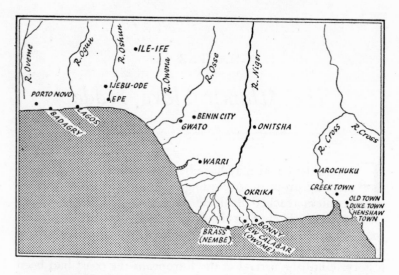

3. Nigeria's slave-trading ports, sixteenth to eighteenth centuries

These voyages are all of historical interest but had little bearing on Portuguese decisions to venture beyond Cape Bojador. It was known even before the fifteenth century that somewhere in the hinterland of the Maghreb gold was obtained by the Arabs from negro peoples. This gold was then sold on the European markets. Not unnaturally Europeans wanted to gain direct access to the source of supply so that they could avoid using the Arabs as middlemen. Furthermore, nations like Portugal and Spain were interested in finding a sea route to India, which would likewise save them from trading for Indian goods through Arab intermediaries. These two economic motives as well as the laudable desire to further geographical understanding led Prince Henry of Portugal, known better as Henry the Navigator, to equip expeditions to sail beyond Cape Bojador and attempt to discover a new route to India. By 1462, as a result of his enthusiasm and imagination as well as the incredible bravery of his sailors, most of the coast from Senegal to Sierra Leone had been opened up to trade with Europe. After his death in 1462 Portuguese enthusiasm for exploration lost something of its initial ardour. In 1469, however, Fernão Gomes, a rich Lisbon trader, was granted the exclusive rights of coastal exploration for six years provided he explored 100 leagues (about 400 miles) along the coast each year. By 1471 the gold trade had been opened up at Mina and trade expeditions were sent out each winter. It was during the winter of 1472–3 that Fernão do Po and Pero de Cintra first explored the Bights of Biafra and Benin.

The Portuguese were not the sole explorers of the Coast, since their neighbours the Castilians were always on their heels. And they were obviously much more worried by this rivalry than subsequent history shows, since they secured Papal Bulls about their rights on the Coast in 1451, 1455 and 1456. Castile only ceased to rival them on the west coast after Columbus had discovered the New World. By 1480 the Portuguese had completed their exploration of the west coast and were able to settle down to its fruits, mainly in gold from Mina and peppers from Benin. Between 1475 and 1479 trade was brought almost to a standstill by the war between Portugal and Castile. England also appears to have profited from this, for in 1481 an embassy was sent by John II of Portugal to Edward IV of England, to request that he restrain his subjects from trading in West Africa, over which Portugal had a monopoly by virtue of its Papal Bull.

In 1483 John II declared himself Lord of Guinea, but in reality his hold over the lands to which he so proudly claimed title was non-existent. The Portuguese were only established at strategic points on the Coast by virtue of treaties with local kings. Apart from hostility on the part of these kings to any penetration inland, there were all the difficulties of climate and disease that were to make later attempts at penetration of the interior so hazardous. Furthermore the Portuguese, hotly rivalled by other European powers, found it easier to concentrate on the erection of stout forts, at which goods could be received and defended against marauders, rather than acquire extensive territory which they were in no position to defend.

Portuguese trade with Benin was largely effected from the small island of São Thomé, where a Portuguese settlement was established. Indeed as early as 1485 John II gave authority to the people of São Thomé to trade with Benin, where peppers were a much-prized commodity. São Thomé, where early attempts at settlement were far from successful, found that Benin could supply its greatest want: a labour force, for it had no indigenous population. Soon Benin was exporting negroes to work on its plantations. Later it was discovered that by exporting slaves from Benin to Mina huge profits could be made, since gold merchants were prepared to pay for them at twice their original cost. The demand for slaves on São Thomé increased after 1493 when colonization of the island was started with deported Portuguese Jews, exiles and convicts. Thus began one of the most remarkable forced migrations in history, whereby the pattern of the world's population was radically altered. The slave trade which followed close on the first visits to West Africa—slaves were on sale in Lisbon as early as 1441—was to make the negro race second only to the Europeans in their dispersion over the world's surface.

The Portuguese built a factory, as trading stations on the Coast were known, at Gwato, the port of Benin, to handle the pepper trade and to purchase slaves. Fortunately through the establishment of this factory we have some amount of information about ancient Benin, though it is often far from accurate. Benin was quickly recognized by the Portuguese as one of the most important kingdoms on the Coast and the King of Benin sent an ambassador to Portugal in the reign of Dom João II (1481–95). In return Portugal sent missionaries and factors (trading agents), together with many presents for the King. The King himself showed little enthusiasm for the new religion, though he ordered his son and some of his chiefs to become Christians. He also ordered a church to be built.

Pina, a contemporary chronicler, records the visit of the Benin ambassador thus:

'This ambassador was a man of good speech and natural wisdom. Great feasts were held in his honour, and he was shown many of the good things of these kingdoms. He returned to his land in a ship of the King's, who at his departure made him a gift of rich clothes for himself and his wife: and through him he also sent a rich present to the king of such things as he understood he would greatly prize. Moreover, he sent holy and most catholic advisers with praiseworthy admonitions for the faith to administer a stern rebuke about the heresies and great idolatries and fetishes, which the negroes practise in that land.'

Early optimism about the value of the pepper trade with

Benin was damped and by 1510 trade with Benin was almost exclusively in slaves. This was to be the pattern for the next three hundred and fifty years, when trade in the natural products of West Africa finally ousted that in humans. Slaves were normally sent over to São Thomé where they joined large caravels, packed with men from the Congo and Mina, and sailed to their destinations.

From the start, however, there was considerable intercourse between the Bini and Portuguese. The Portuguese taught some of them to read, and in 1553 Captain Windam was surprised to find that the King of Benin 'could speak the Portugal tongue, which he learned of a child'.

To this day a section of the Benin royal palace speaks a language, quite unintelligible to the ordinary Bini, which is allegedly derived from Portuguese. That the King of Benin greatly impressed the Portuguese is clear from the report of the Portuguese representative, Duarte Pires, to King Manuel from Benin, 20th October 1516.

'. . . he pays us high honour and sets at table to dine with his son, and no part of the court is hidden from us but all the doors are open. Sir, when these priests arrived in Benin, the delight of the king of Benin was so great that I do not know how to describe it, and likewise that of all his people; and he sent for them at once; and they remained with him for one whole year in war. The priests and we reminded him of the embassy of your highness, and he replied to us that he was very satisfied with it; but since he was at war, that he could do nothing until he returned to Benin, because he needed leisure for such a deep mystery as this; as soon as he was in Benin, he would fulfil his promise to your highness, and he would so behave as to give great pleasure to your highness, and to all your kingdom. So it was, at the end of one year, in the month of August, the king gave his son and some of his noblemen—the greatest in his kingdom—so that they might become Christians; and also he ordered a church to be built in Benin; and they made them Christians straightway; and also they are teaching them to read, and your highness will be pleased to know that they are very good learners. . . .'

Some twenty-five years later, a Portuguese navigator wrote that the men taken as slaves were mainly captives of war, or sometimes children sold by their parents in the hopes that they might find a more profitable life elsewhere. He also gives an interesting account of the burial of the King of Benin, though its accuracy cannot be vouched for since he states in the same account that most negroes live to 100 years old. He was also quick to observe the divine status of the Benin kings:

'The Kings are worshipped by their subjects, who believe they come from heaven and speak of them always with great reverence, at a distance and on bended knees. Great ceremony surrounds them, and many of these kings never allow themselves to be seen eating, so as not to destroy the belief of their subjects that they can live without food. . . .'

After 1520 no Portuguese lived for any length of time in the Niger region, and their agencies were held by half-castes or Africans able to speak Portuguese. The main reason for decline in direct trade with Benin was the growth of Asian trade and the creation of better bases at Fernando Po and São Thome.

The hazards of West African trade are well brought out in Richard Eden's account of Windam's voyage to Benin in 1553, at a time when Portuguese monopoly of the west coast trade was already being whittled away by rival European powers. Eden describes a visit to the King of Benin. 'They were brought with a great company to the presence of the king, who being a black Moore (although not so black as the rest) sat in a great huge hall, long and wide, with walls made of earth, without windows, the roofs of thin boorde, open in sundry places, like unto lovers to let in the aire.'

They traded successfully with the king, who straight away offered them the thirty to forty hundredweight of peppers in his own store, and promised to gather enough to fill all their ships within thirty days. He did this, collecting the phenomenal amount of eighty tons. But the crew drank too much palm wine and caught fevers. Most of them died. So Windam sailed without the pepper, full haste to avoid further disaster, leaving several of his crew behind including one Nicholas Lambert, a son of the Lord Mayor of London. This was one of the last of the major pepper expeditions. It also marked the end of Portuguese monopoly of trade on the west coast.

From then on England was to establish herself not only as a leading trader on the coast, but as one of the chief exporters of slaves, a trade profitable both to Africans and Europeans, though bringing with it untold human misery and degradation.

Some estimates put the total number of slaves exported from West Africa and Angola as high as 24,000,000, of which probably only 15,000,000 survived the notorious Middle Passage across the Atlantic. In the sixteenth century about 1,000,000 slaves were transported to the Americas, in the seventeenth century, some 3,000,000, and in the eighteenth century some 7,000,000 or 70,000 a year. Of these about 22,000 were shipped annually from ports in Nigeria. Benin and its colony of Lagos sent about 4,000 and the ports of Bonny, New Calabar and Old Calabar, which grew up directly in response to European demands for slaves, together with the Cameroons sent some 18,000. Even in the nineteenth century, when many major European powers had abolished slavery, and when the British Navy patrolled the coast of Africa, another 4,000,000 slaves were taken across the Atlantic. Many of these came from Yorubaland, where civil war produced thousands of captives to be sold into slavery.

The stimulus to this colossal traffic in human beings was the discovery of the Americas and the realization of their mineral and agricultural wealth. In 1580 the union between Portugal and Spain opened up the west coast, hitherto a Portuguese monopoly, to the country with a monopoly of the New World. Spain's policy of settling and developing the New World and her stake in west coast trade greatly stimulated the sale of slaves in West Africa. Both in the West Indies and on the mainland the Spaniards found that the indigenous inhabitants, with the exception of the Indians of Mexico and Peru, were unable to adapt themselves to the new conditions imposed on them by their conquerors. In the West Indies the establishment of Spanish rule led to the extinction of nearly the entire indigenous population. This was repeated on the mainland to which the Spaniards moved after the exhaustion of the West Indies mines. There was not enough labour available or willing to leave Europe and live in these new lands, so that when it was found that Africans survived well in the climate, and moreover were adaptable both to working in mines and on plantations, the slave trade that had been carried on in a desultory way at the beginning of the sixteenth century received tremendous new impetus. The settlement of North America and the West Indies in the early seventeenth century by Britain and France led to further demands for slaves, especially with the development of sugar-cane plantations in the mid century. In 1637 the Dutch, who had thrown off the Spanish yoke in 1572, conquered Brazil, and in order to supply the already established Portuguese planters with slaves, set about capturing west coast slaving forts. In addition to these major slaving powers, supplying slaves to their own colonies, there were the purely commercial slavers like the Brandenburgers and Danes who sold to the highest bidders. During the seventeenth century the Dutch were the leading slavers, followed by the Portuguese. But after the Treaty of Utrecht in 1713 Britain and France took control of the traffic, the French mainly operating on the upper Guinea Coast. The British who had acquired the Spanish monopoly of the slave trade under the terms of the treaty were rivalled by the Dutch on the lower Guinea Coast. The British were particularly strong in the Niger Delta ports, where a corrupt form of English became the language of the slave dealers. Liverpool and Bristol owe their growth at that time to the profits of the slave trade.

Thus in the seventeenth and eighteenth century the west coast of Africa became a centre of European enterprise and rivalry with slaves as the prize. There was only one means by which the Europeans could ensure the supply of slaves, and that was to obtain the co-operation of the local population. In certain instances it was feasible to make raids on sea and riverside villages, but the small number of slaves captured by these methods never justified the huge expenditure in fitting up a ship to go to the west coast. It was impossible for the Europeans to penetrate inland, not only because of the tight control the local rulers had on their territories, but also because of the diseases to which they were subjected. It was also in the interests of the coastal middlemen to prevent the European from penetrating inland and trading direct with the slave-supplying areas. African chiefs were not only reluctant to hand over land to European traders, but were also prevented from doing so by customary law whereby, in most cases, land belonged corporately to the people. In such circumstances the European and African slave dealers soon established friendly relations to further their mutual interests.

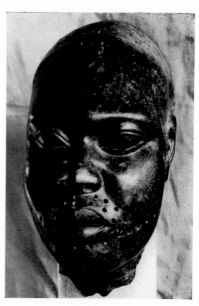

1. Nok terracotta: 'The Jemaa Head'

2. Ife bronze: head of an Oni of Ife

3. Benin bronze: a Portuguese soldier

4. Igbo bronze: detail of drinking vessel

5. Captain Hugh Crow: a Liverpool slaver

6. Survival of the Slave Trade: a priestess of the Yoruba god
Shango in Bahia, Brazil

The Atlantic Slave Trade

The slave traffic raised surprisingly few objections in the minds of either Africans or Europeans. The Europeans, of course, conveniently salved their Christian consciences by suggesting that in fact they were saving 'heathens' for Christendom. Anyway, on many occasions they had profits of the order of £5,000 to £10,000 a trip to dispel any qualms they might have felt. Moreover, the horrors of the Middle Passage were far from the sight of ordinary civilized people. To the African the idea of slavery was not foreign. Most tribes had some form of domestic slavery, though this was very different from that proposed by the Europeans. In the African system slaves, though of inferior status, had certain rights, whilst their owners had definite and often onerous duties towards them. In Bornu, for instance, the kings often sent slaves out to govern their provinces; Hausa kings often ruled through slaves; and in Yorubaland slaves of the Oba attained great power and were much feared by his subjects. In these states slaves had a special usefulness as recruits to high office, since they had no influential lineages behind them, and hence no pressures on them that could be potentially opposed to their ruler's interest. They were also utterly dependent on their ruler, and as slaves could attract no following among the freeborn. In some states eunuchs held similar positions.

Once slavery had been instituted it was hopeless to expect those Africans who profited from it to have any more conscience about it than the Europeans who bought slaves, especially since in this case the Africans were not usually selling their own people, but members of other tribes whom they considered very often not only as inferior, but also as only fit to be slaves. Normally prices for slaves were high, since demand invariably exceeded supply, though occasionally when there were few ships, the price of slaves dropped. The slavers usually anchored some distance away from the slave port, and most of the negotiations were conducted on board after customary presents had been given to the local chief. Slaves would be brought out by canoe and the traders would then present them to the ship's surgeon for inspection; those rejected were as often as not murdered on the spot.

In exchange for slaves the Europeans brought a large and varied list of goods, whose popularity differed along the coast.

The Atlantic Slave Trade

James Welsh, who visited Benin in 1588 on a trading voyage, lists the following items they carried for trade: linen, woollen cloth, iron bars, copper bracelets, or manillas, glass beads and coral. This was not a slaving voyage, and they bought in exchange ivory, palm oil, pepper, cotton cloth. He also reported that cowries were the local form of currency. A century or so later James Barbot visited Bonny where the rate of exchange for slaves was thirteen iron bars for a male slave, nine for females. In 1703-4 the price of slaves in nearby New Calabar was twelve bars for a man and nine for a woman. Often media for the purchase of slaves were copper bars, beads of various sorts, brass belts, cloths, ox horns for drinking cups, pewter tankards, spirits and blue linen.

On board ship the lot of the slaves was terrible. Crammed into the holds of the ships, men slaves were shackled to each other by chains. There was hardly room to move. It was almost impossible for them to excrete, other than where they were lying, so that dysentery soon became rife. Each day the slaves were taken on deck for exercise and left there till evening. The women, boys and men were all separated. The ship's officers had the right to use any woman slave. Strongest precautions were made against attempts at suicide by jumping overboard. If conditions were frightful for the slaves they were almost as bad for the wretched sailors, many of whom were press-ganged into service on the slavers with contracts that forbade them to complain subsequently about their ill-treatment. About a sixth of the slaves transhipped died; probably a greater proportion of the sailors did, being whipped for the slightest fault by sadistic captains who seemed to make a speciality of the slave-trade. Not all slaving captains were of this character. For instance, Captain Hugh Crow from Liverpool was a more thoughtful master, priding himself on delivering his slaves all fit and alive. He was a close friend of King Pepple of Bonny.

The English captains did not always have it their own way. On many occasions slaves revolted on board, for they often outnumbered Europeans ten to one. On the Bonny River a group of slaves just taken aboard an English ship took advantage of the bargaining between the captains and the local chiefs for further supplies of slaves, seized the ship's arms and overpowered the crew. This is one reason for the barbarity of the instruments of torture or discipline kept on the ship. The men were usually all chained together, though on one occasion women, who were allowed the freedom of the deck, saw the armoury unlocked and swiftly passed arms to their men, and together they seized the ship. The lot of the slave was little improved when he reached his destination, especially in the British West Indian colonies, where many of the slaves from the Delta ports were sent. The method of sale today seems almost comic, except when one puts oneself in the place of the slave. Those who seemed about to die were quickly sold at cheap prices to surgeons; the healthy ones were often sold at what was called a 'scramble'. They were enclosed in a pen, obscured from the public view. Prospective buyers paid an agreed price, and were then let into the pen to seize the best they could. The terror of the wretched negroes as a horde of white men rushed amongst them, grabbing them as quickly and in as great a number as they could, can easily be imagined. No one ever thought to warn them of the method of their sale, which, compared with that of the African markets, must have appeared utterly barbaric. Indeed the barbarism of the West Indian colonies was incredible; for misdemeanour on these islands the slaves were subject to the most inhuman of punishments. Trivial offences might mean an ear lopped off, a hand axed, a tongue or nose slit. 'No slave to be buried after sunset,' reads one of the laws. 'Nor in any other than a plain deal board coffin, without covering; nor shall scarfs and favours be worn at any of their funerals. The punishment for transgressing to be 50 lashes, and the scarfs, etc., to be forfeited.' Of course, such laws were largely a result of fear of slave revolts such as took place in Brazil, Havana, some of the French West Indian colonies and Jamaica itself.

The growth of the slave-trade had marked effects on the political structure of the Niger Delta and its hinterland, where a large proportion of the slaves exported from Nigeria were procured. Before the arrival of the Portuguese the Delta seems to have been inhabited mainly by the Ijo peoples, who lived in small, scattered fishing villages in the tidal zone. It appears from their language which is not immediately related to any of the languages spoken by their neighbours that they were probably among the oldest established inhabitants of Nigeria. Most of these Ijo communities have a history of moving down from the north-west, several claiming that they migrated from Benin, or rather away from Benin domination. But these legends refer to a period well before the opening up of coastal trade. These early southward movements, whatever their causes, were unrelated to the slave-trade; possibly they referred to some upheaval in the early Benin Empire.

The arrival of slave-traders in the Delta stimulated the growth of a number of trading states, which were in effect expanded versions of small Ijo fishing villages that happened to occupy favourable positions on the creeks of the Niger Delta. The most important among these were Bonny, Owome (New Calabar) and Brass (Nembe), which grew up in the early seventeenth century. Farther down the coast at the mouth of the Cross River, the Efik trading state of Old Calabar was also organized to meet European demands for slaves. In the western Delta the Itsekiri kingdom of Warri, closely related to Benin, became another major source of supply for slaves.

The Delta states obtained slaves not from amongst their own people but from the tribes of the interior, particularly the populous Ibo, who inhabit most of what is now the Eastern region of Nigeria. The most dramatic change in the structure of the Ijo fishing villages was the rapid expansion of population through the importation of slaves, who were integrated into the community. Ijo culture was not markedly affected by these imports, for in the trading states the criterion was quick assimilation of slaves. In the small fishing villages government was carried out by an assembly of the entire adult male population under the presidency of the *Amanyanabo*. In the new trading states power tended to be concentrated in the hands of the most important traders. Government by an assembly of all adult males thus gave way to government by the heads of the houses founded by the first great traders under the presidency of the *Amanyanabo*, who had become the kings of contemporary travellers' reports. It was a marked feature of these Ijo states that a slave of ability could succeed to the leadership of these houses.

The development of house rule in the Delta states is an interesting example of the response of a primitive community to a new economic situation. The house consisted of a wealthy trader, his children and all the slaves he bought. All lineal descendants of himself and the slaves were members of the house. When he died preference as successor was given to one of his own children as head of the house, though a slave of outstanding ability could succeed. The new head was chosen by a meeting of all freeborn and slave members of the house. The head of house exacted tax from other traders in the house and with this he was able to run the house and equip a war canoe, consisting of thirty men. The capital involved in equipping not only war canoes but trading canoes further tended to concentrate power in the hands of the heads of houses. Ability to equip a war canoe allowed a man to found a house, and the head of an existing house always encouraged members to branch off on their own, since in the assembly this would give him extra voices, for every head of house had the right to a seat in the town assembly.

The head of house had a great deal of authority over his members, in certain cases even being able to settle cases of homicide. Any inter-house dispute became a matter for the town assembly, presided over by the *Amanyanabo*, who also had his own house. The *Amanyanabo* was the initiator of policy. He decided on the conduct of war, and led the battle fleet. He was expected to pay for the conduct of war, and to defray these expenses the town assembly agreed that from time to time he should have a complete monopoly of a particular trading article.

The system of house rule was encouraged by the European traders who preferred to trade through a few men with established reputations who could also vouch for the honesty of their subordinates. Some of these traders took on credit several thousand pounds' worth of goods to exchange for slaves in the interior.

This pattern of house rule was the most characteristic feature of these new trading states, including the non-Ijo states of Old Calabar and Warri. The organization of each state, however, differed considerably. Bonny, New Calabar and Warri were under a strong monarchical system, whilst political authority in Brass and Old Calabar was divided.

In Old Calabar, for example, there was no one supreme person, and ascendancy in the community shifted from the leading house of Duke Town to that of Creek Town. The real power in the community was the Egbo Society. This was a secret society to which only those of age and wealth could belong. Membership cost a considerable sum, but once admitted members shared in the proceeds of payments by other initiates. It gave out laws, settled disputes between various branches of the houses and collected debts. It was, for example, Egbo which in 1850, under pressure from Europeans, passed a law forbidding human sacrifices. As G. I. Jones has written: '... Egbo was the sole authority capable of maintaining peace between the different groups or stopping fights and disturbances once they had broken out, since it alone could apply effective sanctions against offenders.' In Bonny and New Calabar, by contrast, political authority lay with the king in council with his chiefs. In Bonny the monarchy dated back probably to the fifteenth century, and at the height of slave traffic in the eighteenth century the state was under the remarkably capable Pepple dynasty. However, his power was not absolute and, like most African kings, he was bound by restrictions of other important members of the community, in this case the house heads. The power of the various Delta states depended on their fast large war canoes.

The economy of all the Delta states was based on slaves not only for export but as the workers within the state. However, there was a considerable difference in the attitudes of the various states towards slaves. Old Calabar and New Calabar make a striking contrast in this respect. In New Calabar as we have already noted the main emphasis for membership of the state was acculturation, rather than descent from the founding ancestor of the house as it was amongst the Efik. Thus a slave who was successfully integrated into New Calabar could rise to the highest position of state. It was a capital offence to refer to a man as of slave origin. Again, the competition between the three Ijo trading towns of New Calabar, Bonny and Brass (Nembe), forced them to lay emphasis on ability as the major criterion for leadership if they were to survive in the fierce struggle for control of markets. Thus, at a later date in Bonny, when there was strife between two major factions in the state, a slave, Jaja, was able to establish a rival state of Opobo. In the New Calabar state the slaves lived in their masters' compounds, giving them little chance to organize themselves; in Old Calabar they were relegated to plantations, whilst the freeborn stayed in the towns, giving them ample opportunity to organize revolt. In New Calabar there was relatively little oppression and no slave revolts. In Old Calabar there was oppression of the slaves, not only through refusing to admit them to high status in the community, but also by excluding them from any participation in society. In addition once Egbo, the main instrument of government in Old Calabar, had unified the Efik settlements at the mouth of the Cross River the geographical insulation of their route to the markets eliminated the cut-throat competition with other states which would otherwise have turned attention to ability rather than pedigree in the selection of leaders.

James Barbot, in his *An Abstract of a Voyage to New Calabar River or Rio Real in the year 1699*, gives a good picture of trade conditions in the Delta states.

'On the first of *July*, the King sent for us to come ashore, we staid there till four in the afternoon, and concluded the trade on the terms offered them the day before; the King promising to come the next day aboard to regulate it, and be paid his duties. . . .

'The second, heavy rain all the morning. At two o'clock we fetch'd the King from shore, attended by all his *Caboceiros* and officers, in three large canoes; and entring the ship, was saluted with seven guns. The King had on an old fashion'd scarlet coat, laced with gold and silver, very rusty, and a fine hat on his head, but bare-footed; all his attendants showing great respect to him and, since our coming hither, none of the natives have dared to come aboard of us, or sell the least thing, till the King had adjusted trade with us.

'We had again a long discourse with the King and *Pepprell* his brother, concerning the rates of our goods and his customs. This *Pepprell*, being a sharp blade, and a mighty talking *Black*, perpetually making objections against something or other, and teasing us for this or that Dassy, or present, as well as for drams, etc., it were to be wish'd, that such a one as he were out of the way, to facilitate trade. . . .

'Thus, with much patience, all our matters were adjusted indifferently, after their way, who are not very scrupulous to find excuses or objections, for not keeping literally to any verbal contract; for they have not the art of reading and writing, and therefore we are forced to stand to their agreement, which often is no longer than they think fit to hold it themselves. . . .

'We gave the usual presents to the King, etc. . . . To Captain Forty, the King's general, Captain Pepprell, Captain Boileau, alderman Bougsby, my lord Willyby, duke of Monmouth, drunken Henry and some others two firelocks, eight hats, nine narrow Guinea stuffs. We adjusted with them the reduction of our merchandize into bars of iron, as the standard coin, viz: One bunch of beads, one bar. . . .

'The price of provisions and wood was also regulated.

'Sixty King's yams, one bar; one hundred and sixty slave's yams, one bar; for fifty thousand yams to be delivered to us. A butt of water, two rings. For the length of wood, seven bars, which is dear; but they were to deliver it ready cut into our boat. For a goat, one bar. A cow, ten or eight bars, according to its bigness. A hog, two bars. A calf, eight bars. A jar of palm oil, one bar and a quarter.

'We paid also the King's duties in goods; five hundred slaves, to be purchased at two copper rings a head.

'We also advanced to the King, by way of loan, the value of a hundred and fifty bars of iron, in sundry goods; and to his principal men, and others, as much again each in proportion to his quality and ability. . . .'

The supply of slaves to the Delta ports was controlled by the Aro of Arochuku, and in a land of politically decentralized people, they maintained a highly complex and centralized system of trade, coupled with religious-political domination. The power of the Aro, a sub-section of the Ibo peoples, was based on the universal respect of the peoples of Eastern Nigeria for their oracle known as the Long Juju, which was said to be Chukwu, the Ibo supreme deity. Thus the Aro, who controlled the oracle which resided in a cave in their territory, commanded great respect among Ibo and the Delta states. The Aro as representatives of the oracle settled in small colonies throughout the region, ostensibly as mediators between other tribes and the oracle. These colonies very quickly became trading colonies, hedged with religious sanction. In loosely organized Iboland the Aro were the only people who could safely travel from village to village unharmed. Thus Aro hegemony over Iboland, which was directly founded on the proceeds of the slave-trade, provided the mechanism of communication over long distances in Iboland where none had existed before: one could now travel in the company of a recognized Aro agent, a guarantee of safe conduct. The Aro colonies were sited on the main trading routes, and along them passed slaves for the Delta ports. The Delta rulers found the oracle a convenient buttress to community discipline. Slaves would be threatened with being sent to the oracle, where it was believed certain death would follow, though, in fact, the cunning Aro rarely killed a man, but sold him into slavery. In New Calabar it was common for one chief to accuse another of witchcraft, so that he would be sent for 'trial' by the oracle. To avoid certain enslavement the chief would have to pay the oracle keepers most of his fortune, which would consist largely of slaves. He would return a broken man, without followers (i.e. slaves) and therefore without status. The Aro backed up the efficacy of the oracle by hiring mercenaries to raid those who would not respect it. Fines from big men had to be paid in slaves who were supposed to be eaten by the oracle, but in fact were quickly exported.

West of the Aro sphere of influence, the hinterland was unified by the migration eastward from Benin to the Niger of people who drew the indigenous population together into sizeable states. The classic example is the migration of the Onitsha people to the Niger, which is generally believed to have taken place in the seventeenth century. Though classified as Ibo, the Onitsha, as do many other Ibo groups along the Niger, have strong Benin influences in their political structure. They had a monarch, which most Ibo societies did not; and many of their chiefs bear Benin titles.

Benin was the most important slave mart, west of the Niger. The port for Benin was Gwatto, where factors of the King exercised his monopoly on trade. John Ogilby, in *Africa*, published in the seventeenth century, wrote: 'No Foreigner can Trade up the River of *Benyn* without Order of the King; who chuses one Fiadoor, or Counseller of the Kingdom to Treat and trade with them. Neither may those appointed for the Trade, so much as converse with the *whites*, or come into their Slavehouses, much less buy any *European* wares, but are constrain'd to take them at the dearest rate of the *Fiadoor*.' Benin traders were interested in cloths of all descriptions, brass armlets, looking-glasses, iron bars, fine coral, cowries from East India, beads and perfumes. In exchange they exported slaves, local cloths, pepper, jasper stones, leopard skins and ivory.

At that time Benin appears to have been very prosperous, with a large well-disciplined army. But in 1703 when Bosman, the observant Dutch traveller, visited Benin, he remarked: 'Formerly this village was very thick and close built, and in a manner over charg'd with inhabitants, which is yet visible from the Ruins of half remaining Houses. . . .' Benin seems to have overspent itself by the eighteenth century, its constant slaving wars ultimately impoverishing the kingdom. Bosman was nevertheless impressed by its organization. He describes the honesty of the traders, the just code of law, the lack of beggars, and the civility of his own reception.

By the end of the century, Captain John Adams, writing in the period 1786–1800, remarked the decline of the slave-trade in Benin and its concentration farther down the coast in the Delta ports. Significantly for the future he observed: 'Human sacrifices are not so frequent here as in some parts of Africa; besides those immolated on the death of great men, three or four are annually sacrificed at the mouth of the river, as votive offerings to the sea, to direct vessels to bend their course to this horrid climate.'

The last of the great slave ports was Warri, which appears to have been founded by a son of the King of Benin named Ginuwa some time in the fifteenth century. By the seventeenth century it had grown into a powerful trading state, almost independent of Benin. Dapper, in his *Description de l'Afrique*, writes: 'The King of Ouwerre is the ally and in some manner the vassal of the King of Benin, but in other respects he is absolute in his dominions.' There appears to have been considerably more contact between the Portuguese and the Itsekiri of Warri than with Benin, for Dapper records that Antonio Domingo, Olu of Warri in 1644, was a mulatto, his father having been educated in Portugal where he married a Portuguese lady. In 1682 Father Jerom Merolla da Sorrento recorded that the reigning Olu of Warri was married to a Portuguese woman from São Thome. He had married her according to Catholic rite, and many of his subjects had apparently followed his example in adopting the Catholic faith.

The Atlantic Slave Trade

In Nigeria, as elsewhere on the Coast, the first effect of the slave-trade was depopulation, though this is exaggerated when one considers that probably during the early eighteenth century no more than 11,000 people were sent abroad annually from Nigeria, and that even in the heyday of slave-trade at the turn of the eighteenth century Captain John Adams estimated that in twenty years between 1800–22, probably some 370,000 Ibo had been sold into slavery. This may seem a tremendous figure, but it certainly had its economic *raison d'être* since then, as now Iboland's chief problem was overpopulation.

The slave trade tended to bring some equilibrium to the Eastern region which, in parts, was intensely overpopulated, in other parts sparsely populated. There is sufficient evidence to suggest that in fact most slaves came from the overpopulated areas where there was land hunger, being exchanged with the agriculturally richer areas for yams and other farm products.

It is interesting to follow up what happened to the many Nigerians who were forcibly settled in the New World. On the whole they soon lost their tribal identities, especially in those territories where families were broken up indiscriminately and where no consideration was given to the welfare of the slaves. It was difficult for a group in the British West Indies to retain its identity when, as we have seen, common participation even in a funeral, was forbidden. Different tribes reacted differently to the new situation. The Ibo, for instance, were not highly organized like the Yoruba. Their unit of government was the extended family, and though the domination of the Aro Chukwu oracle gave them some political and religious unity, there was little common ground between Ibo from villages fifty miles apart.[1] It must be remembered, too, that a large number of slaves from Ibo territory were already slaves, who had offended their masters and been sent to the Aro Chukwu oracle or else were outcasts from their own societies. It was almost impossible to take Ibo of high status with the Ozo title as slaves, since they always committed suicide. Thus it is not surprising that a de-

[1] Some impression of eighteenth-century Iboland can be gained from *The Interesting Narrative of the Life of Olaudah Equiano, or Gustavus Vassa, the African*, written by himself, London, 1789, and cited in Thomas Hodgkin's *Nigerian Perspectives*, pp. 155–66. It, however, appears to refer to a Western Ibo society.

centralized people like the Ibo did not retain their cultural individuality under the oppressive slave system. This was not the case with the Yoruba, who lived under the rule of the highly centralized state of Oyo, and were not usually captured individually as in the east but as the result of wars, which might cause a large number from the same town to be transported. It must be remembered also that they were shipped through the ports where the Portuguese and Spanish purchased their slaves, and many of them found their way to Brazil, Cuba and Trinidad, where their masters were less oppressive in their attitude, especially with regard to the possibility of slaves practising their own religions. This was far from being an altruistic concession in Brazil, for the government permitted and indeed encouraged the maintenance of cultural traditions, thinking that thus, on the classic formula of divide and rule, they could preserve the ethnic identity of various groups and prevent Africans of various tribes uniting in their misery against them. The Governor of the state of Bahia, writing in the early nineteenth century, said: 'These feelings of animosity between tribes may be regarded as the best guarantee for the security of large towns in Brazil.'

This finds a modern parallel in South Africa, where the official policy of the Nationalist Government has been to emphasize tribal differences to prevent Africans uniting against them.

On the other hand the African as such was not despised by the Latin races, and indeed many slaves attained their freedom and became powerful traders long before the eventual abolition of the trade there in the late nineteenth century. Miscegenation frowned on in British and French territories, was the general rule in Brazil where, as to a lesser extent in Cuba, traditions of the Yoruba in particular survived, since they were one of the major ethnic groups there. Today there has developed in Bahia and other towns that were based on a slave economy a syncretistic religion combining elements of the Catholic and Yoruba religion. Yoruba from Nigeria can still recognize the religious ceremonies practised by their cousins in Brazil. In Cuba, Efik and Ibibio slaves re-created Egbo, whose membership included both black and white. In Haiti Voodoo is a survival of traditional African religions.

A further feature of this cultural interchange between Nigeria and Brazil was the repatriation of large groups of slaves who revolted against the government. Between 1807 and 1813 the Moslems, chiefly Hausa, revolted against not only their white masters but also fellow-Africans who were not Moslems. This was undoubtedly an extension of the Holy War being fought in Northern Nigeria at that time by the Fulani, and is an indication of the close contacts between Nigeria and the New World. Moslem Africans who had been liberated and had become wealthy also joined the revolt, and together they were repatriated, taking with them many ideas learned in Brazil. Today, in Lagos, there are still many of the houses built by those people and the Yoruba who were repatriated after the Nago (Yoruba) and Fon revolts of 1826–35. Unfortunately, some of these repatriated slaves became some of the wealthiest slave-dealers on the west coast of Africa, encouraging the slave-trade when the British were doing their best to suppress it.

The slave-trade, though it brought great suffering to many Africans, both on their way to the coast where they were roughly handled, and on the Middle Passage to the Americas, did not in the case of the Delta bring the political instability that is usually described. Kidnapping and raiding in Iboland were the exception rather than the rule, and in many ways the governments that evolved on the coast were admirably suited to their new economy. One authority has written, probably with more enthusiasm than is justified by the facts: 'From the contemporary personal reports of English Port-Governors and employees, of slaver captain surgeons and ships' officers, it is evident that the African chiefs had a highly developed system of government and a rigid code of laws and that, influenced largely by superstition as they were, they yet lived in ordered communities and were as far removed from the "barbarian brutish nations" of the Liverpool merchants' conception as their cruel witchcraft trials were akin to the religious inquisitions and pogroms of civilized Europe.'

CHAPTER V

The Holy War of Usman dan Fodio

Hausaland and Bornu were almost unaffected by the arrival of Europeans on the coast; their economy remained firmly orientated towards the Sahara desert. By the beginning of the eighteenth century Katsina had won the long struggle for control of the caravan routes from Northern Nigeria to North Africa and for a hundred years she was to remain the leading commercial and cultural centre of the western Sudan. Bornu lived in the shadow of its former glories, retaining control over its vassal states, but being constantly threatened on its northern borders by desert nomads and on its southern borders by the sedentary tribes that served as its slave reservoir. The standard of learning in the state rose, and the Mais who ruled in the second half of the eighteenth century, though they were noted for their scholarship, at the same time tended to lose interest in political affairs and became dominated by the intellectuals in their courts. The structure of the court had become more elaborate, especially now that princes who in ancient days would have ruled provinces were kept under surveillance in the capital or in the nearby summer palace of Gambarou. The growing weakness of the empire was made clear towards the end of the eighteenth century when the Bornu army suffered a disastrous defeat at the hands of the Mandara, a subject tribe.

The first half of the eighteenth century witnessed the rise to power of Zamfara which, though one of the oldest of the Hausa Banza Bakwai states, had never before been of major importance in the politics of the western Sudan. In 1700, however, Zamfara conquered Kano, and by the middle of the century she was rivalling Katsina's supremacy in Hausaland. At the same time the Hausa state of Gobir which, because of its frontier position

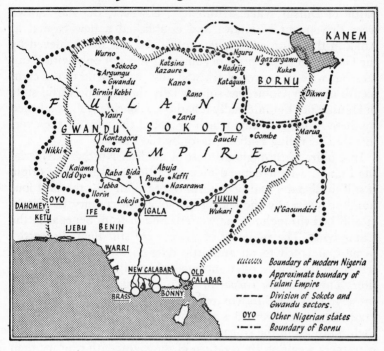

4. The Fulani Empire and Bornu, *circa* 1850

on the desert, had remained rather remote from the general trend of affairs in Hausaland, began to assert its power, and from 1731–43 engaged Kano in a series of hard battles. The Gobirawa were at the time being pressed back on their northern frontiers by desert tribes and were looking for expansion to the fertile lands of Zamfara on their southern borders. At first they infiltrated peacefully into Zamfara, and Barbari, King of Gobir, gave his own sister in marriage to Marroki, King of Zamfara. A treaty was drawn up whereby the Gobirawa were allowed to settle near modern Sabon Birni, for the King of Zamfara welcomed the assistance of the Gobirawa in his struggle for supremacy in Hausaland.

In 1764, however, Barbari attacked and sacked Birnin Zamfara, capital of Marroki, who fled to Kiawa, a Katsina town, where, with the help of the King of Katsina, he held out against the Gobirawa and defeated Barbari's successor, Bawa, at the battle of Dutsin Wake. Ultimately, however, the Zamfarawa were driven out of Kiawa and established a new capital at Anka in the south of their territories. All this was achieved by the Gobirawa at the price of continual war not only with Zamfara but with its powerful Katsina ally. At the end of the eighteenth century Gobir was superficially the most powerful state in Hausaland, but internally it had been considerably weakened by these prolonged wars which prepared the way for the overthrow of its ruling Habe dynasty by the Fulani.

In Gobir, as throughout most of modern Northern Nigeria, the Fulani, a light-skinned race of cattle nomads whose origin is still in dispute, had been settling peacefully for the past four hundred years. By the end of the sixteenth century they were established throughout the western Sudan from Senegal to the Cameroons. The majority of them were still nomadic cattle-owners, devoted to an animistic religion, but a number had settled in the towns, often intermarrying with the local population. These *Fulanin Gidda*, or town Fulani, became the chief proselytes of the Moslem religion in the western Sudan. In Hausaland they were the acknowledged intellectuals, gaining high positions in the courts of the kings. Many of them became extremely wealthy. By the turn of the eighteenth century their increasing political and economic influence in the northern states gave the local rulers considerable cause for disquiet, especially since they formed a class at the vanguard of movements for religious and intellectual reform. They openly criticized what they described as the religious laxity and the decadent standards of learning in the Hausa states. In some areas they were openly asserting themselves, as in the Benue where the Fulani were attacking the Jukun, even before 1800.

The general unrest amongst the town Fulani was focused around an elderly Moslem scholar in Gobir, Usman dan Fodio. He was born at Marata in Gobir, a Fulani of the Toronkawa clan which had migrated fourteen generations before from the old Empire of Mali. He had been educated at Agades where he studied under the famous teacher Mallam Jibril and came in touch with the reformist ideas that were stirring throughout the Islamic world. His education was extremely thorough, consisting of the traditional Islamic sciences of Grammar, Law, Exegesis, Theology, Rhetoric and Prosody. On the completion

7. Reception of the Denham-Clapperton Mission by the Sultan of Bornu

8. Habe Tower in Katsina

9. Nigerian warriors in chain mail

10 (a), (b). Nigerian Explorers: Clapperton, and Crowther who later became Bishop on the Niger

11. Richard and John Lander proceeding down the Niger

of his education he returned to Degel in Gobir where he became a teacher. Nafata, King of Gobir, soon sought him out to become tutor to his own children. As a result he gained considerable influence in the court both with the king and the nobility. In 1802 Yunfa, who had been his pupil, succeeded to the throne of Gobir. He was deeply resentful of the power of his old tutor in the court, and particularly concerned about his radical reformist ideas. He even took drastic measures against the further conversion of his people to Islam. The wearing of the turban was forbidden to men, and the veil to women. This interference, as Mr. M. Hiskett, an expert on the period has written, was almost entirely political for it was 'these customs which gave to the Shehu's party the cohesion and sense of common identity which the Habe kings feared'.

Much was made by the Fulani, in their justification of the Holy War they later declared against Yunfa and all the other Habe rulers of Hausaland, of the reversion to paganism in Gobir and the rest of the Hausa states. It is true that over certain matters Islam, which had been long established in Hausaland, made many concessions to the indigenous religion of the Hausa. This was particularly marked in the institution of monarchy. Indeed, as far as the Habe monarchs were concerned, they practised a calculated syncretism whereby their authority as Moslem monarchs was boosted by, and to a considerable extent depended on, their respect for Habe religious rites and social practices. Thus the Fulani attack on their 'reversion to paganism' was an attack on the very authority by which they ruled. Though the Habe kings made such political concessions, Islamic learning flourished in their courts. They maintained around them a small circle of Moslem divines and scholars. At the court of Gobir, Usman dan Fodio had been amongst the most respected of such scholars.

It becomes clear in this light that the attacks of Usman dan Fodio struck at the very heart of Yunfa's power, and Yunfa's anti-Islamic measures were probably designed to prevent Usman, the reformer, from gaining more adherents. The antagonism between the two was not really that between believer and infidel, even though the Fulani liked to depict Yunfa as an unbeliever, but between radical reformer and a conservative willing to compromise in pursuit of stable government.

The Holy War of Usman dan Fodio

In the *Kitab-al-Farq*, a work on the Habe kingdoms attributed to Usman dan Fodio, and translated by Mr. M. Hiskett, the writer accuses the Habe rulers of imposing illegal taxation on the population of their states. Taking into account any natural prejudice that might come into the writings of one attacking the established régime, there was no doubt much truth in his charges. In the Habe kingdoms *gaisuwa*, or the giving of bribes to superiors, was common; judges were open to bribery; Moslems were pressed into military service; illegal market taxes were imposed. Undoubtedly the indiscriminate, oppressive and frequently excessive imposition of taxes was one of the sorest grievances of the people against their rulers. In particular the Fulani nomads bitterly resented the taxes on their cattle, and here, as much as in the violation of the principles of the Sharia, we may look for the motives which brought both the Hausa commoners and the Fulani nomads into Usman dan Fodio's camp.

As a result of his attacks on Yunfa, Usman was forced to leave court and retreated to his own town, Degel, where he was so outspoken against the Habe régime that Yunfa even planned to have him killed. Revolt only broke out after Yunfa attacked Gimbana where one of Usman's disciples, Abdussalami, had refused to bless some Gobirawa troops passing through the town. This attack on Gimbana was followed by a threat to destroy Degel and heralded the general persecution of the Shehu's followers. Usman fled from Degel to Gudu in February 1804, a period of his life known as the Hijira. The Shehu's brother Abdullahi said at the time, according to Usman dan Fodio in *Tanbikhu 'l-ikhwan*: 'Truly this matter has become intolerable; recourse must be had to arms. There can be no doubt that the situation demands a prince to manage our affairs, for Moslems should not be without government.' Usman dan Fodio was therefore elected leader of the revolt against the Habe King of Gobir, and his followers did 'homage to the Sheik, as is directed by the Kuran and Sunna in such circumstances, and made him the leader of the Holy War'.

Thus in early months of 1804 the elderly Moslem scholar and reformist preacher, Usman dan Fodio, found himself at the head of a great Jihad, or Holy War, that within a few years was to sweep most of the Hausa kings off their thrones, and during the next thirty was to establish Fulani hegemony throughout

82

all Northern Nigeria with the exception of Bornu and certain pagan areas inaccessible to the Fulani cavalry.

The causes and motives of this Jihad are extremely involved. As far as it concerned Usman dan Fodio, who was given the title of Amir al-mu'minin or Commander of the Faithful in acknowledgement of his religious leadership of the revolt, it was a Holy War to establish a purer form of Islam in what he considered a predominantly corrupt and decadent society. This fits into the pattern of reformist movements taking place throughout Africa at that time. As Thomas Hodgkin has written of Usman dan Fodio: 'His ideas and achievements have to be understood in the context of the succession of reforming movements which profoundly affected the Moslem world during the latter part of the eighteenth and nineteenth centuries—beginning with Muhammed Ibn Abd Al-Wahbab in Saudi Arabia, and including Muhammed ibn Ali al-Sanusi in Cyrenaica (Barka), Shehu Ahmadu and Al-hajj Umar ibn Said in the western Sudan and Muhammad Ammad ibn Abdullah (the Mahdi) in the former Egyptian Sudan. These movements, though differing from one another in many respects, had a common objective—"a return to the pure and primitive faith of Islam, purged of heresies and accretions". This implied the attempt to restore the original model of the Islamic State, as it was believed to have existed in the time of the Prophet and the first four Caliphas: a State in which social justice, administered in the light of the Shari'a by God-fearing rulers, took the place of the arbitrary decisions of irresponsible—and effectively non-Moslem—despots.'

Thus, in Usman dan Fodio's *Wathiqat ahl al-Sudan*, which may well have been the proclamation of war in the Jihad, it is declared in paragraph xiv: 'And that to make war against the king who is an apostate—who has not abandoned the religion of Islam so far as the professing of it is concerned, and who mingles the observances of Islam with the observances of heathendom, like the kings of Hausaland for the most part—is obligatory by assent, and that to take the government from him is obligatory by assent.'

The initial motive force of the rebellion came from a small cultured group of Fulani, mostly religious leaders and teachers, who, as Mr. Hiskett has written, 'were able to carry their

The Holy War of Usman dan Fodio

Jihad to a successful end . . . due to their sense of cohesion and intellectual superiority over the surrounding Hausa. This gave them a degree of organizing ability and political acumen above that of the Hausa aristocracy'.

Beyond the primary religious motive lay many political and economic factors. Group feelings were of dominant influence. The Fulani were a small minority amongst the Hausa, and in many ways it was a war between Fulani immigrants and Habe Hausa rulers, although this is too clear cut an explanation, for many of the Hausa *talakawa* or common people joined the Shehu's revolt, whilst as Abdullahi, the Shehu's brother, complained bitterly, many Fulani remained on the side of Yunfa. Certainly the cattle Fulani who joined the Shehu did so largely out of tribal loyalty, for many of them were certainly not Moslems.

Most significant was the large number of talakawa to join forces with the Shehu, who was preaching not only religious reform but a reform of the political affairs of the kingdom, particularly the oppressive system of taxation and the despotic administration of its ruler. Economic fears were also involved; the town Fulani were in many cases extremely wealthy, and this, combined with their political influence, aroused considerable jealousy. Ultimately it is impossible to say whether religious or economic motives, class feelings or tribal loyalties, played the largest part in the revolt.

In its later stages the Jihad became increasingly political and correspondingly less religious in its character. Zamfara, for instance, had considerable cause to regret its early assistance to the Fulani against Gobir when its towns were sacked by Abdullahi and Bello, the son of the Shehu. Later El Kanemi who, as we shall see, effected a religious revival in Bornu similar to that in Hausaland, was to write to Bello asking him why he should want to carry the Jihad into Bornu, which was a Moslem state under himself, a reformist ruler. He also accused the Fulani of seizing political power in the guise of a religious revolt. El Kanemi's letter, and the reply made to it by Bello, not only illuminate the arguments for and against a Jihad, especially when this concerned attacking avowedly Moslem states, but serve as an excellent illustration of contemporary diplomatic correspondence.

The Holy War of Usman dan Fodio

Perhaps the harshest critique of the revolution came from one of the Shehu's earliest disciples. Abdussalami, who it will be remembered had precipitated Yunfa into attacking the Fulani after his refusal to bless the Gobirawa soldiers, had sought refuge afterwards with the Shehu, where he became one of his closest lieutenants. His initial fervour for the Shehu's Jihad declined in later years, and he took up arms against Bello. The reason he gave for this was that the Jihad had lost its early reformist character. He cited the fact that the best posts in the administration had gone to the Shehu's brother and son, whilst he, an early disciple, had been given nothing.

If anything, its complexity of motives gave the Jihad added force. The old régime crumbled before the Fulani armies which were vigorous though hastily drawn up.

The actual history of the Jihad can be divided into three phases: the consolidation of power in Hausaland and the establishment of the Fulani Empire; the attack on Bornu; and the southward expansion of the Fulani Empire.

Once it became apparent to the King of Gobir that the Fulani were proving a real danger to his own security, he sent out forces to attack them. The Fulani retaliated by raiding outlying Gobirawa villages. The first engagement between the two forces was on 21st June 1804 at Tabkin Kwatto where the Fulani, assisted by the Zamfarawa, defeated the Gobir army. It would seem that this was achieved against great odds for Bello records that the Fulani had only twenty horse, whilst those of the Gobirawa were 'numberless'. This was decisive in its effect on the discontented Fulani throughout Hausaland. The Shehu had demonstrated that Habe kings could be overthrown, and despite his subsequent defeat at Tsuntsuwa he was able to keep the loyalty of his forces. In July 1804, hot from victory at Tabkin Kwatto, he sent what amounted to declarations of intended war to the Habe Hausa kings, urging them to purify their religion.

In 1805 he built a permanent base camp at Sabongari, twenty miles north of the Zamfara capital of Anka. Here he received delegations of Fulani from all over the north. He gave a flag to the leaders of each delegation, blessing them and calling on them to rid the country of unbelievers and to establish Islam throughout Hausaland. The Shehu himself was no soldier and entrusted the army to his brother Abdullahi and his son Bello.

The Holy War of Usman dan Fodio

The ranks of his army were swollen by the faithful as well as the usual band of adventurers that followed any Sudanese army. This curious admixture of religious fanaticism and opportunism accounts for the charges of mass slaughter and plunder that accompanied most Fulani victories. The Shehu was quick to condemn such actions on the part of his followers.

Zamfara, which had been alienated by the attacks on its villages by Fulani forces, joined its old enemy Gobir, together with Kebbi and the Tuareg, in an attempt to suppress the rebellion. The alliance very nearly succeeded when it defeated the Fulani at Alwassa and all but took Gwandu, which had become the Fulani headquarters. However, after these initial successes the Habe kings seemed unable to resist the Fulani forces.

What was the secret of the Fulani strength? How was a scattered immigrant minority able to overthrow the powerful Habe states, with their large standing armies? These are questions to which satisfactory answers will not be forthcoming until further research is made into Jihadi documents. One important factor was the lack of unity among the Hausa kings. Even so, it is remarkable how the Fulani succeeded. As Bello wrote, 'We had none of the *Soudanese* on our side except the people of Zamfara, and the reason for their being so was their enmity to the people of *Gobir*.' Yet the town Fulani were able to organize their own army in such a way that they could defeat the formidable alliances of the 'Soudanese' kings. In the first place there was close contact between the town Fulani and the cattle Fulani. The town Fulani were often the representatives of a large clan, acting on its behalf in the capital of the kingdom in which they were accustomed to pasture their herds. Very often the leading town Fulani owned large herds, and therefore indirectly controlled the considerable number of their nomadic brethren involved in their care. Since the cattle grazed right across Northern Nigeria it was not difficult for the Shehu in remote Gobir to the north-west to have close contacts with town Fulani in Adamawa far to the south-east. The call to revolt was quick to spread, for there were stronger loyalties between town and cattle Fulani in those times than is the case today. Granted these close connections, how were these nomads formed into the formidable fighting force they later became? In the eighteenth century, the social organization of the Fulani differed considerably from that of the small groups which we are accustomed to see nowadays wandering freely over Nigeria. In those days the Fulani sacrificed considerations of good pasture in order to live in semi-permanent settlements. In their migrations eastward to Nigeria they had been subjected to frequent attacks by local kings, particularly the pagan Bambara kings and the Tuareg. In Hausaland they were not infrequently the object of cattle raids by the Habe kings. Their encampments were organized on a defensive basis, and each group had its own militia to guard it in times of attack. Thus, when Usman dan Fodio called on the Fulani to join his Jihad he was not calling on loosely organized peoples, untutored in the art of disciplined warfare, but men who had long experience of fighting in their own defence. What is more these nomads had certain advantages over the standing armies of the Habe kings: in particular their light cavalry was far superior to the heavy cavalry of the Hausa.

By 1807 the Fulani army had brought most of Hausaland under control. One of their earliest successes was in the great kingdom of Zaria, where Mallam Musa, after receiving a flag from the Shehu in 1804, joined forces with a Bornuese Fulani called Yamusa. Almost as soon as they reached the city, the pagan king with all his subjects fled southwards to what has since become Abuja. Today the kings of Abuja are still referred to as Sarkin Zazzau, the name of the state of which Zaria was the capital. In 1805 Muhammedu Fodi, King of Kebbi (1803–26), was driven out of his capital at Birnin Kebbi by Abdullahi, though from his new headquarters at Argungu he offered stubborn resistance that the Fulani were never able to overcome. He was eventually killed by the Fulani twenty-two years later, but he succeeded in maintaining the great Kebbi dynasty, descended direct from Kanta, for his brother Karari became the first Kebbi King of Argungu. Hadeija, north-west of Kano and on the borders of Bornu, submitted to the local Fulani leader Umaru without resistance. And shortly afterwards the neighbouring towns of Kazaure, Garin Gabbas, Gatarwa and Auyo surrendered. The great Hausa cities of Katsina and Kano both fell to the Fulani in 1807. The local leader of the Fulani in Kano sent to the Shehu for a flag in that year, and though the King of Kano was able to control his eastern territories, the Fulani conquered the west with ease. When they met in battle

The Holy War of Usman dan Fodio

at Dan Yahaya the Fulani triumphed and the Habe king fled. The victorious Kano Fulani sent to the Shehu to choose a ruler, since there were several factions among them, making choice difficult. The saintly Shehu asked who was the wisest man among them, and when they replied Sulumanu, servant of their general, the Shehu declared that he should be their Emir.

In Katsina three Fulani leaders, Umaru Dumyawa, Na Alhaji and Umaru Dallaji, went to the Shehu for a flag. All three were given flags, though after quarrels between them Umaru Dallaji took over leadership of the Fulani revolt against the King of Katsina, who fled with many of his people to Maradi, some fifty miles north. From there he and his successors were to harass the Fulani for many years to come. Umaru Dallaji became first Emir of Katsina, whilst the son of Na Alhaji became ruler of the Yandaka area, and Dumyawa overlord of Sandam, to which Maradi paid tribute. All three rulers owed allegiance directly to the Shehu. Throughout Umaru Dallaji's reign, which ended in 1835, he was threatened by the Habe kings of Maradi who had Agades and Zamfara as allies. Indeed, until the separation of Maradi and Katsina by the effective establishment in the 1900's of the Franco-British boundary between Niger and Northern Nigeria, there was no peace between the two. In 1808 Yunfa, King of Gobir, died in battle outside his capital of Alkalawa. This marked the end of the Jihad in Hausaland.

With all the important Hausa states under Fulani domination the foundations of the great Fulani Empire had been laid. In the fighting the Shehu had taken little part; he was rather the philosopher of the revolution, whilst Abdullahi and Bello were its executives. The new empire was divided into two: the Western Sector with headquarters at Gwandu came under the administration of Abdullahi; the Eastern Sector was placed under Bello, who ruled it from Sokoto which the Shehu had made his home. The administration was devolved on these two men, whilst the Shehu returned to his studies.

The first serious check to Fulani expansion eastward came from Bornu. In 1805 the Fulani of the Western Province of Bornu rebelled and were attacked by Mai Ahmed, who at first drove back their leader Ardo Lerlima, but finally, when other Fulani groups joined the attack, was defeated at Nguru, the

Galadima's capital, which the Fulani sacked. This led to a general uprising of the Fulani and a number of small emirates were carved out of Bornu by their leaders. Ibrahim Zaki, who came from an old-establish family in Bornu, founded the emirate of Katagum on the eastern frontiers of Hausaland. Buba Yero, who was given a flag by the Shehu in return for his help against Zamfara in the early days of the Jihad, established himself in southern Bornu in the emirate of Gombe. The most serious threat came from within Bornu. In 1808 the Fulani led by Gwoni Muktar drove the Mai out of his capital of Ngazargamu, which they sacked. At that time it seemed as though Bornu would quickly fall under Fulani domination.

The Fulani were eventually repelled by the leader of a similar cattle-owning, nomadic people, the Kanembu, who came from the old kingdom of Kanem. Under the leadership of El Kanemi they had already formed a small army which attacked the Fulani wherever they seemed strongest. This was a curious situation for their acts were apparently quite unofficial, having no sanction from the Mai of Bornu though they were clearly in his interest. It seems that a possible explanation was jealousy between the two nomadic groups. The Kanembu were as reluctant to be ruled by the Fulani as was the Mai. El Kanemi absorbed the remnants of the defeated royal army into his own, and marched on Ngazargamu, retaking it and killing Gwoni Muktar. In 1810 Mai Ahmed died and was succeeded by Dunama. A period of peace ensued whilst the Fulani consolidated their position in the small frontier emirates. In 1811 Ibrahim Zaki was given a flag with the right to take whatever parts of Bornu he could conquer. In a brilliant campaign he took Ngazargamu once again, but Mai Dunama's forces joined with those of El Kanemi and drove him back to Katagum. Despite succeeding wars the *status quo* in Bornu was fixed by the outcome of this campaign.

El Kanemi had thus become the saviour of Bornu. He established himself near the new capital of Mai Dunama, enjoying great wealth as well as the devotion of the masses.

In 1814, Dunama, in an attempt to shake off this shadow ruler, undertook what Urvoy has described aptly as 'a flight to Varennes', intending to establish himself at a firm base in some distant province. He was caught and deposed, and though the

Sef dynasty ruled until 1846 this marked the real end of their power. Kanemi now exercised all the powers of the old Mai. As Clapperton, who visited Bornu in 1821, remarked, 'The Sultanship of Bornu, however, is but a name; the court still keeps up considerable state, and adheres strictly to its ancient customs, and this is the only privilege left them. When the sultan gives audience to strangers, he sits in a kind of cage, made of the bamboo, through the bars of which he looks on his visitors, who are not allowed to approach within seventy or eighty yards of his person.' Denham and Clapperton were most impressed by the ascetic El Kanemi, effective ruler of Bornu. '. . . no one could have used greater endeavours to substitute laws of reason for practices of barbarity, and, though feared, he is loved and respected. . . . Compared to all around him, he is an angel, and has subdued more by his generosity, mildness and benevolent disposition, than by the force of his arms. . . .'

El Kanemi's first task after repelling the Fulani was to consolidate the greatly weakened empire. Between 1815 and 1824 he re-established his suzerainty over Kanem and Bagarimi. By 1826 Bornu was once more a powerful state, deprived only of its former territories of Gombe, Hadeija, Missau and Katagum. El Kanemi was succeeded by his son Omar, who like his father took the title of Shehu, and ruled through the puppet Mai, Ibrahim. In 1846, after a relatively peaceful reign the small state of Zinder revolted and Mai Ibrahim and his followers took advantage of the situation by calling on the assistance of the Sherif of Wadai. But Omar so manœuvred his troops that he was able to put down both revolts and Mai Ibrahim was executed, his sons having perished in battle. Thus came to an end one of the longest and most distinguished dynasties in African history.

South of Bornu the Fulani were more successful. Buba Yero in Gombe subdued all the surrounding tribes and even made expeditions into Jukun country. Yakubu, Emir of Bauchi, who was the only non-Fulani flag-bearer, likewise subdued all the pagan tribes in the Bauchi area, founding the town of Bauchi as his headquarters in 1809. Friction occurred between him and Buba Yero when the latter pushed his frontiers westwards, and Yakubu had to check him at Beri-Beri. Buba Yero was more successful to the south where for a time even the Fulani of Muri came under his jurisdiction.

The Holy War of Usman dan Fodio

The farthest extent of the Fulani Empire eastward was Adamawa where two important emirates were established, those of Yola and Muri. In 1806 Moddibo Adama travelled to Sokoto to receive a flag from the Shehu; on his return he quickly rallied around him the many Fulani who had settled in the area. He overcame the local pagan tribes with little difficulty. Meanwhile, the Fulani Emir of Muri made more inroads into the territory of the once powerful Jukun Empire, and hastened its already rapid decline, which had been assisted by the ravages of the invading Chamba people from the south-east.

The Fulani faced much greater difficulties in the southward expansion of their empire into Nupe and Yorubaland. In both areas they gained footholds only after years of patient intrigue in local politics.

At the time of the Jihad, Nupe was involved in bitter civil war. Muhammadu, the Etsu or King of Nupe, had just died, and his son Majia succeeded him, only to find himself rivalled by his cousin Jumada, who had established himself with his followers at Rajada on the Niger, opposite the Nupe capital of Rabba. As in all northern territories, the Fulani had settled in Nupe, and a certain Mallam Dendo took up the position of leader of the Jihad in Nupe. He had, however, to work with great care. His opportunity came soon after Etsu Majia had defeated and killed Jumada. Mallam Dendo straightway offered his support to Jumada's son Idirisu, and together they drove Majia out of his capital of Rabba. Mallam Dendo then established henchmen as emirs of Lafiagi and Agaie. Idirisu soon found the Fulani an embarrassment and attempted to drive them out. The Fulani, ever skilful at intrigue, then joined forces with Majia who routed Idirisu, gaining himself recognition as Etsu Nupe at Jengi. The Fulani remained at Rabba.

Mallam Dendo never took the title of Etsu Nupe, though he was effective ruler of much of Nupeland. At his death in 1832 the Fulani were still far from secure in Nupe, and their position was made the more precarious by strife between their various factions. These disputes necessitated the intervention of the Emir of Gwandu on two occasions. Eventually the rival Nupe Etsus were pushed back to two small towns, Zuguma and Pategi, whilst the title of Etsu Nupe was taken over by Mallam Dendo's successors, who ruled from Bida.

The Holy War of Usman dan Fodio

In Ilorin the Fulani gained their foothold by similar methods. The great empire of Oyo was in its first stages of decline, and the governor of Ilorin, the Kakanfo Afonja, tried to assert his independence of Oyo in 1817 for reasons which are discussed at greater length in the next chapter. He was not strong enough to achieve this on his own, so he enlisted the support of an influential Fulani called Mallam Alimi, who was renowned in that area for his piety and learning. With the aid of Mallam Alimi's Hausa and Fulani mercenaries, Afonja had little difficulty in gaining his independence, and when the newly installed Alafin of Oyo, Maku, sent him a warning declaring, 'The new moon has appeared,' he replied impertinently, 'Let the new moon quickly set'. Incidentally it did when, two months later, Alafin Maku committed suicide as was required of all Alafins who suffered defeat in battle. But Afonja was in a precarious position since he depended on Hausa and Fulani mercenaries to support his revolt against Oyo.

It appeared that Mallam Alimi himself had little ambition for power, preferring to rule from behind the scenes as El Kanemi was doing in Bornu. When Afonja, seeing his need for as much military support as he could possibly muster against Oyo, called on Mallam Alimi's sons for assistance, the old man is said to have warned him that his sons might soon covet the throne of Ilorin. These shadow rulers are an interesting phenomenon in the history of the Jihad. Probably the traditional influence of the established rulers in the case of both Bornu and Nupe was too strong for a complete take-over; and in the case of Ilorin the status of Afonja, and the natural reluctance of Yoruba to accept a Fulani ruler, no doubt cautioned Mallam Alimi against deposing him. However, when Mallam Alimi died in 1831 his prophecy about his sons came true, for the eldest, Abdussalami, soon asserted himself in Ilorin. Recognizing the danger, Afonja tried to rid himself of the Hausa and Fulani mercenaries, but because of his earlier alliances against them he failed to get support from other Yoruba chiefs and his forces were defeated. He himself was killed and his body, pierced with arrows, was publicly burnt in the market-place. Abdussalami thus became first Fulani Emir of Ilorin.

By 1830 the Fulani were masters of the whole of modern Northern Nigeria, with the exception of Bornu, parts of Kebbi and Gobir, and the hill areas of the Middle Belt. Much has been written of the decadence and corruption of the Fulani Empire in its later years. There is, as we shall see, some truth in these assertions, which have unfortunately obscured the real virtues of the early years of the Fulani Empire. Probably its greatest achievements were the establishment of a uniform system of government through a vast area of Nigeria which for centuries beforehand had been torn by internecine wars, and the stimulation of commerce under what might be called the Fulani Pax.

The empire was organized by the Shehu on the lines already envisaged in his *Kitab al-Farq*. The former Habe kingdoms, now ruled by Fulani emirs, together with the newly acquired pagan provinces, were held together by common allegiance to the Amir-al-mu'minin, or Leader of the Faithful, at one and the same time spiritual and temporal ruler. Each province paid tribute to Sokoto, and all matters of higher administration were referred to the capital. For the next hundred years the Fulani Empire was ruled on the pattern conceived by the Shehu, though the stability of the early years, and the justice and honesty of administration, did not continue through to the time when the British occupied the North.

Under Bello, who became Sultan of Sokoto on the death of his father in 1817, the Fulani Empire was distinguished by its contrast with the corrupt administration of the Habe kings. Hajji Sa'id wrote of Bello in his *History of Sokoto*: 'He gave all of them their just place, for he was upright and pious. He spent from his own earnings and did not spend from the public purse. He had already said to his father at the start of their Holy War, "Shaik, lawful resources are lacking, and it is essential that you should spend for necessary expenses from this money, but, as for myself, I will earn my own living as I am a young man." He was apprenticed to a craft by which means he became independent of the treasury.... He was kind to his subjects, most merciful to them, patient, self-controlled, scrupulous concerning their property in possession of the people, and a good administrator. He scrutinized the judges, reversing their judgments which were dictated by their own interests, nor did he give them free rein in their posts.'

Fair taxation, good law and an efficient civil service were instituted by Bello. Officials toured the empire, checking on the

The Holy War of Usman dan Fodio

administration of the emirs. In his detailed study of *Government in Zazzau*, Dr. M. G. Smith has shown how Sokoto exercised considerable control over Zaria Emirate. The Sultan was intimately concerned in the election and deposition of its Emirs and interfered in the appointment of officials. He received tribute from them twice a year and frequently summoned them to Sokoto.

Barth's account of Kano, written in the middle of the century, gives an excellent picture of the improved state of trade under the Fulani régime. No longer involved in the constant wars of the eighteenth century, the former Habe states could now trade easily with each other. Kano quickly regained its former position as terminus of the Sahara caravans, and became the chief emporium of the Fulani Empire.

'The principal commerce of Kano consists in native produce, namely, the cotton cloth woven and dyed here or in the neighbouring towns, in the forms of tobes or *rigona* (sing. *riga*): *turkedi*, or the oblong piece of dress of dark blue colour worn by the women; the *zenne* or plaid, of various colours; and the *rawani baki*, or black litham (Tuareg veil).

'The great advantage of Kano is, that commerce and manufactures go hand in hand, and that almost every family has its share in them. There is really something grand in this kind of industry, which spreads to the north as far as Murzuk, Ghat and even Tripoli; to the west, not only to Timbuktu, but in some degree even as far as the shores of the Atlantic, the very inhabitants of Arguin dressing in the cloth woven and dyed in Kano; to the east, all over Bornu, although there it comes in contact with the native industry of the country; and to the south it maintains a rivalry with the native industry of the Igbira and Igbo, while towards the south-east it invades the whole of Adamawa, and is only limited by the nakedness of pagan *sansculottes*, who do not wear clothing.

'As for the supply sent to Timbuktu, this is a fact entirely overlooked in Europe, where people speak continually of the fine cotton cloth produced in that town, while, in truth, all the apparel of decent character in Timbuktu is brought either from Kano or from Sansandi. . . . Besides the cloth produced and dyed in Kano and in the neighbouring villages, there is considerable commerce carried on here with the cloth manufactured in Nyffi

94

or Nupe. . . . The chief articles of native industry, beside cloth, which have a wide market, are principally sandals . . . tanned hides ("kulabu") and red sheep skins, dyed with a juice extracted from the stalks of the holcus, are not unimportant, being sent in great quantities even as far as Tripoli. . . . A very important branch of the native commerce in Kano is certainly the slave-trade; but it is extremely difficult to say how many of these unfortunate creatures are exported, as a greater number are carried away by small caravans to Bornu and Nupe than on the direct road to Ghat and Fezzan. . . .'

Finally the Fulani Jihad brought about a veritable literary revolution. Even though the Fulani were accused of destroying the books of the Habe, a much-debated accusation, there was a great revival of learning under Bello. Moslem divines came from far afield to the court at Sokoto. Hajji Sa'id lists among the learned of his reign several women: 'Of women—Zani Gharka, mother of Al-Bukhari; Inna Gharka, mother of Bello and others.' This was apparently true of the following reigns, for under Aliu Baba he lists 'Nanna son of Fodio', Uthmanu his son-in-law, who had married his daughter Miriam, his mother Ladi, his daughter Miriam, who knew the Koran by heart. . . .'

The revolution of Usman dan Fodio had been a radical one, encouraging the participation of women in society. One of dan Fodio's accusations against the society of the Habe kings in the *Nur al-Albab* was that 'men treat these beings (women) like household implements which become broken after long use . . . this is an abominable crime. Alas—how can they thus shut up their wives, their daughters, and their captives in the darkness of ignorance while daily they impart knowledge to their students?' At heart the Fulani revolution was a revolution of radical intellectuals. Inevitably after the first ardour of revolution wore off it became increasingly materialistic in outlook. Slave-raiding became more frequent, and certain areas were devastated of human beings. Corruption was rife in many emirates. Nevertheless, when the British occupied the north in 1900, they took over the administrative system adapted by the Shehu from the old Habe kingdoms to suit the needs of his vast empire and made it the basis of their system of indirect rule.

CHAPTER VI

Yoruba Civil Wars
(1700—1850)

The dramatic collapse of the authority of the Alafin of Oyo over his provincial kings and tributary states at the beginning of the nineteenth century was touched off by the revolt of Afonja, in Ilorin, aided by the Fulani and resulted in civil wars that were to last throughout the century. The speed with which the Alafin lost control of the situation was the result of much deeper causes than this simple rebellion.

It has been suggested that by 1700 the Oyo Empire was already in decline. This does not appear to be true for the eighteenth century marked the height of Oyo's conquests of her neighbours. Throughout the preceding century Oyo had been dogged by political instability, and burdened by excesses of tyranny comparable to some of the more lurid tales of the *Arabian Nights*. King after king was rejected by the people, but none seemed able to learn from his predecessor's mistakes. Thus, by the middle of the eighteenth century, the people of Oyo were ready for the seizure of power made by the newly appointed Basorun Gaha, who proved equally as tyrannous as the Alafins from whom he snatched power, but who did at least give some stability to the empire.

During the eighteenth century Oyo's authority stretched south-west to the Ashanti states and Dahomey, and north-east to the Niger. Nearly all the towns of western Yorubaland were subject to the Alafin. These towns, which sometimes numbered as many as 20,000 inhabitants, were each ruled by an oba chosen from the lineage of the founder of the town by the chiefs of the other lineage groups. The Alafin was usually represented

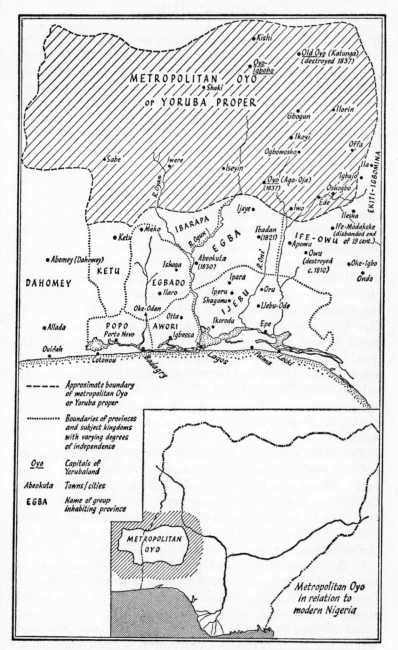

5. Metropolitan Oyo and Yorubaland in the nineteenth century.

by an ilari or intendent who supervised the payment of tribute. Inevitably in a loosely organized empire like that of Oyo many kingdoms were merely nominal subjects of the Alafin, probably only paying tribute in return for the protection Oyo's army could afford them. The position of certain kingdoms, particularly that of Ife, the spiritual home of the Yoruba, is not clear, and much more research will have to be undertaken before it can be established whether Ife was in any way subject to Oyo, or whether in fact it actually exerted an influence on Oyo by virtue of its religious position.

In Oyo the political authority of the Alafin, as we have already seen, was considerably restricted by the Oyo Mesi, or council of notables who exercised right of life and death over him. Should their leader, the Basorun, declare: 'The Gods reject you, the people reject you, the earth rejects you'—then the Alafin was forced to commit suicide. This device was frequently resorted to in the eighteenth century when the rule of the Alafin became excessively tyrannous. Both the Alafin and Oyo Mesi were checked by the Ogboni, a secret society composed of both religious and political leaders, devoted to the worship of the earth. The head of the society had right of access to the Alafin, and the society itself judged any case involving the spilling of blood which was considered an offence against the earth. Furthermore, the society had to sanction certain decisions of the Oyo Mesi, including the rejection of the Alafin.

The Alafin represented authority in its religious, judicial and political aspects through three eunuchs. His decisions were normally arrived at only after consultation with the Oyo Mesi and the various factions they represented. Thus in no sense could the Alafin be compared with the Habe Hausa kings or northern emirs as a fulcrum of power. Attempts to rule on their own were the most frequent cause of rejection of the Alafins.

In the eighteenth century Oyo's main problem was the maintenance of its authority over the young kingdom of Dahomey, founded in about 1625. Its authority depended on its formidable standing army, whose efficacy was described by the Dutch merchant William Bosman in 1698. In that year Alafin Ojigi made war on the tributary state of Great Ardra. Bosman described the army that attacked Porto Novo, the territory's capital, thus:

'These being all Horsed, and a warlike Nation, in a short time mastered half the King of Ardra's territories, and made such a slaughter among his subjects, that the Number of the Dead being innumerable, was commonly express'd by saying, "They were like the Grains of Corn in the Field. . . ." This Nation strikes such a terror into all the circumjacent Negroes, that they can scarce hear them mention'd without trembling: And they tell a thousand strange Things of them.'

Dahomey first defied the authority of the Alafin in 1724 when it invaded Great Ardra in an attempt to gain access to the sea. The Alafin promptly despatched an army, backed up by cavalry, which after initial successes was defeated by the Dahomeyans. Dalzell described the ruse by which Dahomey gained this impressive victory: 'In the morning the Eyeos, seeing the enemy fled, secure of victory, began to burn and plunder the town and to indulge themselves very freely with the treacherous liquor: this soon intoxicated and spread the ground with the major part of their army. At this juncture, the Dahomians, who had timely information of the enemy's disorder, fell upon them with redoubled fury, destroyed a great number, completely routed the rest; and those that escaped, owed their safety to their horses.'

The Dahomeyans were nevertheless frightened of the consequences of this victory and sent presents to appease Oyo. However, in 1727, Dahomey attacked Ouidah in another attempt to gain access to the sea. Ouidah, which had aided Oyo in its attack on Great Ardra in 1698, appealed to the Alafin for help and a second army was despatched against Dahomey. It swept through Dahomey, ransacking its villages, and in 1729 the King of Dahomey sued for peace and promised to pay tribute. This was not paid, and in 1738 Oyo once again invaded Dahomey, laying siege to Abomey the capital. The Dahomeyans tried to make peace, but the Oyo terms were: 40 men, 40 women, 40 guns and 4,000 loads of cowries and corals a year to date with effect from the defeat of 1728. The Dahomeyans would not accept this, but such was the pressure exerted by Oyo that in 1747 Dahomey agreed to pay tribute on these terms.

The subjection of Dahomey coincided with the appointment of Gaha as Basorun by the Alafin-elect, Labisi. Gaha immediately murdered the new king's two chief supporters, so that he was forced to commit suicide. Each succeeding Alafin came increasingly under the influence of this ruthless but capable Basorun. It was not until the accession of Abiodun as Alafin that Gaha met opposition from his nominal master. At first Abiodun accepted his position as figure-head, but quietly plotted against the Basorun with the army commander, Kakanfo Oyabi. On a fixed day all members of the Basorun's family in Oyo and its tributary states were murdered, and the Basorun himself was seized and burnt. According to Dalzell, even pregnant women of the family were 'ripped open and the foetus cut to pieces'.

Abiodun became Alafin in fact as well as in name in about 1785, but though his is recorded as one of the most peaceful reigns in the history of Oyo, the first cracks in the empire were already beginning to show. In 1781 and 1784 King Adahoozu of Dahomey refused to pay tribute. About the same time the Egba declared their independence and successfully repelled the punitive expedition sent by Abiodun. With his death at the end of the century, as Johnson writes, ended 'the universal and despotic rule of the ALAFINS of OYO in the Yoruba country. He was the last of the kings who held the different parts of the kingdom together in one universal sway and with him ended the tranquillity and prosperity of the Yoruba country. The revolution ensued, and the tribal independence with the loss to the Yoruba of the Tapa and Bariba, and Dahomey provinces, and the Popos later on, which has continued to our own day. In a word, with Abiodun ended the unity of the Yoruba kingdom.'

The main reason for the break-up of the Oyo Empire appears to have been the fact that the palace administration of the Alafin and the Oyo Mesi was no longer suited to the vast area and the large number of subordinate and tributary kings they had to control. Furthermore, the axis of the Oyo Empire was shifting southwards. Coastal trade in slaves and European goods was turning the Yoruba away from traditional trade with the north to trade with the coast. The city of Oyo, on the northern borders of the empire, was thus far removed from the new centres of economic power. Not surprisingly the provincial kings itched for their freedom. It seems probable too that tension in the state was aggravated by the infiltration of Islam from Northern Nigeria.

The immediate cause of the disintegration of the Yoruba Empire, as we have seen, was the successful bid by the Kakanfo Afonja to achieve independence for his town of Ilorin. In so doing he was forced to seek the assistance of the Fulani, who further aggravated the tensions. The role of the Fulani in the revolt of Afonja has already been discussed; the Yoruba political aspect is more complicated. Any new Alafin succeeding to the throne was expected to attack a selected enemy who had to be a Yoruba. Thus Abiodun had ordered the destruction of Ijaye, because of an insult flung at him by the Bale's son. Aole, the new Alafin, saw the main danger to his throne coming from Afonja, the army commander and governor of Ilorin, which was strategically placed on the northern borders of Oyo to check the Fulani menace. Aole did not feel strong enough to attack him, nor indeed did he have any valid excuse. However, since Afonja was Kakanfo or army commander and was bound to lead out any army when told to, Aole ordered him to take the almost impregnable town of Iwere. The Alafin was sure Afonja would fail in this task, and knew that if he failed he would have to commit suicide. This order provoked Afonja to murder the royal party which had accompanied him on the expedition and had actually transmitted the Alafin's orders to take Iwere. In this he was joined by a number of other chiefs, for Aole was not popular as Alafin. For a while they procrastinated as to what to do, then they decided to send Aole an empty calabash to indicate that he had been rejected. Aole accepted this and committed suicide, though not before he had uttered a curse that has become memorable in Yorubaland. From the palace forecourt he shot three arrows, one to the north, one to the south and one to the west, crying: 'My curse be on you for your disloyalty and disobedience, so let your children disobey you. If ye send them on an errand, let them never return to bring you word again. To all the points I shot my arrows will ye be carried as slaves. My curse will carry you to the sea and beyond the seas, slaves will rule over you, and ye their masters will become slaves.' Then he smashed an earthenware dish, shouting: 'Broken calabash can be mended but not a broken dish; so let my words be irrevocable.'

From that day for nearly eighty years the Yoruba watched this curse taking horrible effect. Throughout the nineteenth century Yorubaland was torn by civil wars that broke up the old Oyo Empire, obliterated some of the most powerful provincial kingdoms and led to the founding of what today are two of the most important towns in Yorubaland: Abeokuta and Ibadan. Afonja straightway declared his independence of the new Alafin, Adebo. His example was followed by Opele, Bale of Gbogun. Oyo's troubles were further heightened when the only surviving son of Basorun Gaha led a huge force from Bussa country and took Oyo, and would even have taken Ilorin had he not been deserted at the last moment by the Onikoyi. Adebo died while his army was trying to take rebellious Gbogun. Maku succeeded him and was the author of the famous message to Afonja, 'The new moon has risen.' Ironically soon afterwards Maku waged unsuccessful war against Iwo and had to commit suicide.

Every provincial king now seized the opportunity to increase his power and obtain independence of Oyo. Afonja was the only man with anything like the authority of the former Alafins, but as we have seen, to obtain this he played himself into the hands of the Fulani.

Now that the Fulani were effectively in control of Ilorin, they were able to cut off the Yoruba from their traditional supply of slaves from the Niger, and forced them to look for other sources. The breakdown of central authority, and the flare-up of traditional hostilities, were aggravated by the demand for slaves both for domestic purposes and for export. Soon Yoruba were looking to each other for slaves.

Following the death of Afonja there was some attempt to drive back the Fulani who were now complete masters of Ilorin, but so divided were the Yoruba provincial kings that on some occasions they allied with Ilorin against each other, as in the war between Ogbomosho and Ikoyi, when Iwo and Ede joined forces with Ilorin to attack Ikoyi. In 1818 Gezo of Dahomey declared his independence, and by 1821 the Alafin was ruler of Oyo proper alone. The collapse of the central authority of Oyo let loose all the traditional hostilities between towns and the various Yoruba clans. The great wonder is that in this long and vicious series of wars, whose motives and complexities are often difficult to follow, people managed to carry on farming their land, that the unity of Yoruba culture was not destroyed and that indeed the Yoruba remained the vigorous progressive people they are today. Of course it must be remembered that comparatively few people were involved in the fighting, though in the case of the sack of Old Oyo, and the obliteration of Ikoyi and Owu, there were hundreds of refugees.

For a simpler understanding of the complex wars that lasted from 1821 to 1893 it is convenient to name the chief participants. To the north was Ilorin, outpost of the Fulani Empire, intent on carrying the Jihad into Yorubaland. Close by was Oyo, ancient imperial metropolis seeking both to reassert its former authority, and later, after its people were forced to move south, to re-establish itself. To the west was Dahomey, the powerful slaving state, participating in any war which provided opportunities for capturing slaves. To the south and bordering on the coast were the Egba and Ijebu, now placed in a strategic position to act as middle-men for the export of slaves to the coast and for the import of firearms with which to continue the wars. In the east lay many kingdoms, some of which were now independent of the Alafin, some of which had never been under his influence. These, too, became embroiled in the general holocaust, both as slave-raiders and sources of supply for slaves. In the course of the war there emerged two major cities, one of them, Ibadan, destined to be the saviour of Yorubaland from the Fulani, the other, Abeokuta, destined to be the stepping-stone for Christian influence in Yorubaland.

The first of the inter-tribal wars was the Owu war. The Onikoyi, the leading provincial king, ordered the Owu to attack some Ife towns that had been engaging in indiscriminate slave-trading with the Ijebu. This naturally incurred the anger of the Oni of Ife who, thinking that he would easily conquer the Owu, marched against them only to be severely defeated. However, there was some altercation between the Owu and some powerful Ijebu traders, as a result of which the Owu took and destroyed Apomu. The Ijebu then joined forces with the remnants of the Ife army and Oyo refugees fleeing from the Fulani and, armed with guns, drove back the cutlass-swinging Owu. They laid siege to their town and destroyed it (*c.* 1825).

The Owu were chased into Egba territory, where for nearly ten years there ensued a series of battles, invariably alleged to have begun because of some injustice, but more often than not inspired by the desire for slaves. Egba and Gbagura towns were destroyed willy-nilly as undisciplined freebooting armies rampaged across the country-side and thousands were rendered homeless or taken as slaves.

In about 1829 the Ijebu, Ife and Oyo forces settled at the small Gbagura town of Ibadan, into which some of the homeless Egba also moved.

The chief of this polyglot settlement was Maye, an Ife man. He was a considerable leader but was jealous of the Oyo whose leader, Lakanle, was fortunately able to stand up to him. It is not surprising therefore that civil war soon broke out, and when an Egba leader had shot an Ife chief, the Egba decided to leave for what was to become Abeokuta, or 'the town under the Rock', led by Sodeke, a hunter. The new town, founded in 1830, comprised several communities: the Egba-Alake, the Egba-Oke-Ona, the Gbagura and the Owu refugees. They set up a federal form of government, in which the chiefs of each community participated, though Sodeke remained their acknowledged leader. Both the Ibadan and the Ijebu did their best to destroy this new settlement, the Ijebu being particularly jealous of this potential rival to their monopoly as middlemen in trade with the coast. In Ibadan itself there were further disputes, from which the Oyo section emerged supreme. Maye was executed and a civil government instituted. From then on Ibadan grew to be the most important town in Yorubaland, closely associated with Oyo, though never subordinate to it.

The Yoruba might well have defeated the Fulani and driven them out of Ilorin, if only they had not been so divided amongst themselves. They were never able to unite against the enemy. Indeed, if the three powerful kings of Ikoyi, Gbogun and Ago-Oja had for once combined they might have stemmed the Fulani menace, but they chose to make alliances where they saw the greatest opportunity of personal aggrandizement. It was not a paying policy, for very shortly Ikoyi, once the premier provincial kingdom, was captured by Ilorin. The succession in Ikoyi was disputed, the Alafin supporting one claimant, the Ilorin the other. The result was that the Ilorin attacked and killed the Onikoyi approved by the Alafin and appointed their own candidate, Soyenbola, as his successor. The only town now powerful enough to resist the Fulani was Gbogun but the Fulani soon took it, forcing Edun, the greatest Yoruba general of his day, to flee.

Ilorin was thus able to subjugate many of the important towns of Yorubaland. Abdussalami, the Emir, tried to make inroads into Ijesaland, but he was unsuccessful, since the Fulani horse could not operate easily in the hilly and wooded country of that area. Refugees from the northern towns and from Oyo flooded south to Ife, and such was the apparent folly of the civil conflict at the time that the Oni of Ife, with the Fulani at his back door, insisted on humbling the Oyo by making them undertake the most menial of tasks and selling them into slavery. A later Oni however permitted them to settle outside Ife, and there they built the town of Modakeke, defended by a huge wall. With reason, the Ife were furious with their Oni for allowing the Oyo to build a town which they realized might soon become a menace to their own security. They poisoned the Oni and set out against Modakeke, but were repulsed. Once again the Ife attacked, this time to be so severely defeated that Ife, original home of the Yoruba, was deserted.

It is almost impossible to outline the tangled skein of civil strife at this time. The most important event in the decade 1830–40 was the destruction of Old Oyo. Oluewu became Alafin in succession to Amodo who, it is said, died of a broken heart when fire destroyed the Afin (palace) and all its treasures. When Abdussalami tried to force Oluewu to become a Moslem, the latter secured alliances with Borgu and Nikki in a final and bitterly unsuccessful effort to throw off the Fulani yoke. In 1837 Old Oyo was sacked, and today almost nothing remains of 'Katunga', the great metropolis of Yorubaland. Once again the failure of Yoruba chiefs to support the Alafin in his hour of crisis ruined his chances of success even before he had started fighting.

The new site for Oyo was chosen by Atiba, son of Abiodun, who despite his career as a freebooter, was chosen as Oluewu's successor. He selected the town of Ago Oja where he had lived since he was a child. He collected all the Oyo refugees around him, and on pain of death forced all the villages for miles around Ago Oja to move into the new capital. The ruler of Ibadan, also an Oyo, was made Basorun out of deference to his city's immense power. The Ibadan were to protect the north-east and the Ekiti and Ijesa were placed under them. Ijaye was to protect the south-west, whilst the Alafin, who was no longer to go personally to the wars, was responsible for Iluku, Gboho, Kihisi and Saki, where many Oyo refugees were living. The chief of Ijaye was made Kakanfo.

With the foundation of New Oyo, a turn in the fortunes of Yorubaland became evident. The Ibadan defeated the Ilorin at Oshogbo, *c.* 1840, when the latter were laying siege to that town. This victory in fact halted the Fulani advance to the sea, and though there were many battles in the following fifty years, the Fulani were never able to make the easy inroads into Yoruba territory that they had made in the previous three decades. The Alafin failed to follow up this success and even in the hour of triumph civil war broke out once more. Finally the only people who had been able to live in peace in these troubled times, the Ekiti, were brought into the war, when Ilorin attacked them. At the same time the powerful Basorun at Ibadan began plotting to wrest the throne from the Alafin. Though the Alafin was apparently not perturbed by this, Kurumi the Kakanfo of Ijaye, greatest Yoruba general of the day and a man in tent on carving out a kingdom for himself, resented any further increase in the strength of the Basorun, and it was hardly surprising that a move on the part of some Ibadan to occupy a ruined town between Ijaye and Oyo provoked war between the two cities of Ibadan and Ijaye in 1844. This war lasted two years, and so deep were the internal divisions in Yorubaland that the Ibadan at one stage called on their enemies the Ilorin as allies.

In the south-east the Dahomeyans, once tributaries of the Alafin, were expanding their vigorous kingdom, whose main source of revenue was from the sale of slaves. They attacked Otta in 1845. Three years later they captured the town, carrying off its inhabitants as slaves. But their first serious invasion of Yorubaland was the 1851 attack on Abeokuta. Taking advantage of Ibadan's preoccupation with the north in a war against the Ilesha that did not finally come to an end until 1854, the Dahomeyans marched on Abeokuta, a column of Amazons at their head. The Dahomeyan Amazons, a unique feature in the history of West African armies, were originally superfluous wives of the King used first as bodyguards and then to swell the ranks of the army. During the nineteenth century there were usually as many as from 3,000 to 8,000 Amazons, and in the army that attacked Abeokuta 6,000, out of a total strength of 16,000, were women. At the time Abeokuta was in no state to withstand this impressive army, and without the aid of a cunning Oba of Isiaga, through whose town the Dahomeyans passed, the city would certainly have fallen. The Isiaga people persuaded the Dahomeyans to attack the south wall, which was, in fact, the only wall with good defences. At first the Dahomeyans looked like taking the town, and it was really only the discovery that they were fighting women that spurred the Abeokutans into the final resistance that drove off the Dahomeyan army. However, the most significant factor in this was the part played by Britain. Not only had the British Consul, Beecroft, visited King Gézo of Dahomey in an attempt to persuade him to give up slaving, but he had also issued ammunition to the Egba army through the missionaries stationed there. Indeed, without the aid of the British Consul and the missionaries it is doubtful whether the Egba could have saved Abeokuta from destruction by the far better equipped Dahomeyans. British intervention in the first Dahomeyan invasion of Abeokuta marked the beginning of a new era in the history of the civil wars in Yorubaland.

CHAPTER VII

The Suppression of the Slave Trade

The abolition of the slave-trade by Britain in the first half of the nineteenth century laid the foundations of her legitimate commercial relations with West Africa, and eventually led her to establish herself politically along the West African coast, the most important stretch of which was that of modern Nigeria. The abolition of the slave-trade by Britain in 1807 seems paradoxical when it is remembered that at the turn of the century she was the chief carrier of slaves from West Africa.

The decision of 1807 was the climax of thirty years of agitation in Britain against the slave-trade. Before 1772 few people had had any conscience about it. So far removed was the common Englishman from the conduct of the slave-trade with the attendant horrors of the Middle Passage and the cruel system of labour in the plantations, that it is hardly surprising that he rarely questioned its morality. In 1729 the question of the rights of slaves on British soil had been considered by the Solicitor General and the Attorney General, whose opinion was that a slave did not become free by coming to Britain, and remained the property of his master. However, there were a few people in Britain who were not content with this interpretation of the law. And in 1772, as a result of Granville Sharp's one-man crusade against the institution of slavery, a test case was brought before Lord Chief Justice Mansfield to establish whether a slave had freedom under the laws of Britain. This was the case of *Somersett* v. *Knowles*. Somersett, a negro, had run away from his master, who recaptured him and clapped him in irons on board a ship bound for the West Indies. Granville Sharp learnt of this and took out a writ of habeas corpus for Somersett, which was heard by the Lord Chief Justice. In his judgment, Mansfield, who before his elevation to the peerage had been Yorke, the Attorney General responsible for the 1729 opinion, ruled that once a slave set foot on British soil he became free. This was the starting-point of the movement for the abolition of the slave-trade which had for years been fundamental to the plantation economies of the colonies of the great European powers.

In 1776 a motion was moved in the House of Commons that 'the slave-trade is contrary to the laws of God and the rights of man'. It failed, and it was left to ardent social reformers like William Wilberforce, M.P., Thomas Clarkson and Granville Sharp to carry on the struggle against this long-established trade. In 1787 they formed the Society for the Abolition of the Slave Trade, and with Wilberforce as their agent in Parliament began to lobby for abolition. Though Wilberforce gained the sympathy of William Pitt and Charles James Fox, it took him twenty years to secure a majority in the House.

Before it the society had the formidable opposition of the vested interest of the slave-trade. Liverpool and Bristol both depended largely on it for their income, and many members of the government were deeply involved in it. Indeed, eighteenth-century economists believed that the wealth of the West Indies, which depended on the slave-trade, was fundamental to the strength of the British Empire. Certainly the triangular trade between Africa, the West Indies and Britain supplied some of the necessary capital to finance the industrial revolution.

How then did the abolitionists persuade Parliament to do away with what was apparently a vital factor in the British economy? The end of the eighteenth century was a time of new ideas in Europe. America had just broken away from England. The foundations of the French Revolution were being laid by the radical and revolutionary ideas of Liberty, Equality and Fraternity. The rights of the individual, as in Thomas Paine's *The Rights of Man*, were being bandied about in pamphlet and newspaper. Not unnaturally a public receptive of such arguments was also likely to be receptive of the idea that negroes were also men and that the slave-trade was wrong. Certainly they were shocked to read of its brutality in accounts like that of Falconbridge, who had been a surgeon on a slaver. But even then the interests involved seem too great to have been overcome by the zeal of Wilberforce and his small but ardent band of abolitionists. Did Wilberforce really succeed in changing the attitude of a nation? Did he really touch the conscience of Parliament? It hardly seems possible in a nation that carried on public executions of children for petty theft right up till the middle of the century and instituted a system of child factory labour which, in many cases, was far worse than the lot of the slave on the sugar plantation. It is not to belittle Wilberforce and the humanitarians to suggest that in fact by the time of his campaign the odds against him were not so overwhelming as has commonly been suggested. The fact is Britain was really economically ready for this change-over from an economy of mercantilism, based largely on the India trade and slave-carrying between Africa and the West Indies, to that of the first industrial nation in Europe. A good example of this change-over is Liverpool which, at the time of abolition, was already diverting many of her ships to trading in cotton with America. Britain as an industrial nation had greater interests in the opening of markets for her manufactured goods and the slave-trade was not conducive to the expansion of the West African market. Significantly the hostility of the British Government to trading in slaves by other nations did not prevent it from allowing Manchester goods to be used by such nations as their main means of exchange for slaves. Britain had another great interest in stopping the slave-trade: she needed palm oil as a lubricant for her factories and for soap. While slave-trading continued, production in the oil-growing areas of the interior of West Africa would always be hampered. It was therefore very much in the interests of Britain to check slavery in order to permit the economic exploitation of the coast.

It is significant also that neither Bristol nor Liverpool collapsed as a result of the cessation of the slave-trade; and relatively few English ships found it worth while to engage in privateering as slave-dealers after abolition. One notorious French slaver, Théodore Carnot, complained that the British combined suppression of the slave-trade with the promotion of their own commerce in adulterated Manchester goods. Despite these commercial motives, 'the unweary, unostentatious and inglorious crusade of England against slavery', as the historian Lecky has written, 'may probably be regarded as among the three or four perfectly virtuous pages comprised in the history of nations'.

It was one thing for Britain to proclaim the legal abolition of the slave-trade, quite another to persuade other nations to follow suit. Britain tried to bring the slave-trade to an end both by treaty with other powers and by seizing ships actually carrying slaves. In certain cases other nations followed Britain by abolishing the slave-trade. Denmark had actually declared it illegal in 1804. The U.S.A. abolished it in 1808, Sweden in 1813, and the Netherlands in 1814. But official abolition did not stop slavers from operating on the coast. In defiance of the law many American ships crossed the Atlantic with human cargo over the next fifty years. Thus Britain had to undertake the establishment of an anti-slavery patrol on the west coast to capture slaving-ships. In 1817 she secured from Spain and Portugal treaties which agreed to the reciprocal rights of search and the subsequent condemnation of ships if they were found with slaves on board. This often had horrific results, since slavers were liable to discharge their human cargo into the ocean if capture seemed imminent. Later, fortunately, treaties were secured which allowed the condemnation of ships if slaving equipment was found on board. Even so the patrol was largely ineffective in its early years and the figures of slaves exported from West Africa, far from decreasing, actually rose steeply.

Two problems therefore confronted Britain. First was the difficult diplomatic tangle over the right of search; second was the smallness of the patrol for so lengthy a coastline. For operational purposes the coast was divided into three strips: from Senegal to Sierra Leone; from Sierra Leone to Cape Coast Castle; and from Cape Coast Castle to the Line (Equator) beyond which treaty powers ceased. This last was known as the Bights Division. The coast was an unpopular station, and to encourage the anti-slavery patrol the 1807 Act provided for generous rewards for the capture of slavers. But by 1824, when abolitionist enthusiasm was waning under the mistaken impression that the slave-trade was dying a natural death, the bounty was reduced from £60 for a rescued male slave to £10. In 1830 it was further reduced to £5. Nevertheless, the Navy did capture a large number of slavers, towing them to Freetown where they were brought up before the Court of Mixed Commission which was empowered to condemn them. Freetown had been established by the Society for the Abolition of the Slave Trade as a settlement for freed slaves. Despite the inconvenience of taking ships from the Bights of Benin and Biafra on the long leg up the coast to Freetown the British government insisted on keeping it as its base for the suppression of the slave-trade.

The abolition of the slave-trade by the country that hitherto had been its chief practitioner came as a profound shock to many African chiefs who had looked to Britain as their best customer. When the kindly and successful British slaver, Captain Hugh Crow, arrived in Bonny on his last visit, he informed his old friend King Pepple of Britain's decision to abolish the trade. Pepple replied, 'We tink trade no stop, for all the Ju-Ju men tell we so, for demn say you country can niber pass God A'mighty.' And as late as 1842 Lieutenant Levine of the West African Naval Squadron said that Africans in the Delta often asked him whether England was at war with the other nations of Europe. 'They cannot understand why we take them (the slavers). We carried on the slave-trade so shortly before ourselves, that I do not think they clearly understand why we should be so anxious to suppress it now.'

Not surprisingly few of the chiefs took much notice of Britain's change of heart. There were other customers. Indeed, in the ensuing economic war between the slavers on the one hand and the British legitimate traders on the other, 'what determined the side the Africans took', as Dr. Kenneth Dike has written, 'was the importance or otherwise of the trade to the economy of the country'. Certainly the presence of the naval squadron at the various mouths of the Niger did not at first deter Bonny, which had become the leading slaving port on the coast, from dealing with Spaniards, Portuguese and American slavers, as well as a polyglot bunch of pirates and privateers. Bonny was the chief offender, though even she tried to get the best of both worlds. In 1826 12 slavers and 12 British merchantmen were reported in Bonny waters.

Inevitably there was bitter competition between the slavers and the legitimate traders. Life was difficult for the latter, for whenever a slaver arrived, even in Calabar which by the 'twenties had largely devoted itself to trade in palm oil and timber, everyone rushed to meet the slavers' requirements.

The Suppression of the Slave Trade

Farther up the coast Lagos and Badagry flourished as they had never done before on the profits of the slave-trade. Civil war amongst the Yoruba, wars between Yoruba and Fulani, Egba and Dahomeyans kept a plentiful supply of slaves for the markets of Brazil and Cuba. Even here the rivalry between legitimate traders and slavers was keen.

These attempts at the suppression of the slave-trade, despite their early inadequacy, were to bring about a complete revolution in the economy of the African slaving states. A new economic order based on trade in the products of the West African forests was ushered in. However, the old trading organization that was built up to deal with the slave-trade was taken over unmodified to cope with the new trade in palm oil. While Bonny rose to the position of chief slave port on that part of the coast, Calabar compensated for her loss by exporting palm oil. In 1828 she exported 2,000 tons whilst Bonny exported almost none. However, by the 1830's Bonny, which was still the chief slaving state, was whittling away Calabar's early lead. Her traders switched from slaves to oil as the market demanded. New oil markets were developed by the coastal traders, who usually exercised a monopoly over them. In addition to palm oil these traders sold timber, ivory and bees-wax to the British ships.

Britain's growing interest in the promotion of legitimate trade saw a gradual change of both official and commercial attitudes towards the local rulers, who in the past had been accustomed to having their sovereignty completely respected by the European slave-traders. In 1824 Captain Owen, who was significantly given the task of surveying the coast of Africa by the British Admiralty, anchored in Bonny waters, and sent a junior officer to tell King Opobo he had arrived. The King was furious at this breach of etiquette, and resented deeply the fact that British ships had anchored in Bonny waters without his permission. In retaliation he ordered the complete cessation of trade with the British. Though the affair was ultimately settled amicably, it indicated a new trend in British attitudes to West African chiefs. Later in 1836 the Navy, now backed up by the Equipment Treaty which allowed them to take Spanish and Portuguese ships as slavers if they were carrying the appropriate equipment, seized some Spanish ships waiting for slaves in Bonny. A tremendous dispute over this infringement of sovereignty arose between the responsible naval officer, Lieutenant Tryon, and the King, who was naturally supported by the Spaniards. He ordered the arrest of Lieutenant Tryon and threw him into jail. The Navy promptly sailed into Bonny and forced the King to sign a treaty ensuring the protection of life and property of British subjects. This was the thin end of the wedge. Legitimate trade was becoming so important that the British government in order to make it secure was prepared to usurp the power of the coastal chiefs. By 1834 Britain's trade in palm oil was worth £500,000, a huge sum for those days, and she was not going to be without control of its source. Such was the concentration of naval force at the mouth of the River Bonny by the end of the thirties, that Bonny was compelled, at least outwardly, to cease her traffic in slaves. Indeed Britain's treatment of Bonny may be taken as typical of her new attitude to African states. In 1837 the British secured the deposition of Alali, the Regent of Bonny, in favour of the King who had been a minor when Alali took over power. Alali had in fact become very unpopular with the oil-producing tribes of the interior as a result of which trade was becoming very slack. The new King, it was felt, would be more favourable to British trading interests. In 1839 a treaty abolishing the slave-trade was signed with Bonny; but it was never ratified since the Navy believed that the compensation offered for the loss of trade would in fact be used to finance it further. In 1841 a new treaty was negotiated abolishing the slave-trade with the important proviso that 'if at any future time Great Britain shall permit the slave-trade to be carried on, King Pepple and the Chiefs of Bonny shall be at liberty to do the same'. This treaty, too, was not ratified and King Pepple never received his compensation. The existence of the patrol at the mouth of the River Bonny made it difficult for King Pepple to carry on the trade openly, but he and his chiefs cunningly diverted their trade to the small, concealed state of Brass which exported hundreds of slaves to Brazil and Cuba. By 1844 such were British encroachments on Bonny that even King Pepple, who owed his position to the British, was complaining of their interference. That same year a treaty abolishing the slave-trade was ratified on the spot, the only condition under which Pepple would sign.

The Suppression of the Slave Trade

It is significant, too, that in 1842 Palmerston tried to re-acquire Fernando Po as a base to watch over the oil river ports and to give British traders protection. The earlier settlement there had been abandoned at a time when legitimate trade was not so important.

By the 1840's a large section of the British fleet was engaged in the anti-slavery patrol in West African waters. The ensuing decade, 1840–50, was critical both for the suppression of the slave-trade and the establishment of British interests in Nigeria. The growth of legitimate trade during the period in which Britain was busily suppressing slavery is most significant. In 1820 there were 38 British merchantmen trading in the Bights of Benin and Biafra. In 1840 there were 134. Oil exports had increased from 200 tons in 1808 to 13,945 in 1834 and 25,285 in 1845. It is apparent that Britain was looking increasingly towards West Africa as a profitable area for trade.

Despite Britain's growing commercial interest in West Africa, the suppression of the slave-trade nearly suffered disastrous setbacks in the decade 1840–50. In 1839 an English captain and ardent abolitionist called Denman actually destroyed a slaver's barracoon in an attempt to attack the slave-traders at the very source of their supply. In 1841 Captain Nurse followed suit and raised a barracoon on the Rio Pongos, but in the process he destroyed a considerable amount of foreign property. The foreigners declared themselves legitimate traders, and in England, the country of merchants *par excellence*, there was an outcry against Nurse's action on the grounds that it endangered the growth of legitimate trade. Aberdeen, the British Foreign Secretary at the time, then decided that the Navy should refrain from such actions unless the chiefs in whose waters these barracoons were sited agreed by treaty to their destruction. This, then, marked the beginning of a new phase in the suppression of the slave-trade. The Navy started to make treaties with the coastal chiefs to gain their consent to the suppression of the slave-trade. Later this system of treaty-making was to be used in the establishment of the British Protectorate over Nigeria.

All was not well for the abolitionists. In 1846 Peel's Tory government reduced the import duty on sugar which in effect increased demand for it in England and therefore the demand for slaves to work on the sugar plantations of Cuba. Statistics bear this out: it is estimated that in 1842 only 24,800 slaves were exported from West Africa. By 1847 there were 84,356.

In the mid-nineteenth century there was a sharp conflict between humanitarians and traders. All went well when their interests coincided; but when, as in the case of the Sugar Act, they conflicted, humanitarian interests suffered. During the forties the West African Squadron came under frequent criticism, particularly because of its cost. Even those with humanitarian interests attacked it, because at times it apparently worsened conditions for slaves, who would be thrown overboard the moment a ship of the squadron gave chase to a slaver. There was a strong commercial faction that felt that British trade with Brazil would be seriously endangered if Brazil did not obtain slaves, the main prop of her plantation economy. A Member of Parliament called Hutt led these diverse factions in an attempt to have the squadron withdrawn, and in 1849 his Select Committee decided by one vote that the squadron should be called off and diplomatic pressure and missionary enterprise should be used to check the slave-trade in its stead. In the Lords, Bishop Wilberforce managed to set up a rival committee which rejected Hutt's decision. When the reports of both Houses came up before the Commons Lord John Russell made it a vote of confidence in his government to reject Hutt's motion for the withdrawal of the squadron, so that it was defeated.

The result of the defeat of Hutt's motion for the abolition of the slave squadron was, in fact, an increase in zeal for the cause of suppression. There were fresh diplomatic approaches to foreign powers and an increasing number of treaties were made with West African chiefs. One naval captain considered that without a naval squadron on the West Coast 'the coast would become a nest of pirates; the number of slaves exported would be enormous; all legitimate trade would cease, and in a very short time we would have to increase the squadron for the protection of what trade remained'.

By the 1850's slave-trading had largely been abolished in Old Calabar, with whom official treaties had been negotiated. In Bonny, which was increasingly subjected to British political pressure, it had gone under cover. Farther up the coast, Lagos was still a sore spot. By the mid century the slave squadron had completed much of its work. Britain had supplied the slave ports with an alternative trade—that in palm oil. Between 1830 and 1850 legitimate trade had increased by 87 per cent. But the traders in palm oil, known as the palm-oil ruffians, were little different from the slavers themselves. They lived the same precarious existence on the fringe of Africa. They never penetrated inland. A great new field of commerce in the interior still remained to be exploited. This was the result of the enterprise of explorers, missionaries, and traders, African and European. The next three chapters will deal with the role of these three groups—explorers, missionaries and traders—in laying the foundation on which the British government was to build modern Nigeria.

CHAPTER VIII

Explorers and Missionaries

The movement in Britain for the abolition of the slave-trade was accompanied by the desire to find markets for Britain's new industries. At first the marketing of these goods was handled entirely by the African middlemen of the coastal kingdoms, who secured their monopoly on the basis of their exclusive knowledge of conditions in the interior and the fact that the climate was too unhealthy for Europeans to penetrate beyond the coastal fringe. However, as Britain's trading interests grew in Nigeria, so did the desire of her merchants to trade direct with the markets of the interior. The history of the nineteenth century in Nigeria is primarily that of the resistance of African kings and middlemen to penetration of the interior by European traders. That these traders did in fact overcome this resistance was in the first instance largely due to the pioneer work of explorers and missionaries.

It is not surprising when one considers Britain's needs for overseas markets in the first half of the nineteenth century that many of the leading names in the history of the exploration of the West African hinterland should be either British or those of men like the German, Barth, who were sponsored by the British government. The pioneers of inland trade were the great explorers like Mungo Park, Clapperton, the Lander brothers, Barth and Baikie. Their main problem was to discover an inland highway for trade into West Africa. Their attention was focused on the still legendary Niger.

The exploration of this great river dates from the founding of the African Association in 1788. This association represented a multiplicity of interests, such as politicians, scientists and humanitarians. But the chief object of the society was the pro-

118

motion of commerce and significantly one of its founder members was Josiah Wedgwood, an architect of the industrial revolution in Britain. Humanitarians were strongly represented on the board by Fox, Wilberforce and Clarkson. Although there was no direct reference to the abolition of the slave-trade in the objectives of the association, the humanitarians intended to use it to further their own ends, for they believed that the promotion of legitimate trade was necessary to fill the vacuum that would be left by the suppression of the slave-trade.

The importance of the African Association, which was given the backing of Pitt, must be seen against contemporary political developments in the British Empire. Britain had just lost her American colonies, and was looking to India as an alternative outlet for her economic expansion. Australia had just been discovered and British interests in the Far East were increasing. Geographically Africa lay in the path of the main axis of British trade. It was thus of a high strategic interest, heightened twelve years later by the Napoleonic Wars. It was not surprising, then, that the British government gave the African Association its support. But the motives of the association cannot be dismissed as merely political and economic. Its president was Sir Joseph Banks, an outstanding scientist who had accompanied Captain Cook on his voyage to the South Pacific.

The specific object of the association was to organize the exploration of the interior of Africa. At the time West Africa was almost a *carte blanche* and had been used as such by the more imaginative pictorial geographers of the preceding centuries, who dotted the land with mythical cities, and often more mythical lakes and seas that were to confuse considerably the determination of the source of the Niger, which, because it was hoped it might prove a major highway of trade into Africa, became the chief object of the association's attentions. In 1788 it was believed that the Niger flowed to the west, as Leo Africanus had reported several centuries before. The Gambia and the Senegal Rivers therefore appeared as its most obvious outlets. In an attempt to discover the Niger, the association equipped expeditions to cross the desert, all of which were tragically un-successful. Others were sent to the west coast to attack the problem, as it were, from its southern side. Tragedy also struck the first explorer on this route, Major Houghton, who was murdered either by local people in the Gambia or by slave-dealers, but not before he had sent back sufficient information to suggest that the Niger might flow to the east. It was left to Mungo Park, a young Scotsman, whose two journeys into the interior of West Africa have earned for him next to Livingstone the most celebrated place in the history of African exploration, to discover the Niger. Inspired by an incredible determination, which allowed him to suffer the unendurable in the firm belief it was predestined by God, he succeeded in reaching the Niger. Even when he had been robbed of all his belongings, and was sick with fever and deserted by his followers, he did not give up his quest for the Niger. Finally, after a hellish journey, he came 'through some marshy ground where, as I was anxiously looking around for the river, one of them called out *geo affili* (see the water); and looking forwards, I saw with infinite pleasure the great object of my mission; the long sought for, majestic Niger, glittering to the morning sun, as broad as the Thames at Westminster, and flowing slowly to the *Eastward*. I hastened to the brink, and having drunk of the water, lifted up my fervent thanks in prayer, to the Great ruler of all things, for having thus far crowned my endeavours with success.'

This discovery was to set the world of armchair geographers abuzz. Hitherto it had been taken for granted that the Niger flowed to the west.

Major Rennell propounded the theory that the Niger flowed into a great lake—the sink of Africa—where it simply evaporated. However his theory, which gained wide recognition, was opposed by the German geographer Reichard, who correctly stated that the huge delta of rivers in the Bight of Benin was the Niger's outlet into the sea.

The African Association declared that as a result of Park's discovery 'a gate is opened to every commercial nation to enter and trade from the West to the eastern extremity of Africa'. Therefore when Park, who had subsequently become a doctor in Peebles, volunteered to return to the Niger and seek its outlet, the association accepted his services eagerly and the British government put up the money for a lavishly and, as it eventually turned out, farcically equipped expedition. Park set off this time not alone but with a band of forty-five Europeans, fully equipped to construct a boat in which the party would sail down the Niger to its source. The expedition was a disaster, a monument to bad organization. Park, brave and capable of much suffering himself, was incapable of understanding the needs of others, and before he himself was murdered on the Bussa rapids in Northern Nigeria, every man in his party but his Mandingo servant Isaaco had died. Fortunately the devoted Isaaco made his way back to the coast and delivered up Park's manuscript to the British government. At the time Park's achievement of travelling eight hundred miles from Timbuktu to Bussa was not appreciated, since contemporary geographers estimated it at only a tenth of the actual distance.

The problem of the Niger was left aside during the Napoleonic Wars. However, the end of those wars saw a revival of interest in the termination; but an unsuccessful expedition by Major Peddie following Park's old route dampened the British government's enthusiasm, which only really revived in 1821 when Denham, Clapperton and Oudney left for Nigeria across the Sahara. That same year a West Indian planter named M'Queen became a champion of the theory that the Niger's outlet was in the Bight of Benin, deducing this from reports his slaves had given him. Crossing from Tripoli, the Denham-Clapperton expedition at first seemed to justify Rennell's theory, for in 1823 they discovered Lake Chad, supposedly 'the vast sink of Africa'. However, when they followed the river that fed this lake they found that it dwindled to a mere trickle after a short distance.

In Bornu, Denham and Clapperton were received by El Kanemi, who actually wrote to King George IV saying that he would welcome four or five traders from England in his country: 'The Rayes Khaleel (Major Denham travelled under this name) desired of us permission, that merchants seeking for elephant-teeth, ostrich feathers, and other such things, that are not to be found in the country of the English, might come among us. We told him that our country, as he himself has known and seen its state, does not suit any heavy (rich) traveller, who may possess great wealth. But if a few light persons (small capitalists), as four or five only, with little merchandize, would come, there will be no harm. This is the utmost that we can give him permission for; and more than that number must not come.'

The party was greatly impressed by the vast array of chain-mailed horsemen under the command of the Shehu. Clapperton and Oudney, who died shortly after, moved on into Hausa country. Clapperton arrived at the great metropolis of Kano eager with anticipation. He was extremely anxious to look his best on entering this city which frankly, after the tales he had heard from Arab traders, disappointed him. He dressed in his best naval uniform but 'not an individual turned his head round to gaze at me, but all intent on their own business, allowed me to pass without notice or remark'. In Kano he noted that the only foreign goods on sale were French, German and Italian.

Clapperton moved on to Sokoto, the capital of the great Fulani Empire, ruled over by the scholarly Sultan Bello, who was able to tell him much about the country. Though he would not allow Clapperton to leave for the Niger, he expressed a desire to establish commercial relations with the British, and asked that a consulate be established in Sokoto. Clapperton left a happy man and joined Denham, who had gone south along the Shari River which he confused with the Benue, the main tributary of the Niger. Clapperton had every reason to be pleased with himself. He had been promised commercial relations with Sokoto; he had been told by Sultan Bello that he would have no difficulty in reaching the sea by the Niger; and a consulate had been established in Bornu. The party left a Mr. Tyrwhitt, who had joined the expedition in May 1824, as consul in Kuka, the capital of the Shehu of Bornu.

The British government was well pleased with the expedition. The prospects of trade with the interior seemed about to be realized at last, for Clapperton had even been told by Sultan Bello the name of the port at the mouth of the Niger. Clapperton's return to England seemed to herald the end of the long quest for the termination of the Niger. The government promptly equipped a second expedition to be led by Clapperton with the object of reaching the interior from the seaboard, preferably up the Niger.

But on his return to the coast to discover the port, which Sultan Bello had called Rakah, Clapperton met with disappointment. No one had ever heard of such a place. So he decided to trek overland from Badagry to Sokoto, where instead of friendliness he met with considerable hostility from the Sultan. There was now no question of trade, and certainly no question of giving up slave-dealing. It seemed that a rival economic interest, that of Arab merchants from Tripoli and Morocco, had persuaded the Sultan that trade with the Europeans would be foolish. The Sultan also had suspicions about Clapperton's friendly relations with his enemy, the Shehu of Bornu. Bitterly disappointed, and making no headway against the Sultan's new position, Clapperton became ill and died in April 1827. Richard Lander, his Cornish servant, tried to reach the coast along the River Niger, but at the confluence of the Niger and Benue he was captured by local tribesmen and forced to make his way back by land. On his return to England Lander persuaded a reluctant government, which had now come to believe that trade with the interior would never be possible because of the high incidence of disease, to make him a grant to return once more to the coast. He was given £100 for himself and his brother, who was to accompany him, and a further £100 to keep his wife in his absence.

In 1830 the Lander brothers trekked overland from Badagry to Bussa where Mungo Park had met his death. There they were able with much difficulty to secure two canoes. They sailed down the Niger through the confluence with the Benue until at Asaba they were taken captive by local Ibo. Eventually their captors agreed to deliver them to the master of an English brig anchored at Brass on the mouth of the Niger. They were taken downstream and were overjoyed to learn that they had at last discovered the mouth of the Niger. At Brass, Richard Lander was allowed to go on board the brig to negotiate the ransom with its captain, Thomas Lake. At first Lake was most reluctant to pay up, but eventually agreed to do so on delivery of John Lander. No sooner was John Lander on board than he set sail without paying a penny. Thus in 1830, in melodramatic circumstances not untypical of trade in those days, the quest for the Niger was ended by the efforts of Richard Lander, a 'gentleman's gentleman' turned explorer. A new phase of exploration had opened. The route to the interior was known. The great question now was whether life was possible for Europeans in the interior.

Once the mouth of the Niger had been discovered, it was not long before this new knowledge was put to commercial use. With British naval supremacy on the coast, the Niger opened up tremendous and unexplored possibilities to British trade. It was significant that shortly after the return of the Landers a Liverpool trader, Macgregor Laird, financed a commercial expedition to the coast in 1832, though at the time he was virtually the only merchant interested in opening up interior African trade. His two ships, the *Alburkah* and *Quorra*, were the first two iron steamships ever to be built as ocean-going vessels. Commercially however the expedition was a disaster, accompanied by a heavy death toll from malaria. Only nine of the forty-eight Europeans on the expedition survived. Nevertheless, it did sail up the Niger as far as the confluence and beyond. The failure of this expedition postponed further attempts to penetrate the interior for commercial purposes until 1841.

Now a new element was brought in as the motive force behind the development of internal trade: the humanitarians and their delegates, the missionaries.

The humanitarians had quickly come to realize that the prohibition of the slave-trade was not enough. Certainly, as we have seen, the British Navy was not sufficiently strong to prevent traders obtaining slaves for export to the Americas. The answer, they maintained, was to attack slavery at its economic root— that was, to show Africans an alternative method of obtaining money with which to buy European goods. The natural, not the human products of Africa should form the basis of exchange. This was the view put forward by Sir Thomas Fowell Buxton in his book *The African Slave Trade and its Remedy*. The only way to save Africa from the evils of the slave-trade, he insisted, would be to call out its own natural resources. At the same time every effort should be made to save the souls of those whom they were rescuing from slavery. Already missionaries had established a settlement for freed slaves in Sierra Leone, and with the growing militancy of Christian sects in England, thoughts began to turn towards the evangelization of the whole west coast. Africa made an excellent missionary target. In Eugene Stock's *History of the C.M.S.*, published in 1897, Africa is described as ' "one universal den of desolation, misery and crime", and certainly, of all the divisions of the globe, it had always had an unfortunate pre-eminence in degradation, wretchedness and woe'.

Thus early missionaries in West Africa had a dual purpose: to promote legitimate trade between African and European, and to convert Africans to their own religion. This came out clearly in the expedition up the River Niger in 1841. The object of this expedition, sponsored by the Society for the Extinction of the Slave Trade and for the Civilization of Africa, of which Buxton was a leading member, was to promote trade in the interior, to conclude treaties with local chiefs and to establish a model agricultural farm. This farm, originally the idea of Commander William Allen who had travelled with Laird's expedition in 1832, was to serve as an 'exhibition centre' for the surrounding people. The expedition, consisting of 145 Europeans, was given an official send-off at Exeter Hall by no less a person than Prince Albert, Consort of the Queen.

This expedition, which was the brain-child of men who were almost entirely ignorant of conditions in the interior of Africa, came under heavy fire in England. Robert Jameson, in *An Appeal Against the Proposed Niger Expedition*, protested to the government against humanitarian interference in commerce, pointing out that its experiment in Sierra Leone had already proved a failure. Merchants also objected to interference by the government in trade.

Nevertheless the expedition set sail in three ships: the *Albert*, *Sudan* and *Wilberforce*. On board were two missionaries, the Rev. J. F. Schön and Samuel Crowther, a freed slave who later became Bishop on the Niger. He had been taken as a slave during one of the Yoruba inter-tribal wars in 1822. The slaver on which he was being transported across the Atlantic was intercepted and taken to Freetown. On his release he was sent to the C.M.S. school where his great intelligence soon caught the attention of the missionaries. In 1825 he was baptized Samuel, though he always kept his native name Ajayi, which means one born with his face to the ground and destined for a remarkable future. He was then sent to the Parochial School in Liverpool Street, Islington, in London. He took the name Crowther from a distinguished member of the Church Missionary Society.

Crowther and Schön were charged with pursuing the new policy of 'Bible and Plough' on the expedition. From now on missionaries were to play a major role in the exploration of the interior. Hitherto their influence and interest in Nigeria had been marginal, largely because the local chiefs did not permit penetration of the interior, and also because of the difficult living conditions under which most Europeans succumbed to malaria. Furthermore, European slaving interests had naturally been hostile to missionary penetration.

The 1841 expedition was a disastrous failure and set back the promotion of commercial enterprise ten years, for on the expedition over a third of the members of the expedition died of malaria. Ironically the expedition carried plenty of supplies of the one thing that could have cured them: quinine. But they used it only when a patient showed signs of recovery. The model farm, purchased from the powerful Ata of Idah, was a failure, and the expedition returned to England with little to show for their early optimism and enthusiasm.

The Times and *Edinburgh Review*, both of which had criticized the expedition, wrote self-satisfied editorials that prevented its repetition for another decade. And though the foundations of the Niger mission had been laid in 1841, it would hardly have survived as a concept had not Henry Venn been made Hon. Secretary of the C.M.S. in that year. He it was who had such faith in the Yoruba ex-slave Ajayi Crowther, who became first bishop on the Niger, and the first black bishop of modern times. He it was who took the Rev. J. F. Schön's advice, based on his experiences on the expedition, that since Europeans could not easily survive the climate, Nigeria must be evangelized by Africans themselves, of whom there were large numbers ready to offer themselves in the Sierra Leone settlement. As a result of the failure of the 1841 expedition the Niger mission was to start predominantly as an African mission.

Despite the setback which the 1841 expedition represented, missionary penetration of Nigeria really dates from then. Missionaries were to become latter-day, less spectacular explorers, pushing into the remotest corners of the country to spread the Gospel, and thereby to make the hinterland accessible to government and trading interests. Missionary enterprise in Nigeria took the form of a three-pronged attack: the Church of Scotland mission occupied itself with Calabar; the Church Missionary Society established missions in the Niger Delta and up the Niger; the Methodists, the Church Missionary Society, and the Baptists advanced into Yorubaland. In all three areas freed slaves and Africans played an important role in the evangelization of Nigeria.

Africans were very much in the vanguard of missionary activity in Badagry and Abeokuta. In the late 1830's a number of freed slaves from Freetown returned to their original homes in Lagos, Badagry and Abeokuta. As a result of trade between Badagry and Freetown, some of the Aku (Yoruba) Creoles learnt of the great Yoruba cities of Abeokuta and Lagos and decided to return there. Two parties left Sierra Leone, one for Lagos, the other for Abeokuta. The Lagos expedition finished with all 300 members being robbed of their possessions. By 1842 over 500 returned slaves were resettled in Abeokuta. Their appeals to the Church Missionary Society in Sierra Leone to open a mission in Abeokuta brought down Henry Townsend, who had been preceded in the missionary field in Nigeria by a half-caste, Thomas Birch Freeman, head of the Gold Coast Methodist mission, opened a station at Badagry in 1842. He had already established cordial relations with Sodeke, the founder and leader of Abeokuta. Townsend actually met Freeman while he was on his way back from Abeokuta, where the immigrants from Sierra Leone had been well received.

A year later an important event took place in London. Samuel Ajayi Crowther, whose journal of the 1841 expedition had greatly impressed the C.M.S., was ordained a priest. Afterwards preached before Sir Thomas Buxton. When, later, as a result of Townsend's visit to Abeokuta, the Yoruba mission was established, it was only natural then to make the Yoruba-speaking Crowther one of its members. Together with the German missionary Gollmer, Townsend, two catechists and an interpreter, Crowther set off for Abeokuta, only to learn with distress that Sodeke had died. This meant not only that the new mission would be without the protection of this sympathetic ruler, but also that the one unifying force amongst the Egba sub-tribes and immigrants that went to make up Abeokuta had been removed. Matters were further complicated by the dispute over the chieftancy in Lagos, where Kosoko, a well-known slaver, had usurped the throne of his uncle Akitoye. Some Egba war chiefs had given their support to Kosoko, so it became impossible for the missionaries, enemies of slavery, to reach Abeokuta. Further Gezo, the slaving king of Dahomey, had

control of the Badagry–Abeokuta road. The missionaries therefore contented themselves with opening a mission at Badagry.
Schools were built, an experimental farm was established and a
steel corn mill introduced to stimulate legitimate trade. Not
until 1846 were they able to leave for Abeokuta, where they
were well received by the people. Again a church was built and
schools established. However, their work did not easily survive
the death of their first convert in 1848. Funeral rites in most
indigenous African religions are of deepest significance to their
adherents. When, therefore, on the death of an indigenous convert the mission attempted to bury him according to Christian
rites there were naturally many relatives anxious that he should
be buried according to native custom. Feeling ran high and
riots followed, together with a general persecution of the
Christians.

Perhaps one of the most significant results of the establishment
of the mission at Abeokuta was the visit four months later of the
representative of the large trading firm of Thomas Hutton and
Co., with a view to establishing a factory or trading store. Soon
afterwards factories were opened at Abeokuta as well as Badagry
which had become an important trade centre both for slaves
and legitimate commerce.

The prestige of the missionaries in Abeokuta, both Baptists
and C.M.S., rose as a result of their close co-operation in 1851
with the Abeokutans in the defence of the city against the
Dahomeyans. The Amazon vanguard of the Dahomeyan invaders was repelled with Townsend of the C.M.S. and Bowen
of the Baptist mission offering advice. Bowen had in fact been a
contemporary of Davy Crockett, fighting Indians in Texas and
Alabama, before becoming a missionary.

The C.M.S. in London felt optimistic enough to expand its
activities beyond Yorubaland. Hinderer, together with his wife,
who became a great missionary in her own right, arrived initially with the intention of going to Hausaland but, because of
the civil wars, remained in Yorubaland travelling extensively
and gaining warm receptions everywhere except in Ijebuland.

The emphasis in any history of early missionary activity in
Nigeria must be on the C.M.S., since as an offshoot of the Angli-
can Church it had official sanction in days when Nonconform-
ism was still a social disadvantage. No better illustration is

given of this than the close interest of Queen Victoria in the mission's work. She sent two Bibles to the mission, one in English and one in Arabic; and Prince Albert, a year before his Great Exhibition of 1851, not surprisingly made it a gift of a steel corn mill. Later, when Crowther went on leave, he was received by Lord Palmerston, the Foreign Secretary, and had an audience of Queen Victoria, at which he read the Lord's Prayer in Yoruba, described later by the Queen as soft and melodious.

The political influence of the Church Missionary Society, therefore, was much greater than that of any other group. Indeed, as we shall see in the next chapter, one of the main factors behind Britain's decision to depose King Kosoko of Lagos in 1852 was pressure from the missionaries at Abeokuta, who found his slave-trading prejudicial to the development of legitimate trade in Egbaland. And as they were prepared to lobby the British government in furtherance of their policy of 'Bible and Plough', so too they were willing to interfere in local politics. Townsend, for instance, was largely responsible for the introduction of the new supreme ruler of Abeokuta, the Alake, preferring one sovereign chief, with whom he could deal direct, to a multiplicity of chiefs without real power. Later on, as we shall see, this political interference was to bring considerable tension to both Lagos and Abeokuta.

The second prong of early missionary enterprise in Nigeria was on the Cross River in the old slave-trading state of Calabar. In 1846 Hope Waddell arrived in Calabar together with a group of Christian Jamaicans to establish the Church of Scotland Mission. In 1834, on the release of all Jamaican slaves from bondage, the Church of Scotland had established a mission in Jamaica, and it was largely through the moving spirits of these negroes that the mission to Calabar was organized.

In Calabar conditions were as bad as anywhere on the coast. We have already seen that, by contrast with Bonny and New Calabar, the Efik treated their slaves with scant consideration. Human sacrifice on a large and ostentatious scale, associated with the death of chiefs, was prevalent; twin murder was practised; and widows were often forced to remain in total seclusion without washing or changing their clothes for several years. To abolish these practices and the slave-trade, as well as to evangelize the people, was the main aim of the Church of Scotland missionaries. Their mission was granted land between Duke Town and Henshaw Town by King Eyamba V of Duke Town, who with King Eyo Honesty of Creek Town was the most important ruler of Calabar at the time. Shortly after the mission's arrival a leading chief died in Duke Town, and despite the intervention of the missionaries many slaves were killed to accompany him on his eternal journey. In 1847 King Eyamba himself died—this was the signal for large-scale sacrifice.

In Creek Town the missionaries were more sympathetically received. King Eyo Honesty cleared a site for a mission house and school. Pressure from both the missionaries and legitimate traders forced the Calabar chiefs to conduct sacrifices at the death of any of their number more and more secretly. In 1850 ten ship captains, three surgeons and two missionaries met in the mission house at Creek Town to form 'A Society for the Suppression of Human Sacrifices in Calabar'. They wrote to both king and chiefs to inform them that all friendly intercourse with them would cease until the practice was discontinued. As a result an Ekpe society law was passed on 15th February 1850, abolishing human sacrifice. This was not always easy to maintain. The real test was to come later in 1858 when King Eyo Honesty himself died after a long reign. Not one man was sacrificed!

The history of the Niger mission, which was the third prong of missionary attack in Nigeria, once again illustrates the combination of commercial and philanthropic interests that so often went hand in hand in West Africa. Before the highly successful expedition up the Niger in 1854, led by Dr. Baikie, little headway had been made on the Niger. In 1848 an American negro and the principal of the Fourah Bay Institution in Freetown led a mission to the Delta to try and resettle 100 freed Ibo slaves. But the King of Bonny refused them permission and instead they were sent to Calabar. Baikie's expedition was to mark the foundation of one of the most successful missions in West Africa, the Niger mission, the first to start off as an entirely African-staffed mission, following the earlier recommendations of Schön.

The background to the Niger mission was the highly successful expedition up the Niger and Benue in 1854. The British government, whose appetite for expeditions up the Niger had been damped by the 1841 fiasco, was stimulated to a further trial by despatches sent by the great German explorer Heinrich Barth. Still interested in the country around the Niger, the British government had sent James Richardson with two Germans, Barth and Overweg, across the desert for reports on the general conditions in these countries. Richardson and Overweg died, but Barth covered hundreds of miles in Northern Nigeria and wrote eventually a voluminous and fascinating book describing with remarkable observation and scholarship the geography, history and ethnology of the peoples he encountered. In 1852 a despatch from Barth informed the British government that he had crossed the Benue. He speculated that this was the same river as the Tschadda that flowed into the Niger at Lokoja. To ascertain this, and to promote once more trade with the interior, the government financed an expedition to sail up the Tschadda to see if in fact it was the Benue. The expedition was of deepest significance for the future of British commercial interests in West Africa, for not one European died on the 900 miles' journey into the interior to Yola. The use of quinine as a prophylactic against malaria showed that life was possible for Europeans in the interior of Africa. From this date, as much as any other, can be traced the growth of effective British interest in the hinterland of Nigeria, which was eventually to lead to the establishment of a British protectorate over Nigeria and the loss of sovereignty by the various African kingdoms and states that comprised it.

While Baikie and other members of the expedition occupied themselves with the more mundane tasks of the expedition, Crowther set about the reconnoitring sites for the future Niger mission, at Onitsha and Lokoja amongst others. The subsequent history of these missions and their associated trading stations belongs to the next chapter.

The activities of these early missionaries were to have the most profound influence on the future of Southern Nigeria. In the North, of course, they came up against the barrier of Islam, and were able to make little progress except in pagan areas.

Before the arrival of these missionaries, traders, the only other representatives of European culture, had made remarkably little impact on the societies with which they conducted their commerce. New consumer habits were naturally developed as a result of both the slave and the oil trade, but even with the new economic régime brought about by the commercialization of palm oil, the Delta societies remained fundamentally the same. Certainly the traders never sought to alter this situation. They were interested in profits alone. The missionaries, by contrast, came out with the deliberate intention not only of changing the economic habits of a predominantly slave-trading society, but of converting it to a completely new way of life: that of Christ. These missionaries came from a society deeply convinced that their religion and their mode of life, especially with its new benefits of industrialization, were superior to anything else in the world. When they arrived in Africa they quickly came to the conclusion that there was nothing good in indigenous African religion. Almost from the start they condemned the indigenous religions in all their aspects, and required of the African conversion not only to a new religion, but to a completely new way of life. For this they have been frequently attacked, for in so doing they destroyed many of the riches of African culture, in particular ritual art and dancing, with the result that many Africans take as scathing a view of their own traditional society today as the most prejudiced Europeans. On the other hand, it must be said in defence of the missionaries that they made a correct appreciation of the fact that West African religions were much more closely integrated with West African cultures than Victorian Christianity with the rest of Victorian culture. To destroy the one effectively it was essential to destroy the other. In this missionaries were later to be opposed by the administrators, with their policy of indirect rule through traditional institutions. The fact that many Nigerians today still largely retain their traditional religious world view even when they are practising Christians, is in part due to the fact that the missionaries were never able fully to carry out their policy of effacing not only traditional religion, but the entire culture with which it was so intimately bound up.

The most powerful factor of change introduced by these early missionaries was Western education. In traditional society the wealth and power that education could bring introduced education as a new indicator of status. Later, when the occupation of Nigeria by the British brought about a great demand for indigenous employees for the new administration, the benefits of Christian education were seen to be very great. Christian education and knowledge of the English language also gave common ground to members of many of the widely differing groups of which Nigeria is composed. It was from these early converts that the first African *élite* to gain the respect of the white man emerged. It was this *élite* which was to provide the leading members of the professional and commercial world, and which ultimately was to produce the leaders of the nationalist movement for self-government and independence.

CHAPTER IX

The Growth of Legitimate Trade

In 1851 Britain deposed the slave-trading King of Lagos and replaced him by his more tractable uncle. In 1854 *The Pleiad* sailed up the Niger without any European member of the crew succumbing to malaria. Both these events may be taken as symbols of Britain's increasing interest in trade with Nigeria.

In the one case the installation of a king sympathetic to British interests on the throne in place of a hostile king was a classic example of nineteenth-century colonial expansion; in the other it was proved that life beyond the coast was possible for Europeans and this diverted attention from the coastal states to the supposed wealth of the interior. Britain was now prepared to interfere with local rulers if they proved hostile to British trading interests. This becomes increasingly apparent in the years between 1850 and 1865, and makes the subsequent recommendations of the famous 1865 Select Committee that the British government should withdraw from the west coast seem quite paradoxical.

The gradual opening-up of the interior to direct trading relations between European and African, and the consequent breakdown of the monopoly of coastal trade held by the Delta middlemen and the Liverpool capitalists, were to produce a crisis in Delta politics. They were also to encourage the increasing interference of Britain in the Delta. In this period much of the British government's thinking was on the lines that if trade was to be carried on to advantage then the highest authority in the land would have to be that of the British government and not that of the African chief. It was a view that evoked considerable opposition in Britain, crystallized in the findings of the Parliamentary Select Committee of 1865.

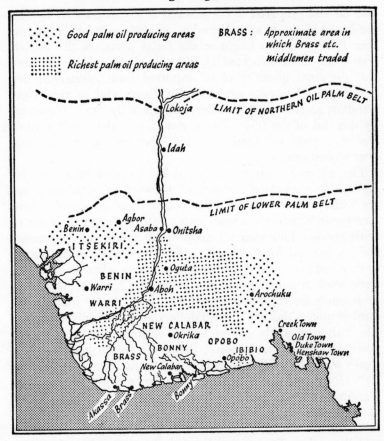

6. Niger Delta oil markets in the eighteenth century

By 1850 British trading interests were concentrating in two regions of what is now Nigeria: Lagos, the gateway to the rich forests of Yorubaland; and the Delta ports, which were the outlet for the trade of the interior of Eastern Nigeria. The chief export was still palm oil. The slave-trade became progressively less important as the African middlemen of the Delta found it more profitable to export palm oil. Only in the area around Lagos where a steady supply of slaves, mainly prisoners taken in the Yoruba civil wars, continued to reach the coast, was it still of a serious nature. During the fifties the Delta was pre-eminent in the palm-oil trade, and Bonny was its richest port.

The oil was prepared in the markets of the interior by boiling the husks in water and skimming off the resultant oil. It was then transported to Lagos or the Delta ports. In the 1855–6 season the Delta exported 25,060 tons of oil, which was over half the total quantity of oil exported from Africa. Of this quantity, 16,124 tons were sold by Bonny and its rival New Calabar; 4,000 by Old Calabar; and 2,280 by Brass. However, by the end of the fifties Lagos, now under the docile rule of Docemo, paid off earlier British intervention by exporting over 20,000 tons.

The oil trade was monopolized by the middlemen of the Delta, who prevented any contact between the producers and the white merchants who came mostly from Liverpool. These merchants supplied the middlemen with credit in the form of trade goods, which were taken up to the markets of the interior and exchanged for palm oil, and to a smaller extent ivory, timber and bees-wax. Credit goods, which were known as 'trust', were often supplied up to the value of £5,000 to reputable middlemen for as long a period as a year. There was no real form of money though Spanish dollars were generally accepted. The value of goods was measured variously in the different ports. In Bonny, for instance, they were equated to iron bars worth about five shillings each. A wide range of goods, particularly cloths, guns, beads, lead and copper rods, were used in exchange. Vast profits were made by the Liverpool merchants through their monopoly. They fobbed off second-rate goods to the Africans who had no standards of comparison, and often sold them ridiculous second-hand clothes pretending that they were those worn by the aristocracy in England. We should not laugh therefore at the amused descriptions by contemporary travellers of the pretentious attire of many African kings, for it was often as not encouraged by the white traders themselves with high profit as the primary motive.

Basically the control of the standards of trade was in the hands of the African authorities, though this became less and less so with the interference of the British consuls. The palm-oil traders were as rough a lot as the old slave-traders, and well deserved their title 'Palm Oil Ruffians'. The African chiefs could not actually bring these traders before their own courts, so they resorted to the expedient of imposing collective punishment on the European community through the banning of trade. This was fairly effective, since conditions on the coast were such that most traders were very anxious to get back to Europe as quickly as possible, and could stomach no delays. The ban on trade was always absolute because of the strict control African chiefs exercised over their subjects. There was no 'scabbing' on the African part, to use a modern trade-union term. On the other hand the Europeans found it difficult to combine effectively, since whenever a European community stuck out for lower prices, there was usually one of their number willing to trade at the African's price.

In 1854 Africans and Europeans in Bonny combined to deal with the problems of local trade by setting up a 'Court of Equity' on which both Bonny middlemen and European supercargoes were represented. Traders offending against the regulations of the court, which was presided over by a different white supercargo in monthly rotation, were subject to fines, which had to have the approval of the King of Bonny. If such a trader refused to pay, a collective boycott was placed on him until such time as he did. This court was so successful that soon similar ones were instituted at New Calabar, Akassa, Benin River, Old Calabar, Brass and later Opobo. Despite this healthy development in the regulation of coastal trade, the European traders still used the power of their local consul to force their own terms on African chiefs. Indeed the growth of British consular power is the most characteristic trend in relations between Britain and Nigeria in this period, and is epitomized by the career of the first of Britain's consuls, John Beecroft.

In 1849 John Beecroft was appointed Her Britannic Majesty's Consul for the Bights of Benin and Biafra. As Dr. Dike has written, it was he who 'laid the foundations of British power in Nigeria and initiated the politics which were to characterize the consular period of Nigerian history'. His very remarkable career in West Africa began on Fernando Po, when it was occupied by Britain as a base for the suppression of the slave-trade in 1827. When it was abandoned by Britain, he stayed on to look after the interests of the liberated slaves who had been settled there. In 1843 he was appointed Governor of the island by Spain. Already he had acquired an unrivalled knowledge of the coast. In 1835 he had travelled as far up the Niger as Idah, and not

one of the Europeans on his expedition died. In 1840 he had
entered the Benin River and proved that it was not the principal
outlet of the Niger. In the following two years he had led further
expeditions up the Cross River. He thus came to know most of
the coastal chiefs intimately, and was deeply respected by them.

From 1844 to 1849 the British Navy employed him on various
political missions, so that he became the obvious choice for
appointment as first British Consul for the Bights of Benin and
Biafra. During his six years as consul he was to wield immense
influence in the Delta and farther up the coast in Lagos. From
the outset he was bent on involving Britain in the affairs of the
coastal states, for as he saw it important British interests were at
stake. He therefore interfered constantly in local politics and
advocated the eventual take-over of the coastal states by
Britain.

Almost immediately after he was appointed consul English
traders in Bonny complained to him about their treatment at
the hands of King William Pepple. Beecroft himself was in
favour of putting an end to Pepple's persecution of British
traders, some of whom had actually been murdered on their
way up the New Calabar River in 1848. He paid little attention
to Pepple's complaints about the series of treaties he had signed
with Britain agreeing to the abolition of the slave-trade and
the protection of British interests; these had not been ratified
nor, more important, had the subsidy promised him been paid.
In the case of Calabar and the Cameroons, Pepple complained
that those treaties had been ratified and the subsidies paid. Why
not his? His bitterness was increased by the fact that his rival
and neighbour, New Calabar, was still trading in slaves and
making a profit out of it. Whereas warships could block the
Bonny River with ease, New Calabar, like Brass, was concealed
in the creeks.

In these circumstances British traders feared a recurrence of
past disturbances, so Beecroft came in to settle the dispute. He
summoned Pepple to come on board his warship, which Pepple
naturally refused to do, inviting Beecroft to come to his own
palace, an invitation Beecroft eventually accepted. No improvement in relations resulted from this visit. Rather did it make
Pepple deeply suspicious of British intentions. He was in a
difficult position, faced with threats of British intervention from

without, and the hostility of the party backing Alali, the former Regent, from within. Alali was only too eager to exploit any difficulties that might come King Pepple's way. The net result of this show of force on the part of the consul was merely to increase Pepple's antagonism towards the British.

The following year Beecroft took what was to prove a crucial step in Britain's involvement with Nigeria and deposed Kosoko, the slave-trading King of Lagos. Kosoko's uncle, Akitoye, was placed on the throne after having guaranteed to suppress the slave-trade in Lagos. The British government took this dramatic step largely because Kosoko was proving one of the major obstacles to the suppression of the slave-trade on that part of the coast. Furthermore his neighbour, King Gezo of Dahomey, had told Beecroft that he would not give up slave-trading while Kosoko still indulged in it. The missionaries at Abeokuta had exerted great pressure on the home government in favour of deposing Kosoko, for while he reigned there was little hope of legitimate trade through the port of Lagos.

The Kosoko dispute has usually been painted as one between a bad slave-trading king and his peace-loving Uncle Akitoye whose throne he had usurped. This is an oversimplification of a very complex dynastic dispute, which dates back to 1811 when the Oba of Lagos died and his second son Adele succeeded him instead of Esilogun who, as eldest son, felt himself to be the rightful heir. This led to a series of disputes and the eventual expulsion of Adele by Esilogun in 1821. Adele turned to the British at Badagry, and in 1825 tried to effect his return with the help of the Navy. It was not until 1833, however, that Adele actually became king again, this time with the aid of the Oba of Benin his overlord. He died the next year and was succeeded by his son Oluwole, who died in 1841 without issue. This led to rival claims, chiefly between Oluwole's cousin Kosoko and his uncle Akitoye. As it was, Akitoye was crowned King of Lagos by the Oba of Benin. Naturally Kosoko resented this and worked hard to undermine the power of Akitoye, and in 1845 he expelled him. Akitoye made an alliance with Abeokuta, in an effort to re-establish himself, and was financed by a well-known slave-trader, Domingo José, which, as Dr. Ajayi rightly points out in his thesis *Christian Missions and the Making of Nigeria*, destroys the picture that Akitoye was an anti-slaver. Had he been King of

Lagos at the time when the missionaries and British traders were trying to promote trade between Abeokuta and the coast, he would just as likely as Kosoko have been an instigator of the slave-trade. As it was, both missionaries and consul saw in him their main hope for establishing a friendly ruler at Lagos.

The missionaries lobbied Palmerston at home, and in due course instructions were sent to Beecroft to deal with the situation in Lagos. He visited the missionaries in Abeokuta, and then went to Badagry, where he held discussions with Akitoye, who was already growing unpopular with the local chiefs. Indeed by this time most of Badagry's chiefs were on Kosoko's side, so that Beecroft was able to take Akitoye to Fernando Po on the grounds that he would otherwise be attacked by the Badagry people. In Fernando Po, Akitoye agreed that if he were restored he would outlaw slavery in Lagos. In 1851, on Beecroft's return, Kosoko's guns fired on a ship flying a flag of truce, and in retaliation Beecroft attempted to seize Lagos with a small naval force, but Kosoko was too well defended and compelled him to retreat. This premature invasion infuriated the British government, particularly Palmerston, the Foreign Secretary, who had already written: 'If Lagos, instead of being a nest for slave-traders, were to become a port for lawful trade, it would become an important outlet for the commerce of a large range of country in the interior, and instead of being a den of barbarism, would become a diffusing centre of civilization.' Instructions had already gone out to the Commodore of the West African Squadron to effect the capture of Lagos, and to have Beecroft instigate a half-cock invasion was humiliating to Palmerston, who was already under fire from Parliament over his West African policy. Fortunately for Palmerston the squadron retrieved the situation by taking Lagos. A month later Kosoko was expelled and Akitoye installed. The latter signed a treaty abolishing slavery, guaranteeing missionary activity and according Britain most-favoured-nation terms. His power was considerably reduced compared with that of Kosoko, and what amounted to a British Protectorate was in fact established. A vice-consul was appointed to supervise the execution of the treaty and the Navy promised support if Kosoko should attempt to recapture Lagos, as seemed very probable at the time.

In the same year Beecroft found cause to intervene in the

slave rebellion in Old Calabar. The Efik, unlike the Ijo states, treated their slaves harshly, and excluded them entirely from participation in the politics and commerce of their community. The majority were relegated to plantations in the interior, from which they might be seized at any time for sacrifice. However, the preachings of the missionaries instilled in them a desire for freedom, and in one plantation on the Qua River, to which all in trouble with Egbo fled, a political organization called The Blood Men sprang up among the slaves. Several of its members were arrested in Duke Town in 1851. This was the signal for the first of a number of uprisings. The slaves ravaged the plantations and threatened to invade Duke Town itself unless they were released. The white supercargoes, fearing a stoppage in trade if there were no authority in Duke Town, called in Beecroft, who effected a settlement that modified certain aspects of Egbo government, but certainly did not put an end to the slaves' grievances. His contention was that without Egbo there would be chaos, and chaos would of course impede the trade of British merchants. The following year Beecroft even presided over the election of the new King of Old Calabar.

In 1852 an event of momentous importance took place. It was also one that was later to necessitate the increasing attention of the Consul. The British government agreed to subsidize a small fleet of steamers owned by Macgregor Laird, which were to form the basis of a regular mail service between Liverpool and West Africa. The introduction of this new service had two important consequences. First, it allowed a large number of small traders to come out to West Africa, who would otherwise have been unable to, since they would never have had the capital to finance a ship. Secondly, it introduced into the Delta competition against the great Liverpool houses. The small traders found that they could undercut the established and highly monopolistic prices of the old firms; furthermore the African middlemen found it cheaper to export oil direct to Liverpool on the mailships, rather than through the old Liverpool firms. By 1856 there were nearly 200 firms operating in the Delta in place of the few houses trading before the inauguration of this service. This caused great bitterness amongst the old-established trading houses who had sunk much capital into their West African trade; it also opened the eyes of the African to the extortionate profits and shoddy goods these houses had so long palmed off on them. Relations between the African middlemen and Liverpool traders were never amicable again.

In 1853 Beecroft's jurisdiction as consul was restricted to the Bight of Biafra, since there was now a consul permanently resident in Lagos. He soon had business in Bonny again. The story of the exile of King William Pepple is a long and complicated one, which has been admirably told by Dr. Dike in *Trade and Politics in the Niger Delta*. Its broad outlines, in so far as it affected trade relations with Britain, must suffice here, for this incident confirmed that Britain was prepared to use action such as she had employed in Lagos to further or secure her trading interests. Pepple was very sick and delegated his power to two regents who were hated by the Alali faction. To boost their authority he persuaded the white supercargoes to support their nomination. In this he was successful, though his policy of forcing all former slave merchants, a prosperous class who tended to back Alali, to pay heavy 'trust' to him, antagonized the white supercargoes who had lost business through it. Tension rose so high in Bonny that some European gigs were attacked and considerable property destroyed. The supercargoes were now suspicious that Pepple himself had engineered these attacks. By autumn 1853, Pepple recovered from his paralysis; but he faced a divided kingdom and hostile supercargoes. He attempted to divert their attention by an attack on his powerful and prosperous neighbour, Amakiri of New Calabar. This attack was a failure, since the Alali faction refused to join the war party. The supercargoes, concerned about the effects on trade, sent speedily for Beecroft who at once came to settle the dispute. Pepple was exiled through the Court of Equity over which Beecroft presided. The official British version of the event was that not only did the chiefs want him exiled, but that he himself had begged the consul to give him safe conduct to Fernando Po. A more realistic view is that, however much even the Alali faction were opposed to him, they did not want him exiled since it was usually difficult to replace legally a deposed monarch, and furthermore, native traders in the interior would not trade with them once Pepple had gone.

Soon after Pepple's departure for England his puppet successor died and poisoning was suspected, though an English doctor vouched that he had died of natural causes. Civil war flared up and the Alali faction took over the town, destroying in the process most of the property of the Pepple monarchy. Beecroft's successor, Consul Lynslager, in a surprisingly conciliatory tone, treated with the Alali party for the institution of a regency council of four. This was not a success. As Consul Hutchinson wrote later in his book *Ten Years' Wandering among the Ethiopians*: 'The experience of five years has taught the British as well as the Native Traders that this government has been no more than a mockery and delusion. . . .' Co-ordination of government was so weak, the authority of the regents treated with such contempt that very soon the European traders who had sought the removal of Pepple were demanding his return. By 1859 they were acutely aware that no one but the legitimate king would be accepted in Bonny, and arrangements were made for his restoration. In 1861 he returned to Bonny having been paid compensation of £4,520. He was accompanied by a number of English men and women who had accepted positions in his court, but since they were not paid they soon left! The British consul and the supercargoes had learnt that they had to be careful in meddling with the institutions of African government, unless they were prepared to take them over altogether.

In 1855 a critical situation developed in Calabar as a result of the introduction of open competition into local trade. The Christian Africans who had come from Sierra Leone to settle there attempted to help the local middlemen avoid the extortionate trading terms of the Liverpool supercargoes, who complained about this to the new Consul Lynslager (Beecroft died in 1854), saying that King Eyo and the Sierra Leoneans were shipping oil direct to England before paying the 'trust' they owed them. Consul Lynslager warned King Eyo to pay off his 'trust' before he shipped oil to England on his own account.

The next year the consul destroyed Old Town Calabar on the grounds that it had broken the law against human sacrifice. In Old Town, where the Church of Scotland had established a mission station, the Chief, Willy Tom Robins, had ordered a large number of people, including his wives, to be put in chains as hostages for what seemed to be his impending death. When he did die many people were sacrificed and, since this was a breach of the agreement between Calabar and the consul,

Lynslager effected the complete destruction of the town. This incurred bitter protests from the Church of Scotland missionaries, who believed that the white traders had merely wanted to make an example of Old Town, where they had no trading posts, so as to bring Duke Town and Creek Town into line. However, Lynslager sent despatches to say that he had destroyed Old Town on the invitation of the missionaries.

The situation in Calabar deteriorated rapidly. The antagonism between the supercargoes and the Sierra Leoneans became so acrimonious that the whites took to beating up the 'interlopers'. There was little that the divided authorities of Calabar could do. (It paid to have a centralized monarchy such as Bonny in cases like this.) Matters came to a head in 1857, when King Eyo Honesty actually chartered a boat, the *Olinda*, to ship oil direct to England. Lynslager's successor, Consul Hutchinson, prevented the ship from setting sail on the grounds that Eyo owed the equivalent of £18,000 in trust. Significantly the trust was owed to the consul's former employers, Messrs. Hearn and Cuthbertson. The Foreign Office was annoyed by this incident, and three years later, with evidence of Hutchinson's bribery mounting, it ordered a Commission of Enquiry into his conduct, as a result of which he was dismissed. This was a severe blow to Liverpool interests in Calabar.

Despite these dramatic shows of force, the British consuls had considerable difficulty in enforcing the punishments they chose to inflict on people who interfered with trade. The local tribes did not recognize Britain's right to force free trade on them, and merely recognized that when warships were around the safest policy was to bow to British demands. Without warships the consuls found it virtually impossible to obtain payment of fines, as in 1862, when some Benin River tribes refused to pay a fine for damaging a trader's store. It was clear that effective regulation of trade could only be secured if some form of protectorate were established over the coastal states. However much the consuls might desire this, there was still considerable opposition in Britain to any extension of overseas responsibilities.

So far, both in the Delta and in Lagos, trade had been restricted to the coast. Trade with the interior was almost exclusively in the hands of the African middlemen, and in the case of the lands beyond the Niger and Benue, no effective trade relations had been established. Baikie's voyage of 1854 changed this situation. Not only did he prove that European life was possible in the interior, but he travelled as far as Yola on the Benue, a distance of over 900 miles from the coast. In 1857 the British government made a contract with Macgregor Laird to maintain a steamer on the River Niger for five years. A subsidy of £8,000 was offered for the first year, diminishing annually by £500. Laird placed Baikie in charge of this expedition which was in fact a failure, since the *Dayspring* on which they sailed was wrecked on the Juju rock at Jebba. Nevertheless, as Professor Dike has written: 'Just as 1854 marked the end of the era of exploration, so in 1857 the traders took over where the explorers left off. Seen in this light the voyage of the *Dayspring* marked the beginning of an era in Nigerian history.'

Factories or trading posts were established at Aboh, Onitsha and Lokoja on the confluence of the Benue and Niger. Laird even issued small copper coins, very popular, to replace cumbersome cowries. Trade was not brisk to begin with, amounting to less than £9,000 in the third year. Laird had to contend with much opposition. His ventures were resented by the Liverpool supercargoes as much as they had resented his earlier introduction of the mail steamers. But whereas the latter venture benefited the African middleman, his attempts to trade direct with the markets of the interior were a deadly threat to the livelihood of the middlemen themselves. Thus Laird had ranged against him both African middlemen and Liverpool supercargoes, who now combined to wreck his commercial adventures. Attacks on the steamers by hostile 'natives' were often alleged by Laird's traders to have been instigated by the Liverpool supercargoes acting through the Delta middlemen, who had long-standing contacts with the tribes of the interior. Heavy guns were positioned at strategic points on the river, and the steamers frequently came under severe fire. Sometimes the steamers were even stopped and boarded, despite punitive measures taken by naval gunboats. In 1859 a number of villages seventy miles inland were shelled for their part in the attack on the *Rainbow* on her return from a successful voyage up the Niger.

By 1860 Laird had largely convinced the government that inland trade could pay, and the government in return offered to escort his ships up the Niger. The instructions to this effect were not carried out by the local naval commander, who felt that the risks were too great to justify such a convoy. As a result Laird's expedition was a disastrous failure, involving heavy loss of capital. From then on until 1870 escorts were provided.

In the meantime Baikie, who had been wrecked in the *Dayspring* on Juju Rock at Jebba, installed himself at Lokoja near the site of the model farm, where he took on the role of unofficial consul, and set about exploring the possibilities of trade with the north. His intentions are best described in his own words: 'The position I have now selected may possibly prove a permanent British Commercial site; and it is most favourably placed both as a convenient rendezvous and as a centre for trade. A direct route to Nupe is now being opened, and other roads lead also to Zaria and the interior of Hausa. As soon as I get a little settled, I shall see about the possibility of a direct route to Lagos.' With the assistance of Lieut. Glover he did establish a direct route to Lagos and won the friendship of King Masaba of Nupe. Baikie demonstrated clearly that the Niger was the real highway to the interior, including Hausaland, of whose potentials Clapperton and Barth had already written. Baikie conceived his task as helping to secure for Britain a commanding position in Africa, and when the Foreign Office ordered his return home, he refused, both because he felt his work was not then complete, and also because he was in debt to King Masaba. In 1862 he trekked to Bida, Zaria and Kano, and died two years later on his way back to England.

Baikie's enterprise on the Niger together with that of Macgregor Laird reflects the vital new interest of Britain in hinterland trade, an interest that eventually led her to annex the whole of Southern Nigeria.

Though throughout the lands of the Niger valley there was a growing hostility to the new-style traders, stimulated by their enemies the middlemen and Liverpool traders; though Laird's factories were attacked and destroyed, by the early sixties trade with the interior was well on its way to supplant the old coastal trade. By 1865 the executor of the will of Macgregor Laird, who had died in 1861, promoted a new Company of African Merchants to trade with the interior. The government even promised a subsidy. The ferocity of the attacks by Liverpool traders on this government decision are a testimony to the seriousness of the economic threat this company and those like it represented to them. After 1865 the pattern of trade in the Delta changed radically, and penetration of the interior became more and more systematic.

Intimately bound up with this expansion of trade with the interior was the founding of the Niger mission. The 1857 expedition led by Dr. Baikie on the *Dayspring* was again a combination of trading, government and evangelical interests. On board was the by now well-travelled Rev. Samuel Crowther, together with the Rev. J. C. Taylor and a party of catechists, bearing a commission from the C.M.S. to found the Niger mission. At Onitsha both trader and churchman negotiated with the Obi or King for land, and the Rev. J. C. Taylor, a freed Ibo slave, was left in charge of the new Onitsha mission station. Crowther sailed upstream founding small stations at both Gbebe and Lokoja, after which his work was called to a halt for a year when the *Dayspring* ran aground on Juju Rock at Jebba. The only mission station to be really successful was Taylor's mission at Onitsha where a school was opened. Soon delegates from many parts of Iboland were asking for stations to be opened in their own towns and villages. The difficulties of the early years of the Niger mission, which is remarkable as an almost exclusively African enterprise, were largely the result of its close association with trading interests. The mission was dependent on the interior traders both for transport and supplies, and inevitably in the minds of the local people it became identified with the traders they so hated. Thus, in 1859 and 1860, attacks on the trading posts at Onitsha brought the mission's work to a standstill. Attempts were made to make it independent of the traders, but this was almost impossible, since the mission relied on them both for supplies and communication with the outside world.

Despite these early vicissitudes, Venn, the Secretary of the C.M.S., did not lose faith in Crowther and in 1864, against considerable opposition from the Yoruba mission under Townsend, he nominated him as Bishop of 'Western Equatorial Africa beyond the Queen's Dominions'. Crowther had been reluctant to accept this great office, but Venn was insistent despite the irate and threatening letters of a disappointed Townsend who had long and justifiably coveted the episcopate now given to

Crowther. Venn was convinced that, with the heavy mortality of Europeans, an African mission was the only solution. Unfortunately Townsend's disappointment at not being selected brought into mission affairs an early element of racial bitterness. Thus whilst the Queen's Dominions such as Lagos and Freetown were excluded from Crowther's diocese, so too was the Yoruba mission at Abeokuta as a special concession to Townsend and the European missionaries.

The fifteen years from 1850 to 1865 saw a general expansion of missionary activity throughout Southern Nigeria. Though the Church of Scotland had been unsuccessful in its earlier efforts to open a mission at Bonny, it established stations up the Cross River. The Yoruba Mission opened stations at Oyo, Iseyin, Saki, Ogbomosho, Ilaro and Isaga. The study of indigenous languages had reached impressive proportions: by 1851 most of the New Testament had been translated into Yoruba; in 1862 Bowen of the Baptist mission supplemented Crowther's earlier work by publishing a *Grammar and Vocabulary of the Yoruba Language*. The Reverend S. W. Koelle of the C.M.S. published in 1854 a *Grammar of the Bornu or Kanuri Language*. In 1849 Hope Waddell published his vocabulary of the Efik language which was supplemented by further studies by his colleague Goldie. In 1862 Schön revised his *Grammar of the Hausa Language*, helped by a Hausa youth whom Barth had brought back with him from Northern Nigeria. In 1864 Crowther published his *Grammar and Vocabulary of the Nupe Language*. The role of missionaries in promoting Western education was cardinal in the history of Nigeria. As early as 1859 the Yoruba mission had published a newspaper called *Iwe-Irohin*, giving news in Yoruba.

In Lagos the overthrow of Kosoko in 1851 had been motivated largely by the exigencies of suppressing slave-trade on that part of the coast; the later annexation of the town was undoubtedly the result of Britain's need for a stable base from which to regulate her trade with the interior. Only against the background of the internal instability of Lagos and the inter-tribal warfare in Yorubaland, which continually interfered with trade, can this expansion of British territorial interests, despite severe opposition at home, be understood.

In 1853 a full-time consul was appointed for Lagos. Benjamin Campbell, the first to hold this office, was certainly more than a consular representative of the British government; he had a large say in local affairs, in which Akitoye acquiesced since he owed his position to the British. Indeed, on his arrival, Campbell found Lagos on the verge of civil war. Kosoko, through his strong faction in Lagos, was preparing insurrection against Akitoye. Campbell promised naval protection, should Kosoko attack. Cunningly Akitoye precipitated the crisis by attacking Kosoko's men, so that the Navy in effect gave support to aggression by Akitoye, when their instructions had been to offer defensive protection only. Though censured by the Admiralty, Campbell decided that the best way of defending Lagos against Kosoko was attack, and he even sent an expedition to seek out Kosoko in his retreat at Epe. A further indication of the new consul's power was the fact that in 1853, when Akitoye died, he arranged the installation of Docemo, who was likely to prove tractable, before any of the other chiefs ever knew of Akitoye's death.

Trade with the interior prospered, though Kosoko proved a major problem through his constant interference with trading canoes plying between Lagos and Abeokuta. Such was Consul Campbell's insistence on the priority of trade that in 1854, against severe opposition from the missionaries at Abeokuta, he completed a treaty with Kosoko, allowing him the port of Palma and a subsidy of 1,000 dollars on condition that he gave up his slaving activities. He installed two pro-Kosoko chiefs at Badagry by force despite the bitter opposition of the Egba who used the port as an outlet for their own trade. The missionaries, remembering the former role of Kosoko, could not easily contemplate any treaty made with him, especially one as advantageous to him as this. But Campbell had his reasons—Kosoko alone was sufficiently influential to extend legitimate trade beyond its present restricted frontiers with Egbaland. The C.M.S. mission lobbied against Campbell at home; Campbell in retaliation despatched a petition against the missionaries signed by leading traders and the local Methodist missionary. The dispute was certainly not one-sided. Campbell, with some justification, felt that the C.M.S. under Townsend interfered too much with the politics of Egbaland and Lagos, which he considered his own proper province. The missionaries felt that their own ideal state, which was to lead the way for the regeneration of Africa through legitimate commerce, should not be sacrificed to the interests of men like Kosoko.

In Abeokuta, too, the missionaries had their own troubles. They had a slaving faction to deal with, and felt that any compromise of principles in Lagos would facilitate the slave-trade. By 1856, however, relations between the missionaries and the consul became closer, when Campbell forced Docemo to expel Madam Tinubu, a powerful middleman operating between Lagos and Abeokuta, who was suspected of being a surreptitious slave dealer as well as a party to the 1856 rising against Docemo. Moreover, the missionaries had so encouraged the growth of cotton and palm oil in Egbaland that trade boomed in Lagos to Campbell's considerable satisfaction. In 1856 alone, 15,000 tons of oil were exported from Egbaland.

In 1857 the French launched a scheme whereby 'free' labour was exported from Ouidah to Martinique in the French West Indies. A contract had been granted by Napoleon III of France to the House of Regis Aine allowing it to obtain labourers for work on its plantations on the condition that they should be volunteers who would be paid for their work. Payment was made to local chiefs for each labourer enlisted, and no questions were asked about his provenance. To the African this was indistinguishable from the slave-trade. Both Consul Campbell and the missionaries associated this scheme with the deterioration of the situation in the interior: tension increased between the Egba and Dahomey, and in 1858 war broke out once again between Ibadan and Ijebu. In 1858 Atiba, Alafin of Oyo, died and was succeeded by his son, Adelu, the Crown Prince. The powerful Are of Ijaye refused to recognize Adelu as Alafin, protesting that he should have committed suicide on the death of his father in accordance with tradition. Ibadan took up Oyo's cause, and it seemed clear that war would soon break out again, with Ibadan and Oyo facing a grand alliance of Ijaye, Abeokuta, Ijebu, Ilesha and Ilorin. The two camps took to battle over a wealthy widow of Saki who refused to pay tax to the Are of Ijaye. The Alafin sent troops to defend her since he claimed that the widow in fact came under his jurisdiction. In the ensuing clash the Are took several dozen prisoners, whereupon Oyo called on Ibadan for help. Ikorodu and Ijebu Remo, both placed strategically on the trade route to Lagos, declared for

Ibadan, thus giving it access to the coast and supplies of arms. Fearing that this civil war would completely disrupt trade in the interior, the new consul, Brand, sent a Lieutenant Lodder to mediate between Ibadan and Ijaye. This mission was a failure and soon after Ibadan made overtures to Dahomey to support them and thereby revenge their defeat by the Egba in 1851.

Kosoko naturally took advantage of the situation and was only kept under control by the presence of a gunboat. Trade dwindled and Consul Brand, who succeeded Campbell on his death in 1860, suggested to the Foreign Office that Britain should take over Lagos as a protectorate. The Foreign Office was not unfavourable to this suggestion, fearing that the French, who had sent a delegation to Docemo, might try to take over Lagos themselves. Brand survived only a year in Lagos, and his successor Foote went even further by suggesting that the only ultimate solution to peace would be the introduction of troops, and the stationing of consuls at strategic towns in the interior. This was opposed by the Foreign Office which was not prepared to undertake such large territorial commitments. Nevertheless, vice-consuls were stationed at Badagry and Lagos. When, soon afterwards, Porto Novo placed an embargo on trade in oil, Foote promptly ordered its bombardment, thereby gaining a treaty guaranteeing freedom of trade for Britain.

The situation for the Egba was serious. On their western flank the Dahomeyans threatened; to the north-east the military power of Ibadan was preparing for another attack, though ominously quiescent. Abeokuta was still the main source of trade for Lagos so that plans were even mooted to supply armed defence for Abeokuta. But McKoskry, the Vice-Consul for Lagos, who succeeded Foote that same year, had a somewhat different approach to the problem, believing that trade should be extended without favour to any one section of Yorubaland. Thus when a contingent of ten men and one officer arrived in Lagos to teach the Egba the art of military defence in pursuance of Foote's policy, they were diverted to the consular guard in Lagos.

Shortly afterwards the Foreign Office sent the consul instructions to annex Lagos 'to secure forever the free population of Lagos from the slave-traders and kidnappers who formerly oppressed them; to protect and develop the important trade of which their town is the seat; and to exercise an influence on the surrounding tribes which may, it is hoped, be permanently beneficial to the African race'. Comparatively little was made of Britain's interest in trade which had been paramount in the actions of all the consuls from 1851 to 1861 and which had led up to the annexation of Lagos.

Thus, on 30th July 1861, Docemo ceded Lagos to Acting Consul McKoskry, popularly known as Apongbon, in return for a pension of £1,030 a year. The handing-over ceremony was concluded by the singing of the British National Anthem by 300 local schoolchildren conducted by two missionaries. A Governor of the Colony of Lagos was appointed and there began a new era in the history of British relations with that part of the coast, an era which inaugurated the new territory of Nigeria. British interests were firmly established in the town. By 1862 there were sixteen British merchants to one French, two Italian, three German and five Brazilian traders. Half in the guise of humanitarian motives, Britain had gained her first foothold on the Nigerian coast primarily to secure her trade.

The history of Lagos subsequent to its annexation in 1861 is closely bound up with the opening up of the interior, largely because its most able and aggressive administrator in the sixties was Glover, who had accompanied Baikie on the 1857 expedition organized by Laird, and shared the ideals of both concerning the penetration of the interior and its accessibility to trade.

The annexation of Lagos was accompanied by a deterioration of conditions in the interior. The Ijaye wars flared up once more. Ibadan, with the assistance of Oyo and Borgu, surrounded Ijaye and cut off its supplies from the south. In this situation Freeman, the new Governor of Lagos, was placed in a dilemma. He had been instructed not to extend British territory, yet he was also to look after trade interest. Freeman, feeling that much of the blame was on the Egba side, since they refused to let Ibadan have a road to the coast, tried to force a vice-consul on them, a move that was quickly rejected by the Egba, who had already seen what happened to Lagos when a consul took up residence. The missionaries complained to the Colonial Office about this interference, and that department made it known that it was against coercion of the Egba. Freeman however pursued a contrary policy, instituting a blockade on Egba trade and annexing Palma and Lekki from Kosoko in return for a pension. He also annexed Badagry so that he could exact a 4 per cent import duty on all goods to help pay for the administration. In the interests of free trade he even destroyed Epe, where the ruler, Possoo, had established himself with the rest of Kosoko's followers who had opposed the cession of Palma and Lekki to the British.

In the interior the situation had become very tense. Kurumi, the Are of Ijaye, had died, thus depriving that town of its most able leader when it was in the direst of straits owing to the successful siege by the Ibadan. Such was their condition that people from Ijaye were even selling themselves to their allies the Egba in order to obtain food. The Ibadan attacked the Awaye people for the help they had given to besieged Ijaye; whilst the Egba attacked the Ijebu Remo for their help to the Ibadan in the Ijaye war. The Egba captured the important Remo town of Iperu, which gave its name to these new wars. They had the singular advantage of having an American sharpshooter called Pettiford, who had fought in the Ijaye wars, and was reserved for picking off Ibadan chiefs in battle. The war was only settled by the intervention of the Alafin, whose influence in Yorubaland was being rapidly reduced by the civil wars. A curious sidelight on this war was the press battle between the missionaries. Townsend championed the Egba through his *Iwe-Irohin*, whilst Hinderer took the part of Ibadan in the *Anglo-African*.

Trade came almost to a standstill during these wars. The new Lieutenant-Governor, Glover, hoped to expand trade in the interior to the friendly country of King Masaba of Nupe. But the inter-tribal wars made this impossible. A further threat came to the Egba from Dahomey in 1863, and at the instigation of Townsend and the C.M.S. prayers were uttered for their deliverance in churches as far afield as Switzerland and Syria. In 1864 the Dahomeyans did attack but were repulsed with great losses.

Peace between Ibadan and the Egba was shortlived. The Egba were jealous of and afraid of the growing power of the Ibadan. The Ibadan likewise resented the heavy tolls exacted by the Egba. In March 1865 the Egba attacked and besieged Ikorodu, a Remo town strategic for Ibadan's supplies from the coast. This was the most important single incident in the long history of the Yoruba civil wars, for it was the first time the British from Lagos actually intervened in them. The Ikorodu traders appealed for help to the Governor in Lagos, who had pressures placed on him by Lagos traders to the same end. Glover had come round to the view that the only way to end civil strife and thus promote trade in the interior was armed intervention. He was also convinced that the Egba were at the root of the trouble, since they were determined to prevent Ibadan trading with the coast. On 29th March 1865 he gave the Egba twenty-four hours to withdraw from Ikorodu, then despatched West Indian troops to deal with them. In a quick action, using screaming rockets, the Egba were defeated and British authority was by implication extended far beyond the frontiers of the colony. Not long after, the King of Dahomey sent Glover an embarrassing gift of a flag on which Dahomey was represented as about to pounce on a deer (Abeokuta), held down by Lagos and Ibadan. Soon Glover found occasion to chastise the oft-bombarded King of Porto Novo. As in the Delta and in the interior, Britain was becoming inextricably involved in Nigerian affairs.

It must come therefore as something of a surprise that in 1865 the Select Committee on West Africa recommended the gradual reduction of British commitments on the coast, and declared itself against any further territorial expansion. To understand this one must look to the history of both England and the west coast. In England anti-imperialist sentiment was strong. It was backed up by missionaries like Townsend who resented the intervention of Lagos in the affairs of Abeokuta. Free trade was an article of faith for many traders, both in England and on the coast, though often the first trader to call in the gunboat when his interest was affected would be the most convinced advocate of free trade. Liverpool trading interests were hardly happy as a result of their experience of government interest in the Coast. Finally there was still a great gulf between the realities of life on the coast and what the government and parliamentarians imagined it to be. If the years 1850–65 proved nothing else, they proved that if the African interior were to be opened up to legitimate trade with Britain, then British authority would have to be paramount.

CHAPTER X

The Consolidation of British Interests

From 1865 until the proclamation of the British Protectorate over the Niger Districts in 1885, British interests in Nigeria were concentrated in three separate areas. In Lagos the trading requirements of the merchants of the Colony necessitated constant interference by the Governor in the affairs of Yorubaland. In the Delta bitter competition for the oil markets between the various states and European traders pushed further the local consul's intervention.

It was however expanding trade in the hinterland of the Delta, with its superb river highway, the Niger, that eventually led Britain to proclaim a Protectorate over the Niger Districts, and thus lay the foundations of modern Nigeria.

Although Britain's official sentiments were against any further commitments in her West African settlements, let alone extension of them, Governor Glover was left in charge of Lagos, and on his past record he was hardly likely to stand aside from Yoruba politics. Under his rule Lagos became increasingly important in the tribal disputes of the Yoruba, and Glover soon assumed the role of mediator-in-chief. The peace between Ibadan and her enemies, the Egba and Ijebu, was very uneasy. Governor Glover certainly believed that the Egba bore chief responsibility for tension in the interior because of their persistent blocking of the roads from Ibadan to Lagos, and he seemed to have little time for Egba complaints that if the warlike Ibadan received arms, they would be the sufferers. And it hardly seemed to the advantage of either the Egba or the Ijebu middlemen to keep the roads closed. Obviously their fear of arms reaching the Ibadan outweighed the economic advantages of keeping the roads open. In an attempt to force the Egba to open the roads Glover blockaded their supply lines in 1865. This policy was to suffer a reversal the following year, when the various West African settlements were amalgamated under a Governor-in-Chief in Sierra Leone to whom Glover was made responsible. Blackhall, the new Governor-in-Chief, was much more in tune with official attitudes in Britain and called off Glover's blockade on the grounds that it constituted interference in affairs beyond the province of the Lagos Governor. Glover went on leave that same year but returned in the autumn. In 1867 the Igbajo war broke out with Ibadan fighting its vassal town of Ilesha. Glover managed to persuade the Ibadan to withdraw from Ilesha. But for this, that town might well have been totally destroyed.

In 1867 the long-standing dispute between Lagos and Abeokuta came to a head. The Egba United Board of Management, a quasi-government of Abeokuta, in which Mr. Secretary Johnson, a coloured British subject, was the most important figure, informed Glover that it was going to set up a customs post on the Ogun River. The E.U.B.M. had been established in 1865 in an attempt to form a compromise government in which both chiefs and educated elements would be represented. 'In fact', as Dr. Biobaku has written in *The Egba and their Neighbours, 1831–1872*, 'the Board was little more than an empty bureaucracy, parading sovereign pretensions, and issuing largely idle threats. Its single positive achievement was that it established a short-lived Customs Department for levying export duties instead of customary tolls at the gates'. It was this preoccupation with raising revenues from customs that was to bring Abeokuta and Lagos into dangerous conflict. Glover tried to use the decision of the E.U.B.M. to set up customs posts as the occasion for the settlement of the boundaries between Lagos and Abeokuta, but this move was rejected by the E.U.B.M. who demanded that Glover withdraw the policemen he had placed at certain points on the frontier. Shortly afterwards a messenger from Glover's old friend, King Masaba of Nupe, was murdered by the Egba *en route* for Lagos. Glover demanded an explanation which only accentuated feelings against European interference which were running high in Abeokuta. At the time Glover even feared an Egba invasion of Lagos and moved troops up to Ebute Metta. However, the Egba vented their resentment on locally stationed missionaries and European traders who were expelled from Abeokuta on 13th October 1867 after the riot called *Ifole*, or housebreaking. Several factors influenced this outbreak. The Egba still resented their defeat at Ikorodu by Glover. There was increasing resentment against European penetration in Yorubaland, and it was hardly surprising that Glover's oppression of Abeokuta should be associated quite wrongly with the missionaries. Anyway, there were factions in Egbaland who wanted the missionaries out of the way: would-be slave-traders; influential Moslems; and the Sierra Leone immigrants. In the end the Colonial Office reprimanded Glover for provoking the crisis through his expansionist aims, which ran contrary both to official British policy and the wishes of the Governor-in-Chief in Sierra Leone.

The expulsion of the missionaries from Abeokuta marked the beginning of a period of stagnation in missionary work in Yorubaland. C.M.S. headquarters was moved to Lagos Island and the Egba Christian refugees settled on the mainland. Lagos itself prospered despite the setbacks to trade brought about by the civil wars of the interior. By 1870 the colony was almost self-sufficient. Over half a million pounds' worth of goods passed through the port annually. The administration recorded a very slight excess of expenditure (£42,379) over revenue (£41,684). Furthermore it occupied a key role in the affairs of the interior; for instance, in 1868, only a year after *Ifole*, the supporters of the two rival claimants for the position of Alake of Abeokuta both sought Lagos's support in their dispute.

However, there seemed no foreseeable end to the civil wars. Indeed the Alafin of Oyo feared that they might soon lead to the extinction of the Yoruba people. After nearly fifty years of fighting, antagonisms ran very deep. The Egba and Ijebu both feared the loss of their position as middlemen. Ironically the increase in legitimate trade also increased the demand for domestic slaves for work on the farms or for carrying produce to the coast. Glover was determined to secure, if not peace, at least a free road from Lagos to the interior unhampered by the interferences or exactions of the Egba and Ijebu. To this end, in July 1871 he presided over a conference of the rulers of the interior in an attempt to secure a permanent and free road for the Oyo and Ibadan. Delegates from Oyo, Ijebu, Ibadan and

Abeokuta were joined by representatives from Benin, Ijo, Ilaro and Ketu. There were five major routes to the interior: the Egba route, i.e. Lagos via Abeokuta to Ibadan; the Remo route —Lagos–Ikorodu–Ibadan; the Ijebu–Ode route—Lagos via Ijebu–Ode to Ibadan: the western route—Lagos–Igbessa–Ilaro–Ketu–Ibadan: the eastern route—Lagos–Ijo–Ondo–Oke Igbo–Ibadan. Glover's aim was to persuade the Egba and Ijebu to keep their roads open by threatening to open up an alternative route through Ijoland and Ondo to Ibadan, which would in effect deprive them of their monopoly. He was not successful in this and in 1871 the Ibadan and Egba were once again at each other's throats over the road to Lagos. Glover offered his mediation in vain, and decided to blockade Porto Novo, the main source of Egba arms supplies. If he could annex this port, so much the better, for then he could cut off all supplies for the Egba and force them to open the road. So exasperated did Glover become that he even considered closing all roads and forbidding any exports through Lagos. This naturally angered the Lagos merchants who quickly expressed their anger to the Governor of the West African settlements, Pope-Hennessy, when he arrived. Glover left Nigeria finally as a result of his alienation from the merchants. Dr. Biobaku concludes: 'Glover's departure marked the end of an era of unauthorized expansionist policies which the Egba, supported by the missionaries and later by Sierra Leone immigrants and their Ijebu allies, frustrated.'

The first five years of the seventies were relatively peaceful in Yorubaland, though in 1875 the Ibadan slave-raided into Ekiti country and reached Nupeland. The Ibadan were then at the height of their power, but they still depended on Benin for their supplies of gunpowder since the direct routes to the coast through Ijebu and Egbaland were closed. In 1877, however, a caravan under military escort was sent to Porto Novo to collect gunpowder, purchased by the Alafin Adelu shortly before his death. The expedition, which passed through Egba territory, was successful, encountering neither Dahomeyans nor Egba on the way. On receiving news of this the Egba retaliated by closing their roads completely to the Ibadan, forbidding even the passage of salt. Despite protests from some of his advisers, the Are of Ibadan closed the gates of the city to the Egba and declared war on them, with these words: 'I am going to perform a task which God has allotted me to do, and those who say that they shall see that I do not accomplish it will not live to see it done, as done it shall be, and when I have finished there shall be no more wars for ever in the Yoruba country.' The Are then sent out raiding parties to ravage the Egba farms on the grounds that the best way to harass the Egba was to destroy their food supplies.

The war between Ibadan and the Egba had some of the elements of the strife in Eastern Nigeria between the Delta middlemen and the interior traders. Essentially what the Ibadan wanted was direct trade with Lagos. The Egba naturally wished like the Ijebu, who soon joined them, to preserve their monopoly as middlemen and to ensure that the already considerable military power of Ibadan was not increased by the free supply of arms from the coast. They attempted to get the Ondo road closed to the Ibadan, and to cut off their supplies of firearms and ammunition. The Ijesha who could control this route, and resented the oppressive rule of the Ibadan, their overlords, gladly joined the Egba together with the Ekiti and Ilorin in the north, who also feared the growing military might of Ibadan. By the end of the year, then, the Ibadan were surrounded by hostile armies—the Egba and Ijebu to the south; the Ijesha and Ekiti to the east; and the Ilorin to the north.

Ibadan did not succumb to this formidable opposition, but in fact drove off the members of the alliance with surprising ease, which lends credence to Egba fears of its increasing power. By 1879, however, the strength of Ibadan's enemies seemed overwhelming. The Ekiti, together with the Ijesha, Effon, Yagba and Akoko, formed the Ekiti-Parapo or Ekiti Confederation against Ibadan. Ife helped both parties, but in reality favoured the confederation. Ibadan was cut off from any source of firearms and ammunition, except through Oke Igbo and Ondo. The chief of Oke Igbo, the Oni-elect of Ife, tried to cut off this route, but the Oyo inhabitants of Modakeke, near Ife, managed to get supplies to them. Soon even the Dahomeyans from the west started to attack the Ibadan.

Trade in the interior was by now at a standstill, so it was not surprising that the Governor of Lagos welcomed the Alafin of Oyo's appeal to him to try and reconcile the warring parties. However, the Governor had no success since, when messages were sent to the various war camps, the Ekiti refused to give any firm reply. In 1882 the Ife came out openly against Ibadan and attacked Modakeke, but were repulsed. The combined Ibadan and Modakeke army then took Ife and destroyed it. It is remarkable how well the Ibadan survived these constant attacks. In 1882 they were engaged in battles with the Ilorin, the Ekiti, Egba, Ijebu and Ife. To the west were the Dahomeyans, ready to take advantage of Ibadan's plight and doing so by raids on their farms.

In December 1882 overtures for peace were made between the various participants. The Ijebu, contrary to the wishes of their ruler, the Awujale, actually made peace with Ibadan, and trade was opened up again with the Ilorin. But no general peace could be arranged. In 1884 the Rev. J. B. Wood of Abeokuta attempted to secure peace between the Ekiti-Parapo and the Ibadan but failed, and the following year fighting broke out again at Modakeke and Offa.

As far as Lagos was concerned the trade of the interior was by 1885 completely disrupted, though the wide area of the war did not make life impossible for the people of Yorubaland. Governor Rowe of Lagos wrote in 1883: 'In the so-called war but little actual fighting occurs, few are killed; capture is the object of the warrior on either side. Man hunting is the real business of these fights. . . . All these tribes trade more or less with the Ibadans, notwithstanding they are at war with them; the most saleable produce the Ibadans can bring to market is slaves; to the Egbas they sell the slaves caught from Ijeshas; to the Ijeshas those caught from the Egbas.

'The Egbas, the Ijebus, the Ijeshas are middlemen. When these tribes talk of making peace with Ibadan—they mean a peace on which Ibadan shall bring its produce to their frontier market on the interior side, but no farther—no Ibadan trader must come beyond that market. On the seaboard they will exchange this produce with the Lagos traders for European goods, but no Lagos trader must come into their country beyond the market place on the seaboard. The Ijebus pay a high price for slaves. They use them for farm labourers, and if the Ibadans cease to catch slaves, the Ijebus must cease to import them. The Ibadans find that the most profitable trade article they can take to market is a slave.'

The Consolidation of British Interests

By 1885 it had become abundantly clear that if the Colony of Lagos were to survive, an end to the inter-tribal wars would have to be achieved. This would necessitate direct British interference in Yoruba affairs, implying a reversal of policy on the part of the British government.

Events in the Delta and along the Niger were, however, to place Britain in a much better position for dealing with the problems of Yorubaland, for it was there that competition between British and French merchants, and the increasing need to maintain peace in order that trade might be encouraged, led the British government to reverse its policy of non-interference and proclaim a Protectorate over the Niger Districts.

In 1865 King William Pepple died and was succeeded by his son George, a man of weak personality. Control of affairs in Bonny thus rested with an ex-slave, Oko-Jumbo, who became chief adviser to King George. Opposing him was another ex-slave, Jaja, who became head of the Anna Pepple house on the death of Alali, the former regent. For the next twenty years Jaja was to dominate Delta politics. He was a man of exceptional ability, combined with a ruthlessness that alone could ensure survival in the cut-throat competition of the palm-oil trade. He had been an Ibo slave, who by his quick identification with Ijo customs was readily accepted in the Anna Pepple house. From an early age he showed considerable ability as a trader and mixed well with the European supercargoes. Thus, when Alali died with debts to the tune of £10,000 or more, it was difficult to find a successor to the headship of the Anna Pepple house, which also involved assuming leadership of the opposition to Oko-Jumbo. Certainly none of the senior chiefs wished to fill it, and it was with a sense of relief that they saw Jaja take the burden on. Jaja quickly paid off Alali's debts and appeared to Oko-Jumbo's party as a potentially more serious rival than Alali had been.

In Bonny the quarrels between the two factions became so intense that in 1867 King George asked the consul to intervene on his behalf. This the consul refused to do, reprimanding him for supporting Brass and Okrika in their attacks on New Calabar. In 1869 the supercargoes sent a message to the consul that civil war was imminent. Oko-Jumbo was itching for an early outbreak of hostilities since the Anna Pepple house would be at a severe disadvantage because of heavy losses they had sustained in a fire the year before. On 13th September 1869, civil war broke out but came to a sudden halt when Jaja and his followers decamped to one of the outlying colonies of Bonny. Realizing his weakness he had wisely retreated to a position from which he could counter-attack with much more devastating results than the heavy guns of Oko-Jumbo could inflict on him. Jaja had chosen as his retreat a place in Andoni country from which he could cut Bonny off from its richest oil-producing areas. By 15th February 1870, Jaja felt strong enough to declare himself independent of Bonny. Despite warnings from the consul and from Bonny, the supercargoes traded openly with Jaja. Bonny war canoes retaliated by firing on British ships. Consul Livingstone tried to settle matters by procuring Jaja's return to Bonny. Having failed in that he sent a man-o'-war to Opobo, as Jaja had named his new state, to force him to open the interior markets to Bonny. After forty-eight hours' bombardment Jaja agreed to treat with Bonny under the arbitration of the kings of New Calabar and Okrika. He delayed as before until once more hostilities broke out. Earl Granville, the British Foreign Secretary of the day, wrote to Livingstone: 'It appears to me, as it did to Lord Clarendon, that the continuance of the present state of affairs is as much owing to the rivalry of the British traders as the quarrels of the natives, and that if it were not for the interference of Europeans the dispute might be easily settled.' The pro-Bonny and pro-Jaja supercargoes both ensured a continual supply of arms to their respective allies. Glover in Lagos was consulted and characteristically advocated direct interference. By Christmas 1870, however, since the Foreign Office refused to countenance interference, Jaja was able to proclaim his new kingdom, which was made up of fourteen of the eighteen houses of Bonny. Jaja had broken Bonny and established what was to be the most important Delta state, until Britain finally declared its protectorate. In 1873 a peace treaty was secured between the two states by Commodore J. E. Commerell, V.C., C.B., with the aid of five warships. Britain recognized Jaja as King of Opobo, who in turn made a few small concessions to Bonny.

The spectacular rise to power of Jaja was paralleled by the unobtrusive but lasting consolidation of British interests in the interior. Despite the ruling of 1865, a consulate was established in Lokoja and the new consul J. M. Macleod set sail on H.M.S. *Investigation* the following year. His ship was attacked by local tribesmen and ran aground. This seemed a signal for local people to give general vent to their resentment against the incursions of the European traders. Bishop Crowther, who was busy extending the scope of the Niger mission, was arrested by an African chief who demanded £1,000 for his ransom. He was, however, rescued in a brilliant sortie by the assistant consul at Lokoja who was himself killed in the fighting. Lokoja was blockaded for six months by hostile tribes, who were ultimately beaten off by allies of the consul. The following year, 1869, the consulate was closed, but the Foreign Office, betraying continued interest in river trade, in 1871 sent W. H. Simpson to negotiate with King Masaba of Nupe for protection of all British traders on the river. Masaba, unlike the chiefs of the river tribes, sought the promotion of trade with the Europeans, since they could provide him with much-needed arms to ward off the many rivals to his throne.

The Lokoja incidents illustrate both the determination of the British to secure trade in the Niger hinterland and the equal determination of most of the river-side tribes to keep the European traders away. Considering the vast investments of the British companies on the Bight of Biafra and along the Niger, which together accounted for over £1,000,000 worth of trade annually, it was unlikely that the British, despite the temporary setback at Lokoja, would give in to their opponents. In 1871 hinterland trade suffered another blow when the government abandoned the naval escort for vessels trading up the Niger and the steamer *Nelson*, having decided to go it alone, was fired on and sank in retreat. Yet in 1872 the consulate in Fernando Po was transferred to Old Calabar, and in 1873 the Courts of Equity, which until then had enjoyed no other sanction than the power of the local chiefs and supercargoes to enforce their decisions, and had at times had those decisions reversed by properly constituted British Courts in Accra, were regularized by an Order in Council. By this Order the consul was empowered to inflict fines of up to £200, imprisonment for 21 days, or order banishment for a year for any breach of regulation between natives and the British. It was clear that, if the British were to

protect trade in the hinterland, a more stable form of administration would have to be maintained in the Delta. In 1875 and
1876 *The Sultan of Sockatoo* was so fiercely attacked that no
steamer dared enter the river. Behind this concerted attack on
the British was the influence of the African middlemen of the
Delta ports, particularly the Brassmen, who resented these incursions into their traditional monopoly of the palm-oil
markets. Slowly it was slipping into the hands of European
traders, who had long since realized that direct trade with the
hinterland was inevitable. Thus the temporary alliance between
Liverpool traders and African middlemen in the Delta was
broken, and the middlemen faced a fairly solid combination of
European interests. But the general interest of the British
traders was often seriously damaged by the cut-throat rivalry
between the various firms. In some small trading stations as
many as five firms had established themselves. By 1878 there
were four major companies trading along the Niger: Messrs.
Alexander Miller Brothers and Co. (Glasgow), James Pinnock
and Co. (Liverpool), West African Company (Manchester) and
The Central African Trading Company (London). They maintained trading posts along the river and brought in over
£300,000 trade a year between them. Their main problem was
the hostility of the interior tribes and their lack of common
policy and direction. The old cut-throat competition characteristic of the Delta was spreading to the interior. By 1878 the
three main companies had established an identical chain of
trading posts on the river. Great losses were also sustained as a
result of attacks by neighbouring tribes, who during the dry
season took advantage of the fact that no steamers could ascend
the river to execute punitive bombardments.

The worst of these attacks was on Onitsha when the trading
houses and the mission station were burnt down. Bishop
Crowther had had a difficult task in maintaining the work of
the Niger mission. Though he had some success in the Delta,
especially in Bonny where the worship of monitor lizards was
officially abandoned in 1867, his missions had been subject to
frequent waves of persecution. Yet by 1880 the Niger mission,
which was entirely in the hands of Africans, had eleven stations.
The mission at Calabar had also extended its work. Two missionaries had reached Oban, Uyanga and Ibami in 1879; and

in 1884 the Rev. Goldie established a mission station at Ikotana on the Cross River. Thus whilst traders were pushing the
boundaries of trade farther into the interior, missionaries were
penetrating remote villages and spreading the Gospel. Most
important of all, they were bringing education to an ever-
increasing number of people. Traders who had for long treated
missionary activity with suspicion, were soon to be thankful for
the supply of clerks that the missionaries produced from their
schools.

Until the 1870's trade both in the hinterland and the Delta
had been almost the exclusive province of British merchants.
Indeed, surprisingly little interest had been shown in West
Africa by other colonial powers. But in the 1870's both Frenchmen and Germans were looking to the west coast for expansion.
Indeed the French were already developing their master plan
for Africa whereby they could link their protectorates of the
north with the west coast and, almost more important, extend
their territory from Senegal to the Horn of Africa. The contem-
plation of such vast possessions had been made feasible by the
success of railways in Australia and America.

Thus the firms trading in the interior were threatened not
only by hostile tribes but, though they did not realize it at that
time, by the possibility of foreign competition. Just at this stage
in Delta politics there arrived in Nigeria a man, subsequently
called 'the Founder of Modern Nigeria', who dealt successfully
with both these threats to the British monopoly of trade along
the Niger. First he set about amalgamating the various Niger
companies, impressing erstwhile rivals with the advantages of
co-operation through sheer force of personality. This was
George Dashwood Goldie Taubman, who had already travelled
in north-east Africa, and had been fired with imperial zeal
from an early age. He had a shrewd appreciation of the ambitions of the French in Africa and was determined that they
should not carry off what he considered the main prize: the
lands of the Niger basin. By November 1879 Goldie (he was
later knighted as Sir George Taubman Goldie) had welded all
the major companies trading on the Niger into the United
African Company, having persuaded their directors that the
only cure for over-competition was monopoly. All ships, stores
and staff were pooled. But this monopoly was soon to be chal-

lenged by the French. In 1878 the Comte de Senelle had visited King Masaba of Nupe's successor, Umoru, with a view to acquiring land for a trading station for his Compagnie française de l'Afrique equatoriale. But though Umoru granted the British a monopoly in 1879, the help given to him against rebels by the French secured for the latter his goodwill. By 1882 this company and the Compagnie du Sénégal et de la Côte Occidentale d'Afrique, were almost of equal strength to the United African Company. Goldie tried to ward off their threat in two ways. First, he proposed that his company should become a charter company so that Britain would establish a protectorate over the Niger through his agency. In 1882 the National African Company was formed with a view to receiving a charter, though the British government refused to contemplate such a move. Secondly, he tried to persuade the French companies to join with his own. When they refused, he undertook a drastic price war against them, using most of his personal fortune and under-cutting their prices by as much as 25 per cent. He forced them out of business in 1884. Goldie did not under-estimate the French menace. In 1883 Jules Ferry, with known imperialist ambitions, became Prime Minister of France, and in 1883 annexed Cotonou, Aghwey, Great and Little Popo and Porto Novo, driving a wedge between the Lagos and Gold Coast settlements of Britain. The French even sent a gunboat to Bonny in an attempt to secure a treaty by which they could establish a protectorate on the mouth of the Niger.

The Germans were active, too. G. L. Gaiser, founder of the present well-known firm, purchased Mahin beach near Lagos, though he was later forced to return it. Goldie anticipated these threats with remarkably clear foresight. The Delta he considered no problem, for with easy access to British gunboats the local chiefs and kings could easily be controlled. The hinterland was a different problem. Since it was inaccessible to warships, it would, he believed, always be possible for another power to gain the interior. Though the British government refused to grant Goldie a charter, it conceded him the right to make treaties with local chiefs. By 1884 he had concluded thirty-seven such treaties. He formed a fleet of twenty gunboats, which proved very valuable as opposition to his company's monopoly increased. Akassa, Brass, Patani and Asaba were all bombarded for attacks on the company's trading factories. On the other hand, when Africans like the Emir of Nupe proved friendly and willing to co-operate, the company was prepared to offer its assistance, and indeed it did give the Emir very substantial help in putting down rebellions in 1881 and 1882. Goldie, in fact, behaved as though he had already been granted a charter by the British government. In 1884, when the Germans sent Herr Flegel to gain treaties with the Sultan of Sokoto and the Emir of Gwandu, it was Goldie through Joseph Thompson who forestalled them.

In July 1884, Germany declared a protectorate over the Cameroons; indeed it was her new interest in West Africa that led to the Berlin Conference at which the European powers agreed on their respective spheres of influence in Africa. At the conference Germany insisted on effective occupation as the basis of delimitation. It was then that the real value of Goldie's work became apparent to the British government, now seriously concerned that the French and Germans might gain too much of the continent. Goldie attended the conference as an official delegate, having broken the rival French company only a fortnight before, and armed with a sheaf of treaties with local rulers. Goldie almost saw his work ruined when Germany proposed the establishment of an international commission to ensure free trade on the Niger, whatever power controlled the territory through which it flowed. However, in exchange for Britain's promise to recognize Leopold of the Belgian's Congo Association, Bismarck supported a revised Niger Navigation Act, which, while it insisted on the principle of international free trade, made no provision for a commission to ensure its observance.

As a result of Goldie's work, Britain had little difficulty in laying claims to the area around the Niger. She formally proclaimed a Protectorate over the Niger Districts in the *Gazette* of 5th June 1885, thus reversing her declared policy of 1865. The Niger Districts were proclaimed 'the territories on the line of coast between the British Protectorate of Lagos and the right or western bank of the Rio del Rey' and the 'territories on both banks of the Niger, from its confluence with the river Benue at Lokoja to the sea, as well as the territories on both banks of the river Benue, from the confluence up to and including Ibi'.

The Consolidation of British Interests

From now on Britain was deeply involved in the affairs of Nigeria. Any hesitation about interfering in the affairs of Yorubaland and the more remote Fulani Empire were cast aside as trading and government interests fused as a result of threatened foreign competition. No consideration to African interest was given either by Britain or the other powers attending the Berlin Conference. West Africa was parcelled out in terms of European political rivalry.

CHAPTER XI

Company and Consuls

The states of the Oil Rivers found the new British Protectorate of the Oil Rivers little more effective than the consular rule that had looked after British interests until the Berlin Conference. It was rather the Niger Company which showed the chiefs of the Delta states that the Berlin Conference had changed irrevocably the *status quo* in Africa. In 1886, as a result of Goldie's determined work over the preceding eight years, the Niger Company was granted the Royal Charter that it had been refused in 1881. Under the terms of this charter the company obtained political authority over those territories with which the company's agents had signed treaties placing them under British protection. The company was to 'discourage and as far as may be practicable, abolish by degrees any system of domestic servitude existing among the inhabitants'. On the other hand the company was enjoined to interfere as little as possible in the affairs of native chiefs. Most important of all were the words, 'Nothing in this Our Charter shall be deemed to authorise the Company to set up or grant a monopoly of trade.' The company's subsequent failure to observe this injunction was to incur the animosity of both African and European traders.

The charter was quite explicit about freedom of trade: 'and subject only to customs duties and charges hereby authorised, and to restrictions on importations similar in character to those applicable in our United Kingdom, trade with the Company's territories under Our protection shall be free and there shall be no differential treatment of the subjects of any power as to the settlement or access to markets, but foreigners alike with British subjects will be subject to administrative dispositions in

169

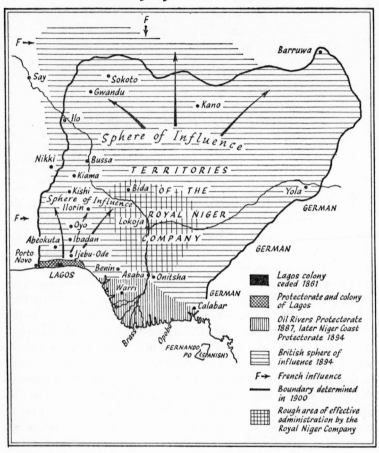

The map legend reads:

- Lagos colony ceded 1861
- Protectorate and colony of Lagos
- Oil Rivers Protectorate 1887, later Niger Coast Protectorate 1894
- British sphere of influence 1894
- F→ French influence
- Boundary determined in 1900
- Rough area of effective administration by the Royal Niger Company

7. The growth of British influence in Nigeria

the interests of commerce and good order.' This conformed with the condition laid down by the Berlin Conference that, while Britain had demonstrated clearly her occupation of the lands along the Niger, that river should be free to navigation by other powers. The history of the administration of the Royal Niger Company, over whose territories British Protection was officially placed in 1887, is largely that of bitter rivalry with its African, British and foreign competitors who all justifiably complained that the company was using its political authority to secure a monopoly of commerce.

The company straightway established its headquarters at Asaba on the Niger, setting up a constabulary, a High Court of Justice and the necessary abministration to run both the territories under its control and its numerous trading posts along the Niger. The northern limits of the Royal Niger Company's territories were not in fact marked. To the south they were bounded by the Oil Rivers Protectorate. A thin strip of land connected Asaba and the hinterland with the company's port at Akassa. Economically the company now controlled the trade of the hinterland where the middlemen of the Delta states as well as the Liverpool traders used to make their living. This would have been acceptable if the company had not exercised monopolistic powers. Indeed the extent of this monopoly was not realized in England until the publication of Sir John Kirk's report on the disturbances at Brass in 1896. Under the regulations of the company, Brassmen were considered as foreigners since Brass lay without the company's territory. Brassmen were therefore required to pay £50 a year for a licence to trade and £10 for each station they traded in. A further £100 a year had to be paid if they required to trade in spirits, 'without which', Sir John Kirk added, 'trade in the Delta is at present impossible'. On top of this the Brass traders had to pay company duties, which it was permitted to levy under the terms of the charter in order to defray the cost of the administration of the territory.

Remembering the value of £100 in the 1880's, it is not surprising that African traders unfortunate enough to live outside the company's territories bitterly resented its policy. Furthermore, by insisting that all trade within its territories pass through Akassa, it dealt a fatal blow to the Delta ports.

No less resentful were the Liverpool merchants in the Delta, as Mary Kingsley, who knew them well and was equally a friend of Goldie, revealed in her *West African Studies*. French and German complaints not unnaturally tended to be biased since both powers were busily extending their colonial interests in other parts of West Africa and regarded the company's territories with covetous eyes. Sir George Goldie had good reason to be suspicious of them. Free navigation of the Niger for foreign powers was all very well if such powers respected the patently tenuous hold of the company over its territories. This it was clear neither the Germans nor the French were prepared to do. In 1887 a German merchant called Hoenisberg entered the Niger with a cargo of salt, with the deliberate intention, it is said, of annoying the company and of 'busting up their Charter'. He had apparently infringed the customs regulations, so his cargo was seized. He then travelled on to Nupe, where it is alleged he intrigued against the company. He was arrested, tried at Asaba and deported. A year later Von Puttkamer, a nephew of Bismarck and German Consul in Lagos, went to Nupe to investigate the case. In fairness to the foreign traders it must be admitted that as with African and Liverpool traders, the company deliberately obstructed their activities. However, the German threat was not the most serious, and indeed boundary agreements were drawn up with Germany in 1886, 1890 and later in 1893. The constant threat to the company came from the French, still fired with the ambition of creating an enormous African empire. Indeed Sir George Goldie himself declared in an interview with Reuters in 1889: 'The only stroke of fortune we have had was the reaction of France in 1884 against colonial enterprises in consequence of those disasters at Tonkin, to which M. Jules Ferry, the great Colonial Minister, owed his downfall and the nickname "Le Tonkinois". But for this reaction in France, which lasted until the Paris Exhibition of 1889, and which she has long and rightly deplored, we might have been pushed out of Nigeria.' The more arbitrary interpretation of the charter by the company as regards its monopolistic control of the territory may better be understood when it is realized just what a threat to the Niger territories the French were.

The French were established on the frontiers of the territories in which the company was interested, both to the west and the north. Technically they also had free access from the south by sea. From their base on the coast of Dahomey they were already trying to establish themselves in Yorubaland.

In 1887 a French mission visited Abeokuta and alleged that it had secured a treaty, never put into effect, permitting it to build a railway from Porto Novo to Abeokuta, and thus drain away the palm-oil trade that was the life-blood of Lagos. There were indications that they were intent on securing a similar treaty with the Alafin of Oyo, so the Governor in Lagos hastened to draw up a treaty of friendship with the Alafin in 1888. In 1889 a Lieutenant Mizon, with a party of Frenchmen and Africans, actually sailed up the lower Niger on a warship armed with a Hotchkiss gun. The party was attacked by the Patani tribe and finally gained succour at Akassa. They then sailed on to Yola, where Mizon attempted to make a treaty with the Emir of Yola. On his return to France Mizon became a national hero as a result of the attack by the Patani, which was not unnaturally attributed to the machinations of the company. Two years later he returned amidst violent protests by the company, but with permission from the Foreign Office, to take an armed party through the company's territories. He reached Muri, where he drew up a treaty with the Emir. As an expression of gratitude, Mizon, against protests from his officers, shelled the local pagan town of Kwang, which the Emir then raided for slaves to sell in the markets of the north. France conquered Dahomey on Nigeria's western borders in 1892, and was rapidly taking the western Sudan under control. To stave off French colonial expansion, particularly towards the Fulani Empire which he had secured by treaty for the company, Goldie put forward the idea that a narrow triangle of hinterland extending to Lake Chad, the modern Cameroons, should be given to Germany. But the real crisis of Anglo-French relations in West Africa came in 1894 with Lugard's famous race to Nikki.

Whilst the Royal Niger Company was established firmly on the Oil Rivers, and as far up the Niger as Jebba, there was a very fluid position in what was known as Borgu. Though France and Britain had made treaties agreeing the boundary between Dahomey and Lagos, this boundary did not go effectively much farther than 100 miles inland. Far to the north a boundary marking the southernmost limit of France's North African possessions was drawn from Say on the upper Niger in a straight line eastwards to Barruwa near Lake Chad, much the same as the present boundary between Northern Nigeria and Niger. A large area of indefinition existed in Borgu, bounded to the north by the Niger, to the east by Nupeland and to the south by Yorubaland. To the west it stretched into modern Dahomey. It was not at all clear which power had rights in this area. It was also not clear whether the Say-Barruwa line merely determined the northern limits to British territory. France chose to read into it that she could expand wherever possible to the south of the line.

The Royal Niger Company was particularly anxious that France should not get a foothold in Borgu since, if she could claim territory to the south of Bussa, she could have a port on the Niger; for the Bussa rapids were the last obstacle to navigation on the river. In 1892 France had declared a protectorate over Dahomey, a development which caused Goldie considerable concern. He claimed Borgu belonged to the company since he made a treaty with the Sultan of Sokoto, suzerain of Borgu. The French, with some historical justification, denied that Sokoto controlled Borgu. Goldie countered this by producing two treaties made with the King of Bussa, who styled himself 'Lord of all Borgu'. The French quickly replied that the King of Nikki was the real suzerain of Borgu. In this there was again some truth for although Bussa was the ancestral home of the Nikki rulers, who had to acknowledge spiritual overlordship from its King, in terms of real political power Nikki was the more important. At that time no one had visited Nikki or knew its exact location. It was even a possibility that the Germans, busily establishing themselves in Togoland, might make a dash to Nikki. The French rushed off an expedition under Decoeur to gain a treaty with Nikki; Goldie was not caught unawares and arranged for Captain Lugard, who had already distinguished himself as a pioneer of Empire in East Africa, to make the treaty with Nikki on Britain's behalf.

Although the exact location of Nikki was unknown, the French expedition had the easier task for their base in Dahomey was a straight march to Nikki. Lugard, who arrived in Nigeria in August 1894, had to start off at a great disadvantage from the company's base at Akassa several hundred miles down the coast. (His task would have been easier if he could have left from Lagos.) With a small caravan of Hausa and Yoruba soldiers, he sailed up to Jebba thus starting what was to become a very long association with Nigeria. Lugard made a quick call on the King of Bussa, feeling that if he were really the 'Lord of all Borgu', he would be able to provide an excellent introduction to the King of Nikki. After some delay Bussa promised to send envoys and letters to the kings of both Kaiama and Nikki in exchange for gunpowder. Lugard returned to Jebba to make preparations for immediate departure with a caravan for Borgu, hoping that Decoeur would be delayed because of the rains which made travel extremely difficult at that time of the year. On 28th September Lugard, with a caravan of 320 carriers and soldiers, set out on what was later to be called the Nikki Steeplechase. Under appalling weather conditions, more often as not low with fever, Lugard pushed westwards to Borgu. At Kishi in the very north of Yorubaland, and but a few yards from the frontier of Borgu, he made a treaty with the local sovereign who gratefully remarked to Lugard that 'the British had introduced law and order into all Yoruba and at last it had come to them'. Despite descriptions of the wildness of Borgu, Lugard was given a very friendly reception by the King of Kaiama with whom a treaty was drawn up. Kaiama warned Lugard of the dangers of Borgu, and advised him on no account to travel beyond Nikki. As he neared that town a messenger arrived to say that the King had been told that if he looked at a white man he would die within three months. Lugard replied that if he did not receive a favourable message within two days he would move in another direction. The loss would be Nikki's not his. This ruse seems to have paid off, for two days later the messenger returned to say that the King would admit the strangers. His reception of them was very unfriendly. Lugard, however, was relieved to find that he had beaten the French. Eventually after much procrastination Lugard obtained the treaty, five days before the arrival of Decoeur's party.

Lugard returned to London to find that his treaty was fast becoming the cause of an international incident. The French hotly contested its validity. In her biography of Lugard, Margery Perham has written of the international background: 'The European nations at this time were not unlike a lot of greedy, quarrelsome children in a school playground; none quite big enough to dominate all the others, kicking and then making up to each other, sulking, coaxing, telling each other secrets and then "splitting", combining for a moment and then breaking up. Britain was the rather aloof child in the corner, a little superior, unwilling to join wholeheartedly in the rough games and yet warily watching lest too many of these quarrelling school mates combined against her.' The Nikki question very nearly developed into an international incident. Both Chamberlain, the British Colonial Secretary, and his French opposite indulged in what had by then become determined brinkmanship to ensure that they retained as much of Africa as possible.

The Royal Niger Company under Goldie extended its frontiers northwards by its conquest of the Emir of Nupe, who had been slave-raiding into the company's territories. To the west it also conquered Ilorin, which had aided the Emir of Nupe and had been a constant thorn in the flesh of the British administration in Lagos. Ilorin lay just to the south of Borgu, where France still had ambitions. The French then stationed a Resident at Ilo, on the Niger, with instructions to occupy territory as far south as Bussa. The French also took Kishi, with which Lugard had signed a treaty. They also placed Kaiama under their protection. It thus became imperative for Britain to stop France's advance along the Niger. But Britain was severely handicapped by the fact that the government had delegated its authority to a chartered company, whilst the French could bring down the full weight of governmental administration behind their ambitions. It was clear that sooner or later a stand would have to be made against the French. Chamberlain favoured conceding the right bank of the Niger to a point thirty miles south of Bussa, which would have allowed the French their port. This Goldie hotly contested, citing his treaty with Bussa. Eventually Chamberlain decided on the creation of a military force under the command of Lugard, which would hold the position of the Royal Niger Company in the hinterland. Lugard returned to Nigeria in the spring of 1898. By 16th April he was at Lokoja where the 1st Battalion of the West African Frontier Force paraded before him.

Lugard immediately set about organizing his small force to deal with the French who were by then established at both Ilo and Bussa. Lugard's task was to take as much of the territory in this area of undefined sovereignty as he could without precipitating actual fighting. The French had been given roughly the same order—so that both sides were really playing an elaborate game of political chess. While this tense campaign of non-violence, in which any single false move might have meant war, was played out in the dry savannah of Borgu, negotiations in

12. James White preaching before King Akitoye of Lagos

13. King Jaja of Opobo

14. King Pepple of Bonny

15. King Obie of Aboh visiting the steam vessels *Alburkah* and *Quorra*

Paris and London were bringing settlement closer. Chamberlain eventually secured a favourable agreement with France, gambling on the strength of Lugard's force and French reluctance to start a war. On many occasions there were very real dangers of fighting, yet by his brilliant brinkmanship Chamberlain, against the opposition of his own Prime Minister, Lord Salisbury, secured a most favourable treaty with France. The French did not get access to the navigable stretch of the Niger, although the British were pushed down the Niger 100 miles from Say to Ilo. The French were given Nikki and the northern boundary of Nigeria was determined as a slight variation on the Say–Barruwa line.

British encroachments on Nigerian territory did not go unresisted by the local population. The Delta middlemen in particular demonstrated their resentment of the increasing power of the Royal Niger Company. This opposition was epitomized by the actions of Jaja, King of Opobo. The year before the Treaty of Berlin, Jaja had made his own treaty with the British by which he placed his country under the protection of the British Crown, but he ensured that the usual clause guaranteeing freedom of trade was omitted. He had suspiciously asked for a definition of the word Protectorate. Hewitt, who as consul had negotiated the treaty, defined it thus: '. . . the Queen does not want to take your country or your markets, but at the same time she is anxious that no other nation should take them. She undertakes to extend her gracious power and protection, which will leave your country still under your government: she has no wish to disturb your rule . . .' (Letter 8th January 1884). This concession was probably made because the French and Germans were also attempting to gain a foothold on territories already under British Protection.

Jaja had at first been treated with considerable sympathy by the British consul. In 1875 he had even sent a contingent to the Ashanti war, as a result of which he was awarded a sword by Queen Victoria. On the other hand he was a bitter opponent of free trade, preventing any European trader dealing direct with his sources of supply. Indeed any tribe that dared to trade direct with the European merchants was punished swiftly, as the Kwa Ibo learnt in 1881 when Jaja captured and executed hundreds of their number. His men fell on the group of villages known as Ibuno (Ibeno). Mr. Holt, the Liverpool trader, writing to Earl Granville, described the incident thus:

'. . . at daylight on the 11th April last he suddenly invaded them with a force of about fifty fully manned canoes, armed with breech loading cannon and rifles, by means of which he bombarded seven of their villages, which he plundered and afterwards burnt, destroying their crops and stores of food, and taking prisoners upwards of 100 people, whilst the natives of Qua Eboe, unable to protect themselves, and without any means of defence, took to the woods, where many of them greatly suffered from want and exposure.

'Jaja's canoe remained in the river several days, broke into Mr. Watt's Factory, scattered his goods about, and either took away or destroyed a number of barrels and hogsheads of oil belonging to him which were in the native towns that were looted. With their plunder and their prisoners, consisting chiefly of women and children, they returned at length to Opobo, where their unhappy victims were cruelly slaughtered, Jaja's own children being made to cut off the heads of some of the Qua Eboe children, to entitle them to wear the "eagle plume" a mark of distinction bestowed only on those who have slain an enemy.'

Whatever the terms of Jaja's 1884 treaty, the international Treaty of Berlin, made far from the sombre creeks of the Oil Rivers, had handed over his country to Britain, and inevitably there was soon to be a clash. Jaja was already involved in a major trade dispute during which European traders had formed the Amalgamated Association to break his monopoly. Oil prices had risen very favourably in England in 1883 and 1884, and this had led to a rise in prices in the Delta, which trimmed the extra profits the English traders had hoped to make. Their boycott to force down Jaja's prices failed since the firm of Alexander Miller Brothers and Co. of Glasgow agreed to trade at his prices. In June 1885 the new consul, H. W. Johnston, who supported the association, explained to Jaja that as a result of the 1885 Berlin Treaty freedom of trade in the Oil Rivers was now guaranteed. This encouraged the excluded firms, who bitterly resented the fact that Jaja was now shipping oil direct to England, to seek markets up-river. However, Jaja was well prepared and his agents threatened vengeance on any tribe that traded with the Europeans. This was no idle threat to anyone who remembered his expedition against the Kwa Ibo in 1881.

In 1887 the consul, by way of retaliation, forbade Jaja to exact his 'comey' or customs duties on the grounds that his direct shipment of oil was unjust competition with those who paid the duty. Jaja protested to the Secretary of State for the Colonies, and sent a delegation of chiefs to Britain. Consul Johnston decided to take drastic action against Jaja whom he believed to be the instigator of the attacks on English merchants in July. He threatened Jaja with gunboats unless he called off his trade war. Under such a threat Jaja agreed to open trade, but in fact did little to alter the situation. On news of trouble in the markets Johnston sailed up river only to find a boom blocking his way. He then telegraphed London for permission to deport Jaja, and on receiving what he considered an affirmative reply, which was in fact probably the reply to an earlier and quite unrelated telegram, he arranged for Jaja's expulsion. Johnston sailed to Opobo on H.M.S. *Goshawk* and invited Jaja to meet him on the beach of Messrs. Harrisons, which Jaja refused to do unless he had the consul's pledge that he would go free after the meeting. Johnston agreed to this in these words: 'I hereby assure you that whether you accept or reject my proposals tomorrow no restraint whatever will be put on you—you will be free to go as soon as you have heard the message of the Government.' But, once there, Jaja was told that if he did not go to Accra for trial he would be considered an enemy and Opobo would be bombarded. Under the cover of H.M.S. *Goshawk's* guns, there was little Jaja could do, so he sailed for Accra where he was found guilty of blocking the highway of trade, and of failing to honour Article V of his treaty of Britain whereby:

'The King and Chiefs of Opobo hereby engage to assist the British Consular or other officers in the execution of such duties as may be assigned them, and further to act upon their advice in matters relating to the administration of Justice, the development of the resources of the country, the interests of commerce, or in any matter in relation to peace, order and Government and the general progress of civilisation.'

He was deported to the West Indies on a pension of £800 a year, and when at last in 1891 he was allowed to return home he died on the way.

Jaja's was the most brilliant, but by no means the last, stand against the British.

Until 1891 no effective government was instituted by Britain for her new Oil Rivers Protectorate, especially none that could deal with situations such as had arisen at Opobo. The energetic consul, H. H. Johnston, tried unsuccessfully to develop the Courts of Equity into a system of governing councils. He also endeavoured to bring the Protectorate as much under British control as possible. He had secured the friendship of Nana, an important trader on the Benin River, whom he appointed Governor of the Benin River. Trade was expanding rapidly. Thus, in 1891, when Sir Claude Macdonald, and not he, was appointed Governor of the Oil Rivers Protectorate, Johnston felt justifiable disappointment. Macdonald had already gained first-hand knowledge of the Delta when he headed an inquiry into allegations made against the Royal Niger Company in 1889. His policy as Commissioner General and Consul General was to avoid the inclusion of his Protectorate in that of the Royal Niger Company. He believed firmly in free trade, and rightly deduced that the Delta kings would not tolerate government by the company. Unlike Johnston, he believed the Delta middlemen could be used to advantage. Thus, on 1st January 1891 Britain established an effective government for her protectorate, with a revenue in the first years of nearly £90,000 derived from import duties. In 1893 the Oil Rivers Protectorate became the Niger Coast Protectorate and included all those areas that had made treaties with Britain and were not included in the Royal Niger Company Protectorate. It was governed by a Consul General responsible to the Foreign Office, under whom served a number of vice-consuls responsible for individual areas. Its administration included customs, postal, marine and medical departments as well as a small army of 200 men. But the extension of this power, even under an enlightened administrator like Macdonald, did not go unchallenged. In 1893 an Akuna chief on the Cross River brought trade to a standstill by deliberately provoking an inter-tribal war. He had murdered some Ibo traders who had been trading with his own people. As a result the newly formed constabulary was sent to end the war, and bring the chief to justice. He was tried and hanged. A much greater challenge to this newly con-

stituted authority came from Nana, Governor of the Benin
River. At first he had co-operated with the Protectorate government. But he also created a monopoly on the Benin River and
carried on a surreptitious trade in slaves. In 1894 Acting Consul
General Moor informed the Foreign Office that Nana had
strangled trade on the Benin River and that he had continually
defied his authority. Moor sent despatches to Nana summoning
him to answer charges against him, but Nana made excuses.
Moor then forbade Nana's men to trade on the river, and once
again summoned Nana, who not unnaturally refused to go,
remembering what had happened to Jaja.

Nana defied all edicts that the river should be made free to
traders and placed a bar across the creek leading to his headquarters at Brohemie. The gunboat *Alecto* was sent to blow up
the barrier, but while it did so it was fired on by Nana's troops.

On the 28th H.M.S. *Phoebe* came to the rescue of *Alecto* with
200 men and 150 members of the constabulary. Nana put up
so strong a fight against this new party that H.M.S. *Philomel*
and H.M.S. *Widgeon* had to be brought up in support. On the
25th September 1894 a strong attack was made on Brohemie
which was captured without casualties, the explanation for
this being that Nana had seen the red light and tried to escape.
He had even made an ingenious, if desperate, effort to cut a
canal from Brohemie to a creek behind the town to evacuate all
his goods. These, as the attackers found, consisted of thousands
of pounds' worth of merchandise, including 8,300 cases of gin.
The town was a veritable arsenal with 106 cannon, 14 tons of
gunpowder, 445 blunderbusses adapted for use on war canoes,
and a machine-gun. Nana gave himself up to the authorities in
Lagos, where he was tried and deported to the Gold Coast. The
importance of Nana at this stage of Nigerian history was considerable. Like Jaja he stands out as one of the few who offered
serious resistance to the encroaching British power, and, as
Mr. E. L. Cook has pointed out in *British Enterprise in Nigeria*,
he established the principle of removing native chiefs who
opposed British penetration, rather than seeking their co-
operation.

The real bitterness felt against the Royal Niger Company by
those it deprived of trade did not come to a head until 1895
when the Brassmen raided Akassa, the company's port. After

years of ineffective resistance to the company's authority, the Brassmen resorted to violence. This had been contemplated before, and the British government was sufficiently aware of the fact to have sent Macdonald to investigate certain allegations made about the company's monopolistic practices. Though he sympathized with the Brassmen, he found that the company had acted within the terms of its charter. The Brassmen took every measure to evade the stringent rules of the company, but by 1895 the situation had become so intolerable to them that they made a direct attack on the company. On 27th January the vice-consul at Brass received an anonymous letter informing him that the Brassmen were to raid the company's port at Akassa. The vice-consul, who did not give much credence to the warning, nevertheless sent the letter on to the company's Agent General at Akassa, who likewise thought the whole affair far-fetched.

He took the precaution of sending off a patrol and setting a machine-gun at a commanding position on the river. Under cover of darkness, and cloaked by the heavy evening mists of the river, the Brass canoes by-passed the patrol, and attacked Akassa. They destroyed the stores and captured sixty men whom they took to Nembe, for which Brass was the port, eating forty-three of them. None of the European traders was taken.

Though the attack had been made on the company, Brass fell within the jurisdiction of the Niger Coast Protectorate and the Consul General was left to deal with the situation. The Brassmen, who were asked to surrender all their chiefs and armaments, refused to do so, stating that their quarrel was not with the Queen, whom the Consul General represented, but with the company. All they wanted was free access to their old markets. In effect they were complaining as bitterly about the company's monopoly as the Protectorate administration had complained of Nana's.

The Consul General then informed the Brass chiefs that if they did not obey his orders they would be punished. They played for time whilst they prepared their defences. A naval force with a contingent of Protectorate troops broke the barrier on Nembe creek, landed on Sacrifice Island and, despite fierce resistance by the Brassmen, captured it. Another ultimatum was issued to say that the town would be destroyed if the chiefs did not comply. They continued to hedge, so the punitive force attacked Nembe and against stiff resistance captured and burnt it.

The Protectorate government had now established its authority over all the traditional centres of trade except Benin. That proud and ancient kingdom had withdrawn increasingly from overseas trade and its king had actually issued a decree forbidding his people to trade with Europeans. Furthermore, the old kingdom had gained a notorious reputation because of the prominent role human sacrifice had played in its religion in recent years. In 1862 Sir Richard Burton, the consul at Fernando Po, had tried to persuade Oba Adolo to abolish human sacrifice, but he did not fully appreciate the very deep religious role sacrifice played in the life of the Bini. Gods had constantly to be propitiated through human sacrifice, for if this were not done disaster would follow for the kingdom. However, in 1892 Galway, Vice-Consul for the Benin River District, did visit Benin and persuaded Oba Ovenramwen to sign a treaty by which Benin was placed under British protection and human sacrifice and slavery were abolished. Trade was also opened. This did not last for long and in 1896 Acting Consul General Phillips decided to visit Ovenramwen to press his compliance with the treaty. Early in 1897 Phillips set off for Benin at the time of the great Ague festival during which the Oba should see no man who was not a Bini. For the Bini this was a festival of the greatest importance for it marked the time of rededication by the Bini to their king. It was also a time for extensive human sacrifice.

Phillips informed Oba Ovenramwen of his intention to visit him, but did not wait for a reply. Ovenramwen was considerably embarrassed, for he knew that to refuse would be to incur the wrath of Britain, but to accept would be to incur the even more dire wrath of the gods. Phillips did not wait for a reply and set off from Gwato, the port for Benin, and was met by the Oba's messenger, led by Ologbosere, who ordered him and his party to turn back. In the ensuing dispute tempers appear to have been lost, and six of the British party of nine, including Phillips, were killed, together with most of their escort of about 200 men.

Company and Consuls

Within six weeks of the massacre a punitive expedition of 1,500 was sent to Benin. Ovenramwen had feared this outcome and human sacrifices were increased in a desperate attempt to ward off the inevitable. This, at least, would explain the otherwise staggering number of sacrifices described by Ling Roth, surgeon to the expedition, in Great Benin. The Bini were conquered, the town burnt and nearly 2,500 of its magnificent bronzes taken by the British back to Europe. Ovenramwen fled, but after threats by the British he was delivered up six months later. He was tried on 1st September 1897, and deported to Calabar. The fall of Benin was the last major act in the British occupation of Southern Nigeria and marked the end of one of the greatest and most colourful of West African kingdoms.

In Lagos the Governor still viewed with considerable concern the strife in the interior which caused constant interruption to trade. By 1888 palm-oil trade was worth £1,172,840 in the first six months, three-fifths of it was in British hands and much passed through Lagos. Moreover, the French were active in Dahomey, and threatened to interfere in Yorubaland if he himself did not. In January of 1886 Lagos was detached from the Gold Coast and became self-administering. Governor Maloney almost straightway sent delegations to the various parties warring in the interior. The two delegations, led by the Rev. S. Johnson, author of the *History of the Yorubas*, and the Rev. C. Phillips, were initially successful. A cease-fire was arranged between the Ekiti-Parapo and the Ibadan, but the Ilorin were still reluctant to call off battle unless the Offa, with whom they were fighting, did so first. Johnson and Phillips then went southeast to Ife where they negotiated peace between that town and its Oyo rival and neighbour, Modakeke.

The various factions then sent representatives to Lagos where a peace treaty was signed including all Yorubaland except Ilorin, which still refused to negotiate. Under the terms of the treaty Ibadan was to be independent of Oyo, and the various members of the Ekiti-Parapo were to have their independence. The Alafin of Oyo and the Owa of Ilesha should be as an older to a younger brother; Modakeke was to be rebuilt within Ibadan territory; and the two war camps should be disbanded. A small Hausa force, led by the Acting Colonial Secretary, Henry Higgins, set off to supervise the dismantling of the war camps. Here is how Higgins described the last major act in the long drama of the civil wars:

'The rains ceased before the meeting took place and, the mist clearing away, the sun shone brilliantly on the scene. Thousands of people were to be seen posted on the huge boulders of rock which were scattered through the Kiriji camp, and crowned the summit of the mountain (the Oke Mesin camp was not visible from the place of meeting, there being a slight rising in the ground between) and, as we learned afterwards, the sound of the gun which was to announce that peace had been concluded, and that the people could go to their homes, was most anxiously awaited in both camps and received, when heard, with cheers and hurrahs.'

The main problem of the peace settlement was Modakeke, the Oyo refugee town near Ife. This had by now grown into a huge town of 60,000 inhabitants, difficult enough to disband at the best of times, let alone at the height of the rainy season. Yet this was what the treaty implied, and it is little wonder that the Modakeke refused to move.

Peace was still not finally restored to the harassed Yoruba, for in the north the Ilorin were fighting with the Offa who were in alliance with the Ibadan. The Ibadan themselves tried to mediate a settlement, but failed, and after their withdrawal the chiefs of Offa submitted to the Emir of Ilorin who had them all murdered. He then raided south to Ikirun in search of slaves. Meanwhile, the Dahomeyans were still a menace on the western frontier, invading Oyo in 1887. To the south the Ijebu tightened their control over the roads once again. All Oyo and European traders were forbidden to enter Ijebu territory. The situation was further complicated by the arrival of a French mission in Abeokuta, where arrangements were made for a treaty whereby France would build a railway from Porto Novo to Lagos. The apparent advantages of the peace arrived at between the Ibadan and the Ekiti-Parapo must have seemed completely lost to the Lagos Governor, especially when he heard that the French intended securing a treaty with the Alafin himself. Thus, as we have already seen, the Governor hastened to make a treaty with the Alafin by which it was agreed Oyo should cede no territory, open trade to all and levy no tolls, except with the agreement of the Governor in Lagos. All this was to be granted in exchange for 200 bags of cowries a year. Even so the war between the Ibadan and Ilorin appeared to have no end in sight. Ibadan became even more loth to call a cease-fire when she caught some Egba traders carrying arms to the Ilorin. In 1890 Governor Maloney despatched yet another mission to the Ilorin, and Samuel Johnson was sent off to see the Alafin, who gave him little co-operation. But the other Commissioners, in an attempt to get the Ibadan to agree to be more loyal to the Alafin, obtained the consent of the Ibadan that any dispute over the limits of their territory should be settled by the Alafin and the Governor. As Samuel Johnson observed, the Alafin, by agreeing to such an arrangement was in effect conceding part of his sovereign rights to the Governor. The Alafin became more co-operative with the Lagos government in his attempts to stop the war as a result of the Dahomeyan menaces on his western frontier. He approached the Ilorin who indicated initial interest but carried on their raids, thereby making a settlement impossible. In the south the Egbado, long oppressed by the Egba, appealed to the Governor to place them under British protection.

Not trusting the French, who were dangerously near Egbado territory as a result of the delimitation of French and British spheres of influence reached in the 1890 agreement, Maloney established a small British garrison at Ilaro, the Egbado capital. For the first time Britain had gained a foothold in Yorubaland. So furious were the Egba that they embargoed all trade with Lagos, and for a time the city came to a commercial standstill, though eventually the Egba themselves recommenced trade, due to economic pressures in Abeokuta. Following closely on the Egba decision to reopen the roads came more trouble with the Ijebu who closed their roads in an attempt to prevent the British in Lagos trading with Ibadan, via Shagamu, which they foresaw would deprive them of their position as middlemen. This position the Ijebu abused cruelly: Johnson, who it must be remembered was an Oyo himself, described at great length the injustices inflicted by the Ijebu on the Ibadan and Oyo trading through their territory to Lagos. They were able to do this with impunity since they knew that Ibadan depended on them for its supply of arms. The Ijebu position remained intact under Governor Maloney, who, Johnson assures us, was not a man of action. 'It was said that he was too fond of writing letters to and drafting treaties for men who hardly appreciated the one or comprehended the other nor knew the force or value of their marks or signature.

'During his five years of administration he never once visited the people and scene of which he so much writes: a single visit from him would have cleared up many difficulties in his way and enabled him to understand much, and he would have acted more to the purpose. No wonder then that matters remained *in statu quo*.'

On Maloney's retirement, Denton, the Colonial Secretary, became acting Governor and attempted to visit the Awujale of Ijebuland to secure a peaceful solution to the problem. The Awujale agreed to the visit, but on Denton's arrival at Ijebu-Ode he was roughly received by the chiefs, and though the Awujale showed some signs of friendliness the chiefs did not attempt to hide their deep hostility to the interference of the Lagos government, and refused to accept the customary presents the acting Governor brought them. This Denton rightly diagnosed as a calculated insult.

This incident led the British government to decide on coercive measures against the Ijebu, and Sir Gilbert Carter arrived as next Governor, determined to bring peace to the interior once and for all. He demanded an apology from the Awujale for his treatment of acting Governor Denton. This was agreed to, as well as a treaty abolishing human sacrifices and opening trade routes in return for a subsidy of £500 a year to cover loss of revenue from tolls to the Awujale. As we have already seen, the chiefs of Ijebu-Ode were deeply opposed to any form of treaty with the British, and under their influence the roads were soon closed again, especially since the ordinary Ijebu did not benefit from the £500 paid to the Awujale in lieu of tolls. The Awujale then took action that may be construed as seeking to placate the Ijebu chiefs. The Awujale, picking a quarrel with the Ibadan, accused the Rev. D. Olubi of the C.M.S. of bringing the Europeans into the interior, and passing European goods through Ijebu-Ode by means of his son. The Awujale demanded the heads both of Olubi and of the Rev. T. Harding, his English colleague. The Ibadan were so frightened by the Awujale's threats that it seems clear that both Olubi and Harding would have lost their lives had not Sir Gilbert Carter decided to send a military expedition against the Awujale in May 1892. The punitive force landed at the port of Epe on the 13th and with difficulty battled its way through to Ijebu-Ode which was found deserted except for the Awujale and a few chiefs. The speedy defeat of the Ijebu was the most significant step in the British occupation of Yorubaland. As Johnson wrote: 'The people felt instinctively that a new era was about to dawn on them. A new and foreign power had entered into the arena of active politics in the country, and everyone was exercised in mind as to how the country would be affected by it.

'To the vast majority of the common people it was like the opening of a prison door: and no one who witnessed the patient, long-suffering, and toiling mass of humanity that week by week streamed to and from the coast with their produce could refrain from heaving a sigh of gratification on the magnitude of the beneficial results of the short and sharp conflict.'

For the first time in years caravans passed freely through Ijebu-Ode. 'They brought cloths of native manufacture, cotton indigo, palm oil, palm kernels, beads, cattle, poultry, yam flour, pots and plates of native manufacture, calabashes in large quantities, turkeys and pigeons, rubber, etc., and took back mostly salt, cloths and other articles of European manufacture, trade rum, gin, matches, etc.'

The speed with which Ijebu was subjected was not lost on the rest of Yorubaland. The Egba sent emissaries to the Governor to present their apologies for their past closing of the roads. Early in 1893 Sir Gilbert Carter set off on his famous trek in which he effectively brought Yorubaland under British influence if not control. At Abeokuta he made a treaty with the chiefs whereby all disputes between Egba and the British were to be settled by the Governor, human sacrifice was to be abolished, and roads were to be closed only with the consent of the British. In effect a British Protectorate had been established. On the other hand a special clause was inserted in the treaty to stipulate that as long as the terms of the treaty were observed there would be no question of annexation without the consent of the Egba.

From Abeokuta Sir Gilbert Carter trekked north to Oyo where, after certain difficulties, the Governor was able to draw up a treaty with the Alafin. The British were given free access to all parts of Yorubaland (i.e. under the Alafin's control) and the roads to Lagos were to be kept open. Christianity would be tolerated and human sacrifice abolished. There would be no agreement made by the Alafin with other powers unless by permission of the Governor as representative of the Queen of England. Any disputes between the parties to the treaty were to be referred to the Governor in Lagos. This treaty clearly compromised the Alafin's sovereignty in favour of Britain. From Oyo the Governor continued what was to be a triumphal trek through Ogbomosho to Ilorin, where he succeeded in persuading both Ilorin and Ibadan to break up their respective war camps. Thus ended sixteen years of bitter war.

The only check to this progress through Yorubaland was in Ibadan. The Ibadan refused to sign the agreement Carter drew up for them on the grounds that most of them as warriors had been absent from their town for many years and found it impossible to negotiate such a treaty without giving it deeper consideration. Furthermore, they objected to the idea that they should have a European Resident stationed in their town.

Carter returned to a triumphal reception in Lagos, for his brilliant diplomatic tour had brought an end to nearly a century of fighting, and had once and for all secured the trade of the interior for Lagos. But he could not resist a few words of bitterness about his failure at Ibadan. He even suggested that it was due to the machinations of someone in his own retinue. Johnson rightly dismisses this: 'His Excellency might have allowed such men as govern a town like Ibadan and all its dependents some credit of knowing their own minds and not be swayed by a mere clerk in his office.' Ibadan accepted the treaty, however, in August 1893, after careful assurances by the Governor that he had no intention of interfering with the government of Ibadan.

The treaty with Ibadan declared that although the Alafin would continue to be recognized as 'the King and Head of Yorubaland' Ibadan should become its headquarters; the treaty made with Oyo should be recognized; land should be provided for a railway; and a Resident plus a small constabulary should be appointed. After this treaty there was peace in Yorubaland. A small fracas with Oyo was quickly dealt with by the first resident, Captain Bower, when he had to take a punitive expedition to Oyo after the Alafin had carried out the emasculation of a man found guilty of a crime for which that punishment was normally meted out. But only Ilorin really remained a thorn in the flesh of the Lagos administration. As we have seen, that problem was finally settled by a punitive expedition despatched by the Royal Niger Company.

The peace Carter achieved was followed up by measures to promote the trade which Britain had always avowed was her main reason for interfering in the politics of Yorubaland. Roads were built and the railway from Lagos to Ibadan was started. Whatever the motives of the British in interfering in Yorubaland, there is no doubt that at the time the Yoruba must have been one of the few African peoples who really welcomed such intervention, for it brought them peace after a century of some of the most complex and seemingly futile wars on the African continent.

CHAPTER XII

Emirs and Maxims

The system of administration employed by Britain over its various protectorates in Nigeria had so many defects and so many anomalies that it was inevitable that some change should be made. The unpopularity of the Royal Niger Company in the south, and the difficulties of establishing administrative competence over those territories of the north assigned to Britain, led to the withdrawal of the company's charter. In a letter to the Secretary of the Treasury on 15th June 1899, Lord Salisbury gave these reasons for his change of policy:

'The Marquess of Salisbury has for some time past had under consideration the question of approaching the Niger Company with a view to relieving them of their rights and functions of administration on reasonable terms. . . . There are, however, other cogent reasons for the step now contemplated. The West African Frontier Force, now under Imperial officers, calls for direct Imperial control; the situation created towards other firms by the commercial position of the Company, which, although strictly within the right devolving upon it by Charter, has succeeded in establishing a practical monopoly of trade; the manner in which this commercial monopoly presses on the native trader, as exemplified by the rising in Brass, which called for the mission of inquiry entrusted to Sir John Kirk in 1895, are some of the arguments which have influenced his Lordship. . . .'

Probably much more important in Lord Salisbury's reasoning was the critical international situation that had arisen on the Niger, culminating in the French occupation of Bussa in 1897. It became clear that direct governmental control would have to be exercised over the area if the situation was not to get out of hand.

The Niger Company was fully compensated for the loss of its privileged position. The administrative buildings were bought up and a sum of £450,000 was paid as compensation. What is more, the government undertook to impose royalties on all minerals won in the region bounded by the Niger and a line drawn from Zinder to Yola, and to pay half of these royalties to the company for ninety-nine years. In return the British government took control of all the company's territories on 1st January 1900. The whole of Nigeria was then reorganized into three administrative areas under the Colonial Office instead of the Foreign Office. The Niger Coast Protectorate which had been transferred to the Colonial Office in April 1899, was included in the new Protectorate of Southern Nigeria which absorbed former company territory as far north as Idah; Lagos remained an official colony together with a small Protectorate; and a new Protectorate of Northern Nigeria was established bounded by the frontiers agreed at the Anglo-French Convention of 1898. The name Nigeria was chosen by the British government in preference to such suggestions as 'Niger Sudan', 'Negretia' and even 'Goldesia' in honour of Sir George Taubman Goldie.

In the south the new Protectorate was sufficient of a reality for the administration to set about establishing itself in earnest, though a series of punitive expeditions had to be made before the administration became effective in certain areas. The Protectorate of Northern Nigeria was nothing but a cartographical claim. As Margery Perham wrote of Sir Frederick Lugard's appointment as High Commissioner, 'a colonial governor can seldom have been appointed to a territory so much of which had never even been viewed by himself or any other European'. The British held positions along the banks of the Niger alone and, as the cunning Emir of Kontagora slyly assured his people, were really a species of fish unable to live away from the Niger. It fell to Lugard to prove to the powerful emirs like Kontagora that the white invaders could indeed live a mammalian existence.

Northern Nigeria had been profoundly influenced by the Holy War of Usman dan Fodio, and because of the coherent

| Glover | Goldie | Lugard |

| Macaulay | Macpherson | Robertson |

| Azikiwe | Abubakar | Awolowo |

| Sardauna | Akintola | Okpara |

16. MAKERS OF MODERN NIGERIA

17. Onitsha: a large trading port on the Niger

18. Modern Ibadan, capital of the Western Region

organization of the Fulani Empire presented a formidable resistance to the small forces at Lugard's disposal. In the sixty years that had followed Sultan Bello's death, the Fulani administration had lost much of its reformist character, becoming increasingly materialistic in outlook. Conditions varied from state to state. Some, like Kontagora, lived entirely on the proceeds of slave-raiding, and in the process depopulated vast tracts of land. Others, like Kano, lived on commercial and agricultural prosperity. There has been a strong tendency to talk of the decadence of the Fulani administration in its later years. Certainly it fell off from the high standards set by Usman dan Fodio and his son Sultan Bello. In cases like that of Kontagora, often used as a justification for British intervention, affairs were lamentable. In 1880 Ibrahim Nagwamatse, son of the founder of the small Emirate of Kontagora, set out on a ruthless plan to expand his lands. In the course of his conquests he captured thousands of slaves for sale in the northern markets and devastated hundreds of villages, killing off anyone unsaleable as a slave and leaving a once populous land so desolate that even today it is one of the most sparsely populated areas of the north. When later he was captured by the British and asked to renounce the slave-trade, he taunted: 'Can you stop a cat from mousing? I shall die with a slave in my mouth.' Certainly the example of Kontagora did much to colour British views of Fulani administration. Major Sharpe, Resident of Kontagora, described his province as denuded of all its inhabitants except old men and babies. It is a contrast therefore to read the notes made by Major Burdon, an early resident in the north, which show a marked enthusiasm for the Fulani and their administration. He writes: 'What is the attitude of the British Administration towards these states? Briefly it is construction not destruction. Our aim is to rule through existing chiefs, to raise them in the administrative scale, to enlist them on our side in the work of progress and good government. We cannot do without them. To rule directly would require an army of British magistrates . . . which both the general unhealthiness of the country and the present poverty forbid. My hope is that we may make of these born rulers a high type of British official, working for the good of their subjects in accordance with the ideals of British Empire, but carrying on all that is best in the constitution they

have evolved for themselves, the one understood by, and therefore best suited to the people.'

These are not the words of a man who has recognized an
empire about to collapse. Unpopular it may have been, but the
system of administration was still effective and developing. The
materialism of later years should not be confused with ineffi-
ciency. After the death of Sultan Bello there was in fact a tendency to greater centralization on the twin capitals of Sokoto
and Gwandu. The Emirs of Zaria, for instance, were selected
by the Sultans of Sokoto, who usually chose them from among
the three families in Zaria, on the recommendations of the
electoral council of Zaria. The Sultan was even able to depose
the Emir of Zaria in 1860, substituting his own nominee, a man
who was not even a member of the families that had so far
provided the rulers of Zaria. The Emir of Zaria paid homage as
a vassal at the court of Sokoto twice a year, bringing tribute in
the form of slaves, Zaria cloth, horses and cowries. When Zaria's
own vassals had complaints they could always seek the intervention of Sokoto. The Waziri (Vizier) of Sokoto, as head of the
imperial administration, made frequent tours of Zaria and other
vassal emirates, assessing tribute, regulating disputes and checking internal administration.

Many of the abuses of the later Fulani Empire were often the
very ones on which its prosperity was founded. The slave-raiding in the southern emirates was essential to the agricultural and
commercial prosperity of the north. Slaves were used on the
northern farms and were a major item of commerce in trans-
Saharan trade.

There is not enough space to go into the detailed history of
Sokoto after the death of Sultan Bello, and we must content ourselves with those events that affected the British occupation of
Northern Nigeria in the period between 1900 and 1906. Whilst
the Niger Company had made treaties with Sokoto and a number of its subordinate rulers, no effective administration had
been established in Fulani territory before 1897. In that year
the Royal Niger Company constabulary was sent against both
Nupe and Ilorin on account of their persistent raids into company territory. A force of 500 men and 25 officers quickly subdued the Nupe forces and a new emir, likely to be favourable to
the company's interests, was installed. The force then marched

on to Ilorin, where a treaty was signed whereby the Emir recognized company sovereignty in his state. The Emir of Nupe was forced to concede to the company the southern half of his kingdom which became the province of Kabba. This was the first inroad made by the British into the great Fulani Empire.

It was not until the 1st January 1900, however, when the British flag was hoisted at Lokoja, that real attempts were made to establish British control over those territories north of the Niger and Benue assigned her by the Berlin Conference. Though both the Fulani Empire and Bornu came within this sphere, the company had control over neither. True, they had drawn up treaties with Sokoto and Gwandu, to whom all other emirates were politically subordinate, but these were mere scraps of paper useful only for the purposes of international diplomacy. At first the new administration headed by Sir Frederick Lugard was in a difficult position, since the bulk of its defence force, the W.A.F.F., had been seconded to the Ashanti campaign. Only Ilorin, Borgu and Kabba were under effective occupation and even there Lugard had continually to assert British authority. To the north lay the slave-raiding kingdom of Kontagora and the emirate of Nupe whose puppet ruler had been deposed by its former ruler, Abu Bekri, a man naturally deeply hostile to the British. These two made plans to attack the W.A.F.F. troops in their Wushishi garrison.

At the same time as he was preparing to deal with Kontagora and Nupe, Lugard was equally engaged in trying to assemble an administration for the vast country he was about to take over. The old company administration was at his disposal but, as Lugard himself complained, this was very rudimentary and certainly not equipped to administer a huge country of nearly 15 million people. Furthermore, nothing he could prepare on the small sum of £135,000 available to him would be sufficient to cope with the administration of so vast an area. To deal with this seemingly impossible situation he formulated his famous policy of indirect rule, that is, rule by the colonial administration through the existing native institutions.

From the very outset Lugard decided that indirect rule was the only method by which the country could be governed, and as a result he has often been credited as its originator. This is an incorrect assumption. It had been used in India and Fiji. His close friend Goldie had already propounded it as a suitable method for governing Nigeria. But Lugard ennobled indirect rule from being just an expedient in times of financial hardship and lack of staff to a complete philosophy of government for Britain's colonial peoples. Before he even reached Nigeria he had decided that his political officers should be called residents, thereby giving them the status of diplomats rather than administrators. In his first annual report he outlined his system. 'The Fulani rule has been maintained as an experiment, for I am anxious to prove to these people that we have no hostility to them, and only insist on good government and justice, and I am anxious to utilize, if possible, their wonderful intelligence for they are born rulers. . . .' In later years he and his successors were to embroider this makeshift policy into a complete theory of administration.

The immediate problem, as Lugard saw it, however, was still the spread of an effective administration and the promotion of trade. In 1900 he was already advocating the building of a railway without which the North could never be commercially developed. Such a railway would also facilitate the movement of troops. A campaign was therefore first undertaken against the hostile emirs of Kontagora and Nupe, the main obstacles between him and the conquest of the rich northern emirates. Nupe and Kontagora, having failed to bring Ilorin in on their side, put up stiff resistance against the British, until a full-scale campaign was launched against them in 1901 after the return of the W.A.F.F. troops from the Ashanti campaign in the Gold Coast where they had fought with great distinction. Willcocks, Lugard's right-hand man and commander of these troops, was highly impressed by them. In a letter quoted by Margery Perham, he wrote to Lugard: 'I never served with such fellows. How I love them! Always cheerful, plucky, brave and uncomplaining.' With these well-trained troops Kontagora and Nupe were quickly conquered. Abu Bekri fled northwards and the old company emir was reinstated. Lugard, at the same time, wrote to the Sultan of Sokoto, informing him of this and asked him as overlord of Kontagora to nominate a successor to Nagwamatse. To this letter the Sultan did not reply. By April 1901 eight provinces were established and brought under Lugard's control: Borgu, Ilorin, Kabba, Kontagora, Bida, Zaria, Lower Benue (Nassarawa) and Upper Benue (Muri).

In Yola the Emir, whom Lugard described as 'a fine type of the Fulani ruler, well educated, but possessed with a religious fanaticism, which rendered him entirely intolerant of European "infidels" ', ordered the representative of the Niger Company to haul down the Union Jack, despite his earlier treaty with the company. An expedition under a Colonel Morland was therefore sent to deal with him. The Emir put up such resistance as he could with the aid of two cannon, but the British forces with their Maxim guns were too great for him. The Emir fled and was murdered by pagans in Adamawa, after attacking German forces in Kamerun. Lugard wrote regretfully of his death: 'I should have wished, had it been possible, to have afforded domicile to this brave though fanatical chief, but he was wholly irrecoverable. . . .'

North of Yola lay Bornu, most of which had been assigned to the British under the terms of the Berlin Conference, though no treaty had been drawn up with the ruler of the thousand-year-old state. Whilst affairs in the Fulani Empire had remained largely static since the death of Sultan Bello, Bornu had suffered great upheavals with the invasion of a Sudanese adventurer called Rabeh, who defeated the Bornu army in 1893. By 1896 he had brought the whole state under his control. Rabeh had had a chequered career in the Egyptian army and later in the service of the notorious slave-raider, Zubair Pasha, who was imprisoned by the Egyptians for fear of the growing power of his private army. Half of this army was taken over by Rabeh who set off on a whirlwind career of conquest and slave-raiding. Before he won the great prize of Bornu, he had conquered Wadai, Dar Kuti and Baghirmi. In Bornu he proved himself as competent as an administrator as a general, dividing the newly acquired state into strictly controlled districts which paid him fixed tribute. His army consisted of 20,000 men, nearly 5,000 of whom were equipped with firearms. In 1892 he attacked Baghirmi, disturbed by the presence of the French officer Gentil in that kingdom. In 1899 he massacred a column led by a Frenchman Brettonet, and ordered the strangling of a Frenchman on a mission to Dikwa, which he had made his headquarters.

Rabeh was fervently anti-European and advocated Holy War against Europe. Well he might have been, for just as he was about to found a third Bornu dynasty, under a much improved administrative system, the final partition of Bornu between the colonial powers of Britain, France and Germany was determined by the Anglo-French Convention of 1898. Zinder, Kanem, Baghirmi and the lands east of the Chari were to be given to France; Dikwa and the territories between the Chari and the Yesderam to the Germans; and the rest to the British. In 1900 the French sent columns to make good their claims to Bornu, and engaged Rabeh in a fierce battle in which he was killed by one of his former soldiers now serving the French. Gentil then restored the Kanemi dynasty to Dikwa. However, Rabeh's son, Fad-el-Allah, still claimed the throne of Bornu, and appealed to the British for recognition, promising that he would co-operate fully with them. Major McClintock, who had visited Bornu on Lugard's behalf in 1901, was in favour of recognizing Fad-el-Allah, though Lugard doubted whether it would be politic to recognize an avowed enemy of the French. Any indecision on this matter was brought to an abrupt end by a French raid against Gujba, 150 miles within the borders of the agreed British sector of Bornu, in which Fad-el-Allah was killed. The French then demanded 80,000 dollars from Abubakar Garbai, the legitimate Kanemi Shehu, for defeating Rabeh and his son. Only 6,500 dollars remained to be paid when a British task force arrived to take over Bornu. On the way this force subdued Bauchi and established a garrison in the town, hindered only by a self-proclaimed Mahdi, Jibrella of Gombe, who put up extremely brave resistance against the British. In Bornu the British did not have to fight, since they promised Abubakar Garbai the throne of Bornu if he would cease paying the indemnity demanded by the French and submit to their rule, a proposal he gladly accepted. He was eventually established as Shehu at Maiduguri where a British garrison was installed.

The occupation of Northern Nigeria was slow. An expedition had to be undertaken in 1902 against Abuja, where the Emir, descendant of the Habe rulers of Zaria, had closed the trade route to the north. The Magaji of Keffi was the next to be attacked. As the Emir of Zaria's representative and most influential member of the old King of Keffi's court, he slaved openly in defiance of the laws abolishing slavery promulgated by Lugard in April 1901. He actually killed Captain Moloney, the local resident, with his own hands when the latter tried to persuade him to stop his nefarious practices. He then fled to Kano by way of Zaria, whose emir still wavered between declaring allegiance to the invading power, or affirming that to his traditional ruler at Sokoto. At the end of the expedition against Keffi, Lugard confidently predicted in his second Annual Report that there would be a great increase in trade due to the pacification of Bornu, Yola and the Benue provinces. But two tasks still confronted Lugard: to render trade routes safe from raiders and to conquer the emirates of the far north. As Lugard remarked in the Annual Report for 1902: 'Trade cannot, indeed, be established on a satisfactory basis until the northern Hausa States are included in the "Provinces" of the Protectorate and the trade routes rendered safe for small traders.'

Both Sokoto and Gwandu, the traditional capitals of the Fulani Empire, remained hostile to the new administration. When the Sultan of Sokoto eventually communicated with Lugard, the terms of his reply made it clear that the north would only be taken by force.

'From us to you. I do not consent that any one from you should ever dwell with us. I will never agree with you. I will have nothing ever to do with you. Between us and you there are no dealings except as between Mussulmans and Unbelievers, War, as God Almighty has enjoined on us. There is no power or strength save in God on high.

This with salutations.'

Dated: May 1902.

Lugard therefore collected together a force to attack Kano where the Magaji of Keffi had been given asylum by the Emir, who observed hopefully, 'If a little town like Keffi could do so much, what could not Kano do?' Lugard was well aware that the whole of the Fulani North, including those states already captured, was awaiting his trial of strength with Kano and Sokoto. As long as Kano retained its reputation for invincibility, and Sokoto remained independent as spiritual overlord of all Fulani emirs, so long would there be hope of escape from the new administration. If Lugard, who had pathetically small forces at his disposal, showed any sign of wavering, he might have a general uprising on his hands, which it would be impossible to contain.

Lugard had two things in his favour. First, in the words of Hilaire Belloc:

> *Whatever happens we have got*
> *The maxim gun and they have not.*

Secondly, Lugard firmly believed that once the Hausa peasantry saw that he was the real master, they would not put up much of a resistance on behalf of their Fulani rulers. Even so Kano presented a formidable objective. The great city, encircled by enormous walls, deep thorn-filled ditches and cunningly constructed gates, could, under a determined leader, withstand almost indefinite siege. Kano was first to show its cards. The Emir despatched a force against Lugard's garrison at Zaria, only to withdraw on the news of the death of the Sultan of Sokoto. Lugard then sent a force of 1,000 local troops and 50 Europeans, commanded by Colonel Morland, against Kano, despite the strong reservations of the Colonial Office about such an expedition. Thus, in January 1903, after shelling the first town that offered resistance, Lugard's forces marched in triumph to the gates of Kano, each town capitulating without struggle. The test came at Kano, whose defence had been entrusted to two slaves of the Emir, who had himself gone to Sokoto to draw up another army. The town was quickly taken, and it appeared that the inhabitants, who were Hausa as distinct from their Fulani overlords, were barely concerned about this change of masters. The army brought up by the Emir of Kano was of little effect since his brother, the Wombai, detached his half and refused to fight. The Emir fled across the French border, leaving his army under the command of the Waziri. On 26th February, the Wombai submitted to the British and was installed as Emir. This was the beginning of the end of Fulani resistance. Katsina's intention of submission was then received and *en route* for Sokoto the British took over Gwandu, capital of the Eastern Empire. On the 14th March the Sokoto army was defeated, and since the Sultan had fled, the Sokoto Council of Notables selected Atahiru as his successor. In a speech approving Atahiru's appointment Lugard made it clear that the old Empire of Usman dan Fodio was now at an end.

'The old treaties are dead, you have killed them. Now these are the words which I, the High Commissioner, have to say for the future. The Fulani in old times under Dan Fodio conquered this country. They took the right to rule over it, to levy taxes, to depose kings and to create kings. They in turn have by defeat lost their rule which has come into the hands of the British. All these things which I have said the Fulani by conquest took the right to do now pass to the British. Every Sultan and Emir and the principal officers of State will be appointed by the High Commissioner throughout all this country. The High Commissioner will be guided by the usual laws of succession and the wishes of the people and chiefs but will set them aside if he desires for good cause to do so. The Emirs and Chiefs who are appointed will rule over the people as of old time and take such taxes as are approved by the High Commissioner, but they will obey the laws of the Governor and will act in accordance with the advice of the Resident. Buying and selling slaves and enslaving people are forbidden. . . . All men are free to worship God as they please. Mosques and prayer places will be treated with respect by us. . . . It is the earnest desire of the King of England that this country shall prosper and grow rich in peace and in contentment, that the population shall increase and the ruined towns which abound everywhere shall be built up, and that war and trouble shall cease. Henceforth no Emir or Chief shall levy war or fight, but his case will be settled by law, and if force is necessary Government will employ it. . . . You need have no fear regarding British rule, it is our wish to learn your customs and fashion, just as you must learn ours. I have little fear that we shall agree, for you have always heard that British rule is just and fair, and people under our King are satisfied. You must not fear to tell the Resident everything and he will help and advise you.'

Meanwhile the ex-Sultan had joined forces with the Magaji of Keffi, and announced his intention of making a pilgrimage to Mecca, obviously in the hopes of stirring up trouble. He was pursued across country by British forces and was run to ground at Burmi, where both he and the Magaji of Keffi were killed.

After the conquest of Sokoto, Lugard was able to get down to the more fundamental task of administration. One cannot but be impressed by the meticulous annual reports he submitted each year, showing how much thought he gave to every problem of administration. Slavery was abolished, but rather than upset the whole social structure of the country, only those who ran away from their masters were deemed free. A dual system of law was instituted. The organization of the provinces was streamlined. Roads were pushed through the bush. Every effort was made to stimulate trade. All this was the more remarkable since for the first three years of his office Lugard was tied down by military expeditions, and handicapped for the whole period by acute shortage of funds. Nevertheless, his policy of indirect rule matured well. The emirs seemed to appreciate the honesty with which Lugard carried out the promises he had made to Atahiru, on his installation as Sultan.

Suddenly, in 1906, it seemed that all Lugard's work was to be destroyed overnight, when news arrived by telegram from Sokoto:

'. . . whole of C Company Mounted Infantry, defeated and annihilated in Satiru. . . . Hillary and Scott, Residents, Blackwood, West African Frontier Force, are I fear killed. Dr. Ellis severely wounded, Sergeant Slack, R.A., and myself and doctor only men remaining most urgent. Signed, Gosling, Sergeant.'

This was a severe blow to Lugard. At a time when his administration seemed to have taken root, white men had been murdered in the heart of the Fulani Empire. Would this be a general signal for revolt? Would the emirs, especially those like Gwandu and Hadejia who had never really accepted the new administration, now try and overthrow it? They all knew that his forces were tied down suppressing an outbreak of rioting among the Tiv, who had come to the aid of their neighbours the Jukun in a quarrel with local Hausa traders, many of whom had been enslaved. Most serious of all, Major Burdon, the highly competent Resident of Sokoto, was trekking southwards on his way home for leave. What was more, the Sokoto rebels had captured a precious Maxim gun.

It was only later that Lugard learnt the full story of the rising. Two years before, the chief of Satiru, a town some fourteen miles distant from Sokoto, had declared himself the Mahdi. He had been arrested and had died in prison. However, an outlaw from across the border, Dan Makafo, had now persuaded the chief's son, Mallam Isa, to proclaim himself the prophet

Jesus. In their excitement the people of Satiru had risen against neighbouring enemy villages, so the acting resident went with a small force to quell the rebels. When he tried to treat with them, they rushed his troops, inflicting the casualties outlined in Sergeant Gosling's telegram. It was a touchy moment for British Imperialism in Northern Nigeria. For the first time the white man had been conquered, and a general rising, if led by the Sultan of Sokoto, could well have broken the hold that Lugard had maintained so effectively till then on his shoe-string army. Indeed everything depended on Sokoto. 'Had he shown the slightest indecision', wrote Burdon later, 'I have no doubt that the bulk of the "talakawa" (peasantry) would at once have joined the enemy.' As it was, Sokoto remained loyal, possibly because he realized that ultimately the British could always draw on more reserves, possibly because he saw that the success of a revolt led by a 'prophet' would be a threat to his own religious pre-eminence. Maybe he really did feel some loyalty to Lugard.

With Sokoto's decision to support Lugard, the rising was as good as quashed. A military expedition defeated the rebels, whose ringleaders were put to death. The village of Satiru was razed to the ground, and cursed by the Sultan. The Emir of Gwandu, who had wavered on the side of the rebels, was deposed, and an expedition was led against the long recalcitrant Emir of Hadejia, who died in the fighting.

Shortly after the Satiru rebellion, Lugard was appointed Governor of Hong Kong. He left behind him a country now firmly under British control. In a final trial of strength the emirs had proved remarkably loyal. Undoubtedly this had much to do with Lugard himself, for he held them in deep respect. It was for his successors to consolidate the vast gains he had made and to regularize the makeshift administration he had so rapidly and successfully established.

CHAPTER XIII

The Unification of Nigeria

O n the withdrawal of the Royal Niger Company's charter, the Niger Coast Protectorate and all the company's territories as far north as Idah were amalgamated into the new Protectorate of Southern Nigeria. The Lagos Protectorate, like the Protectorate of Southern Nigeria, was brought under Colonial Office jurisdiction, and comprised all of Yorubaland except the Emirate of Ilorin which was included in the Protectorate of Northern Nigeria. By 1900 the major areas of resistance to British authority had been overcome, but in some areas of the Eastern provinces British authority was only extended village by village. Yorubaland had been brought under British rule by treaty, Benin had been conquered and the Delta states had all been subdued in the interests of trade. However, it took many punitive expeditions to bring the whole of Iboland effectively under British administration.

The first major operation undertaken by the new Protectorate government was against the famous Aro Chukwu oracle, which had held such sway over the peoples of Eastern Nigeria in the eighteenth and nineteenth centuries. Its guardians, the Aro, naturally hoped to retain its influence as long as possible, both because of the profits derived from the sale of slaves and the trade tolls they were able to exact because of their privileged position both in Iboland and the Delta states. The British government could obviously not tolerate the oracle's continued existence, not only because it encouraged slave-trading, but because it represented a rival source of authority.

Since the Aro refused to cease slave-trading and were impeding the establishment of free trade in the hinterland, the British had the excuse they needed to destroy the oracle in the famous expedition of 1902. This expedition was only the most spectacular of the many expeditions despatched in order to establish British authority in the Eastern provinces. Numerous columns, named after the areas they patrolled, were kept on a standing basis. In Ogoja, Owerri, Ibibio and Western Ibo, the new government had its most difficult task, often extending control village by village. The local people had the initiative despite their primitive weapons. Great rain forests, meshes of streams and rivers merging into swampland, made rapid communications almost impossible and put the villagers at a great advantage over their well-armed enemies. Thus for the first six years of the Protectorate's life the new administration, particularly in the Eastern provinces, was concerned primarily with the assertion of its authority.

Though some parts of Iboland were not finally brought under British control until as late as 1918, the year 1906, when the Lagos Protectorate was merged with the Protectorate of Southern Nigeria and the north was finally pacified, can be taken as marking the beginning of effective British administration in modern Nigeria. Before then cultural contact with the European, with the exception of the coastal ports and certain towns in Yorubaland, had been of marginal significance. During the three centuries that Europeans had been visiting Nigeria they had made remarkably little cultural impact on the bulk of the local population. This is in marked contrast to the trans-Saharan contact in Northern Nigeria, which, as we have seen, resulted in extensive changes in religion, law, architecture, technology and concepts of social stratification. It was only after 1906 that the way of life of the invaders had any appreciable effect on Nigerian society. From then on can be traced the rapid breakdown of the structure of traditional society, as the various peoples of Nigeria were brought under an administration which if not uniform in its application was at least controlled by a single power. Before then the British had been but a handful and their main interest in Nigeria had been economic. With the exception of the missionaries they had neither deliberately nor unconsciously attempted to alter native society except in so far as customs hindered trade, or where practices such as human sacrifice were openly repugnant to them.

The period 1906–12, which preceded the amalgamation of

The Unification of Nigeria

the Northern and Southern Protectorates by Sir Frederick Lugard, is one of the most crucial in the history of Nigeria, for it marks both the beginning of effective administration and the beginning of the rejection of standards and customs that had endured almost intact for many centuries. It was the first time that Nigerians were subjected in any large measure to Western influences, which in the next fifty years were to have such a great effect on Nigerian society. A whole new economic world was to be opened to Nigerians. Christianity, as the official doctrine of the colonial masters, began to spread throughout the pagan areas of both Southern and Northern Nigeria. New forms of administration and justice were introduced. Finally, education in the Western way of life was made available to a wide range of Nigerians as a result of the spread of missions. So although this period appears from the annual reports as a static one, it was in effect the beginning of silent revolution in Nigeria.

Since Britain's overriding interest in Nigeria was economic, it is not surprising that one of the dominant factors tending towards the disintegration of traditional society was the growth of Western-oriented trade. A comparison between trading figures in 1908 and 1910 gives an indication of the extent of this growth in Southern Nigeria. In 1908 exports were valued at £3,094,175 as compared with £4,320,000 in 1910, whilst the figures for imports were respectively £3,076,309 and £5,122,000. Exports consisted mainly of palm products. Trade figures for the North were substantially lower, amounting to little more than £200,000 worth of exports in 1910. Yet significantly in 1911, when the railway reached Kano, figures for groundnut exports were 19,288 tons compared with a mere 1,179 tons the previous year.

The rapid growth of the Nigerian economy was to have profound effects on the traditional structure of Nigerian societies. The installation of the British administration created a huge free trade area, eliminating the dangers that had beset most traders in the past, and depriving many societies of their occupation of exacters of trade tolls. Under British protection traders could move about the country freely with the result that not only did the volume of internal trade rise steeply, but exporting and importing became easier. The most significant innovation by the new administration was the introduction of a new communications system. The slow caravans that trekked from north to south and back, passing along narrow footpaths, often heavily armed against attack, were now replaced by the railway, which if not fast by modern standards cut days off the old journey, and reduced the cost in human carriers. This growth in the internal market was facilitated by the introduction of a common system of portable currency, which, though in many areas it took a long time to replace traditional forms of currency like cowries and iron bars, necessarily overcame many of the obstacles previously presented by inter-ethnic trading. Systematic taxation gave Nigerians motives for producing more than was normally necessary to maintain the family. The introduction of European goods soon stimulated new wants so that in many parts of the country people were beginning to produce a surplus for exchange.

The new money economy brought with it many changes, more marked in smaller societies than, for example, in Hausaland where a developed export trade had been conducted across the desert for many centuries. Wealth soon began to compete with traditional status. Heredity began to give way to acquisition of wealth as the arbiter of influence in the community. New towns began to spring up, or else traditional towns expanded in response both to the demands of trade and the new administration. Here peoples of many tribes mingled, dealing in the same markets, living side by side, and dropping former tribal hostilities and differences in the interest of trade. However, the old static corporate life was slow to be replaced by a life of economic individualism, for it was not undermined to nearly the same extent as in the German Cameroons or certain French territories where efficient plantations were established by alienating indigenously owned land and transferring it either to expatriate individuals or companies. In Nigeria traditional land laws were observed and Europeans were unable to purchase land. Since corporate ownership of land by lineages was fundamental to the traditional structure of most Nigerian societies, the observance of customary land law proved a bulwark against the disruptive elements of the new economic order. At the same time it prevented the economic exploitation of the land by individual Nigerians.

Western economic forces have contributed to the unity of the arbitrary block that is modern Nigeria, and the various ethnic groups comprised within its frontiers have necessarily become more and more dependent on each other as the economy has expanded. Superficially, however, unity was given to the new Nigeria by the establishment of the British administration. Nevertheless, after Lugard's amalgamation of the Northern and Southern Protectorates in 1912, the administrative distinction between the two was maintained. However, many local variations there may have been in the administrative system, there was one ultimate factor: there had been a diversion of power from the traditional authorities to the incoming colonial administration. Even in the Northern region where the principles of indirect rule were applied most intensively, the Emir was no longer sovereign and held power by grace of the colonial government. His authority was considerably reduced by the knowledge that, if he stepped over the uncertain boundary of rules for good government laid down by the British, he could be deposed. On the other hand he was no longer subject to the authority of his overlords in Sokoto or Gwandu or to threats of deposition from within by rivals.

In the North, Sir Percy Girouard and Sir Hesketh Bell, who succeeded Lugard, whilst they consolidated the principle of indirect rule, also spent much time in streamlining native authorities. Courts were regularized and native treasuries known as Beit-el-Mal were put on a solid basis, so that the Emir's traditional authority was considerably restricted. In the South the Yoruba oba and their courts were equally subjected to the new concepts of what was good government, and a diminution of their authority inevitably ensued. In those parts of the East that had been brought under British control the local administration assumed much greater importance than in any other part, and must have proved a revolutionary concept for societies which had conceived political organization at the village level on a largely democratic basis where no one man or group had exclusive power. Furthermore, the introduction of the British system of justice for a large number of matters in the South naturally detracted from the authority of traditional chiefs and broke down many of the sanctions of traditional society. It also provided a place of appeal outside the traditional social system.

Neither the economic nor adminstrative policy of the govern-

The Unification of Nigeria

ment set out deliberately to upset the traditional social structure. Indeed the core of the philosophy of indirect rule was the ensurance of minimum interference with 'native society'. It attempted only to create favourable conditions for trade and to ensure what it considered the basic essentials of human behaviour. By contrast the missionaries, who were excluded from the Moslem areas of the North by Lugard's agreement with the Sultan of Sokoto that he would not interfere with Moslem religion, approached Nigerian societies with a very different attitude. They were convinced that their own society was superior, and also that conversion of the local people would have to be not only from the traditional religion but from the whole way of life which was intertwined with it and supported it. They therefore deliberately set out to change the very structure of traditional society. Until the beginning of the twentieth century they had made only comparatively small inroads into Nigerian society.

Something of the ardour with which the early missionary pursued his self-chosen task is indicated by the career of that remarkable woman missionary Mary Slessor, who is remembered vividly to this day by many of the peoples of Eastern Nigeria. Like her fellows she saw almost nothing that was good in African society, though she never treated the African himself as a man of inferior quality as many other missionaries did.

Mary Slessor left her home in Scotland, where she had worked as a mill girl and had seen the most sordid sides of the nineteenth-century industrial life, to serve the Presbyterian mission in Calabar. She arrived there in 1876, and soon became interested in the conversion of the Okoyong people of the Cross River. For the nineteenth-century missionary they presented a considerable challenge: they practised twin murder and human sacrifice on a large scale. Their country was some of the wildest in Nigeria. Nevertheless, against the advice of the other missionaries, Mary Slessor went to live among these people, eating their food, sharing their life so completely that after many setbacks she was able to persuade them of the undesirability of their practices. Such was her standing with the Okoyong, that in 1890 she was appointed Vice-Consul for Okoyong by Sir Claude Macdonald, since it was felt that no official could gain their co-operation. In the years that followed she worked in many different parts of the Cross River, earning the deepest respect of the people, for although she was uncompromising about those practices she found repugnant, she had a deep love and respect for the people she was trying to convert. When she died she had made a great impression on a very large number of Eastern Nigerians, many of whose children and grandchildren are amongst the best-educated Nigerians today.

The career of Mary Slessor not only shows what missionaries were fighting, but also how they appreciated that total conversion was necessary. Such an attitude was bound to be disruptive of both those elements which were undesirable on the European scale of moral values and those which gave cohesion to society. The impact of missionaries was more intimately felt by Nigerians than that of administrators. Like Mary Slessor they penetrated the most remote regions, bearing with conditions that would have been intolerable to any other than one who was so wholeheartedly dedicated. In every case they hacked prodigiously away at the very roots of society. Since chiefs or elders were invariably resentful of these intruders, missionaries were often forced to turn to the socially low placed or outcast, who had no deep vested interest in traditional society. Thus a slave, or mother of twins, would be more receptive than a young man destined for important position in the community. Conversion implied for the African a complete rejection of his society. Dancing and drumming were even included in the list of undesirable associations with traditional life. Marriage payment, forming a great bond between two families, polygamy, initiation ceremonies, the basis of a man or woman's education into adulthood, ancestor worship which symbolized the continuing existence of the community, all these were rejected by the true convert. This naturally tended to undermine the structure of the old community. Parental authority, social sanctions were broken down. The convert was necessarily alienated from his community, and indeed was taught to look on its every aspect with contempt. In accepting Christianity he accepted the individualism implicit in its doctrine, which conflicts radically with the corporate concept of African life. He was also taught to believe in the fundamental equality of man before Christ, and the Christian of slave status could use this in argument against his traditional superiors. Later, of course, the Christian convert was to use the same argument in demands for equality with the Europeans. Christianity, whose influence was in the early years restricted to the South, and today affects little more than 20 per cent of the population, had a profound influence on the attitude of the convert towards his own society, for as James Coleman has written, in a searching analysis of missionary impact on tradition society (*Nigeria: Background to Nationalism*): 'Once the genuine African convert had embraced Christianity, the difficulties of individual adjustment to a socio-political structure incapable of realizing Christian ideals became insuperable.'

Whether the break need have been so dramatic is open to doubt. Subsequent missionaries have felt these early endeavours were too unaccommodating, and implied too great a rupture with the past. Bishop Crowther, who headed the first major experiment in an Africanized mission, believed that it would be possible to convert communities *en bloc*, rather than tackle individuals. But most early missionaries felt that conversion was purely a personal matter, and that no wholesale conversion could be a true conversion. They were not prepared to compromise principles in the light of particular situations. The Moslem proselytizers, on the other hand, probably approaching the problem a little more sceptically, and with a greater appreciation of the realities of African society, made a bee-line for the chief, realizing that once he was converted, the rest of the community would the more readily follow suit. However nominal the conversion might be for the first generation, the succeeding generations would be more likely to be devout Moslems. Bishop Crowther, whilst he never took so calculated an approach as this, undoubtedly as an African realized the difficulties confronting men when asked to give up all their past ways. It was not surprising that his episcopate ended with the Society criticizing him for laxity in supervision and for tolerating heathenish practices amongst his clergy. The mission was purged by a European bishop, and led to a secessionist movement in the Delta, which established the United Native African Church in 1891.

The most radical influence on Nigeria introduced by the British was the Western system of education. Until the end of the nineteenth century education had been conducted at various levels in Nigeria. In the Moslem societies of the North academic education of the Koranic type was fairly widespread. In other societies education of children was essentially directed towards enabling them to take their proper places in the community. There were no societies in the South where reading and writing were understood, so that traditional education was essentially directed towards the acquisition of skill in crafts and agriculture. But since the missionaries were not prepared to modify their educational programmes to suit African needs, academic rather than technical education was given to children. Early suspicion of education was naturally overcome when it was seen that education was the key to success in the new economic order. The revolutionary effects of education were widespread: English was established as a *lingua franca* so that different tribes now had a common means of communication. Education soon came to be seen as a means not only of economic betterment but of social elevation. It opened doors to an entirely new world, the world of the white man. Since missionaries had a virtual monopoly of schools, they were able to use them as a means of further proselytization, and continued to warn their pupils of the evils of their former way of life.

The North was almost entirely insulated against the revolutionary effects of education by Lugard's promise that missionaries would not be allowed in the Moslem emirates without the Emir's consent. Since the government was neither interested in nor had the money to provide education, for the first years of British administration the only form of education available in the North was that of the Koranic school, except for small schools provided by the C.M.S. missions in Zaria and Bida, and the government school opened outside Kano in 1912.

These revolutionary forces were essentially let loose between 1906 and 1912, a period that in terms of events is really rather dull. They were to influence the subsequent development of Nigeria very profoundly. But one man, in a short but dramatic governorship, was to provide the mould in which the jelly of upheaval was to set. This was Sir Frederick Lugard, nominated in 1912 as Governor General of Nigeria with the task of amalgamating the Northern and Southern Protectorates. The decisions he made in those years were to influence the canalization of these new forces until, after the Second World War, control of government was slowly taken over from the British administration by the Nigerian nationalists themselves.

The immediate reason for the decision to amalgamate the two Nigerias was economic expediency. The Northern Protectorate was running at a severe deficit, which was being met by a subsidy from the Southern Protectorate, and an Imperial Grant-in-Aid from Britain of about £300,000 a year. This conflicted with the age-old colonial policy that each territory should be self-subsisting. Apart from the fact that it seemed logical to amalgamate the two territories, the one land-locked and the other with a long seaboard, it was felt that the prosperous Southern Protectorate could subsidize its northern neighbour until such time as it became self-supporting. Furthermore, there was the pressing need to co-ordinate railway policy, which at the time was practically non-existent. The Southern track had been started in 1901 and reached the River Niger in the Northern Protectorate at Jebba in 1909. It was to continue to Minna, where a Northern line was being constructed to reach Kano. At the same time, Sir Percy Girouard, the Governor, was intent on extending the Northern line to Baro on the Niger, where goods would be shipped down to the sea on barges. By 1912, then, there were two competing systems, the Minna-Baro-Niger system rivalling the Minna-Jebba-Lagos system, though the former proved less effective than was originally hoped. Ironically Girouard's railway had been built with Southern revenues. Since a new line was envisaged from Port Harcourt through Enugu to the North it was essential that there be more effective co-ordination of railway policy and this could best be ensured through amalgamation.

Amalgamation was finally achieved on 1st January 1914. But in preparing for this day Lugard took a number of decisions that were to influence the whole future of Nigeria. Though the two territories were to be amalgamated, Lugard chose to maintain the distinction between North and South, against the better judgment of men who knew Nigeria well. E. D. Morel, at that time editor of the *African Mail* and a persistent critic of colonial policy, advocated the division of the country into four large provinces. It is essential to take careful note of the schemes proposed to Lugard, for much of recent Nigerian politics has been coloured by dissatisfaction with the present political division of

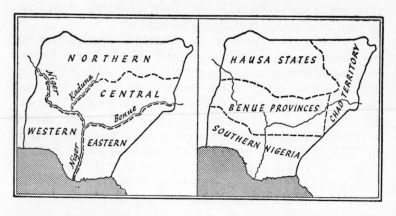

8. Proposed administrative reorganizations of Nigeria, 1914

the country, which might have been different if Lugard had listened to Morel or Temple, his Lieutenant-Governor for the North, who himself advocated the division of the country into seven provinces. Morel suggested that the four provinces should comprise a Northern Province, consisting of Kontagora, Sokoto, Katsina, Kano, Zaria Emirate and Bornu; a Central Province corresponding roughly with the Middle Belt state advocated by the Action Group party today and consisting of Bauchi, Plateau, Adamawa and parts of Niger and Benue provinces; a Western Province consisting of the present Western region, Ilorin and Borgu; and an Eastern Province that would take in Benue Province as far as the Benue River, as well as the whole of the present Eastern region. Temple, who as Lieutenant-Governor of the North was virtually doing himself out of a job by advocating the breakdown of the country into seven provinces, suggested the division of the North into three provinces, and the maintenance of the existing provincial system in the South—Lagos Colony, Eastern, Central and Western Provinces. Neither of these plans was adopted by Lugard, who preferred the existing division partly because he really did not want the break-up of the administration he had devised for the North, partly because he did not want too great an administrative burden thrown on himself. With two responsible Lieutenant-Governors in command of day-to-day administration, he as

214

The Unification of Nigeria

Governor General could carry on with general reform. Furthermore, Lugard planned his administration as a continuous one, uninterrupted by leave. During his first tour he spent six months in Nigeria and six months in London at the Colonial Office, and afterwards eight months in Nigeria and four in London, thereby never once letting slip the reins of government. To achieve this unique type of government he had to delegate the main burden of day-to-day administration to his Lieutenant-Governors.

The Northern and Southern Provinces of Nigeria together retained their status as a British Protectorate, whilst Lagos, the capital, remained a British Colony and its inhabitants had the rights of British citizens. The treaties made with the various Yoruba rulers, except for that with the Alake of Abeokuta, were considered void; for the Chief Justice had found that 'His Majesty had now acquired such complete jurisdiction throughout the Protectorate, with the possible exception of Egbaland, as to be able to legislate in any direction, not only for Europeans and resident non-natives, but for the natives themselves.' Lugard, as we shall see, soon had occasion to bring the semi-independent enclave of Egbaland into line with the other Yoruba kingdoms.

In the general reorganization of Nigeria great powers devolved on the person of the Governor General. Lugard reduced the already limited powers of the Legislative Council, which in 1906 had been extended to all Southern Nigeria, to a mere cipher by restricting its authority to Lagos Colony alone, and in its place set up an unwieldy Nigerian Council with a majority of officials, and only three nominated Africans from the North and three from the South. As an advisory body, meeting but once a year, it could hardly act as a check on Lugard's powers. Lugard centralized only those departments that he felt necessary for control of overall policy. At every turn he avoided acquisition of a large administration, so that administration was effectively regionalized under the Lieutenant-Governors, a process that only exacerbated the growing differences between the two regions. He amalgamated the Treasury, Railways, Survey, Judiciary, Military, Posts and Telegraphs and Audit. Otherwise everything was left to the Lieutenant-Governors who merely referred to Lugard any matter that seemed to affect Nigeria as a whole. Their budgets were prepared locally and then incorporated in the general budget for the territory. By centralizing the Treasury, Lugard was able to divert revenue that earlier had been properly the South's to balance the Northern deficit. He had few qualms about this since the bulk of the revenue of the South came from a liquor duty, of which he disapproved and which could not be raised in the Mohammedan North. He even hoped to shift his government headquarters from the South to the North which was his spiritual home.

The administration of the North remained intact, but the Southern provinces, which had been acquired piecemeal in widely differing circumstances, were reorganized to bring them in line with the North. The three large provinces of the South, where the Provincial Commissioners seemed to have too much power, were broken down into nine provinces with roughly the same population as their northern counterparts. A Resident was placed in charge of each. Bringing the South even more in line with the North, Lugard completely remodelled the judiciary, which had until then been theoretically independent of the executive, though administrators had been commissioners in the district courts of the supreme court, and up till 1914 had presided over native courts, which subsequently they supervised. A supreme court for the whole of Nigeria was established with two divisional courts for the South, one for those provinces west of the Niger and one for those east of the Niger. Under the divisional courts came the provincial courts, presided over by the Residents. A Native Court Ordinance introduced native courts for the South in which cases of native law were heard. Admittedly this system sorted out the judicial chaos that had reigned in the Southern Protectorate before amalgamation, but it raised great objections both in Britain, where the separation of executive and judiciary was held fundamental to good government, and in Nigeria where Lugard's ruling that barristers could not appear in the provincial courts angered the small but vocal group of Nigerian lawyers. Lugard gave as his reason for this ruling that it was designed to restrict 'the fomenting of litigation by lawyers' touts which, by a consensus of opinion, has become a public scandal in the Southern Provinces, with a natural corollary of rendering litigation extremely costly, to the detriment of litigants and the benefit of lawyers'. The greatest objection to Lugard's new scheme was that while it regulated law in the South, it put an end to the attempt to develop a legal system based on that of Britain.

Lugard's most lasting contribution to Nigeria was his development of native administration. Having successfully applied indirect rule in the North, he tried to work out a similar system for what he regarded as the chaotically administered South. Let us look first at the development of native administration in the North.

In his *Amalgamation Report*, published in 1919 just after his retirement as Governor General, Lugard defined Indirect Rule in Northern Nigeria: 'The system of Native Administration in the separate Government of Northern Nigeria had been based on the authority of the Native Chiefs. The policy of the Government was that these Chiefs should govern their people, not as independent but as dependent Rulers. The orders of Government are not conveyed to the people through them, but emanate from them in accordance, where necessary, with instructions received through the Resident. While they themselves are controlled by Government in matters of policy and of importance, their people are controlled in accordance with that policy by themselves. A political Officer would consider it as irregular to issue direct orders to an individual native, or even to a village head, as a General commanding a division would to a private soldier, except through his commanding officers. The courts administer native law, and are presided over by Native Judges (417 in all). Their punishments do not conform to the Criminal Code, but, on the other hand, native law must not be in opposition to the Ordinances of Government, which are operative everywhere, and the courts . . . are under the close supervision of the District Staff. Their rules of evidence and their procedure are not based on British standards, but their sentences, if manifestly faulty, are subject to revision. Their prisoners are confined in their own gaols, which are under the supervision of the British Staff. The taxes are raised in the name of the native ruler and by his agents, but he surrenders the fixed proportion to Government, and the expenditure of the portion assigned to the Native Administration, from which fixed salaries to all native officials are paid, is subject to the advice of the Resident, and the ultimate control of the Governor. The attitude of the Resident is that of a watchful adviser not of an interfering ruler, but he is ever jealous of the rights of the peasantry, and of any injustice to them.'

The basic pattern laid down by Lugard was developed by his successors, who extended it to the pagan areas of the North. Here, of course, its application was more difficult, for in the absence of a powerful emir some petty chief or influential elder was raised to the status of local ruler and agent for the British administration. Inevitably this meant that the local District Officer or Resident had considerably greater power than his counterpart in the emirate. If anything, Lugard's successors developed indirect rule in directions that Lugard did not feel desirable. Indeed he quarrelled bitterly with Temple, his Lieutenant-Governor in the North, over the question of the independence of Native Treasuries. Lugard felt that the revenues of these treasuries should be included in the general budget for Nigeria, since this would give him control over them. Temple and the Colonial Office opposed this, believing that the essence of indirect rule was minimal interference on the part of the British government. Inevitably, treasuries that did not come under the control of some central authority gave greater autonomy to individual native authorities, and lessened central control over the emirs.

The approach of many Northern officers to indirect rule was a static one, which resented any alteration in the system of government of the emirates, whilst Lugard's approach was essentially dynamic, believing as he did that the native administrations could be developed into more and more efficient units of government. Miss Perham, Lugard's official biographer, rightly considers this a fundamental issue in the development of indirect rule in Northern Nigeria and concludes that 'Lugard's policy was at least well worth attempting since, if the new direction he tried to give to policy had been steadily followed by his successors, the Northern region today might have been more uniform in its administration, more centralized, with more fully developed central services. Secondly, it would have presented today rather less of a political contrast with the Southern regions. Thirdly, as the system which many British governments in Africa and elsewhere soon came to regard as the archetype of native administration, it would have been a little less remote both in spirit and form from the more modest realities of these other colonies.'

When Lugard toured Yorubaland and Benin it seemed clear to him that the answer to what he considered the administrative chaos of Southern Nigeria was the introduction of indirect rule on the Northern pattern. The Oba and his court surely corresponded to the Emir and his council. Lugard, of course, misconceived the position of the Oba in Yoruba society. Whilst the Emir was to a certain extent limited in powers by his counsellors, he was effectively ruler of his emirate. On the other hand, as we have seen, the Yoruba Oba was circumscribed in his authority by a large number of checks and balances, effectively only giving voice to a decision that had been arrived at after an intricate process of negotiation and consultation. Certainly he did not possess traditional executive authority that could in any way be construed as measuring up to that possessed by an emir. No Yoruba oba had ever collected taxes from his people on a regular basis, whilst the Hausa had accepted his ruler's rights to taxation for several centuries. Since the levy of taxation was fundamental to the native authority system it meant Lugard had not only to translate his oba into an emir, but also ask him to levy taxation, hardly a popular measure for a people unaccustomed to it. Lugard sent Richmond Palmer, a trusted Northern Resident, on a tour of the Western region to report on the feasibility of introducing taxation. Despite protests from Southern officials, which he dismissed as conservatism, Palmer recommended the introduction of taxation to Oyo, Benin and Abeokuta. Lugard received this report with pleasure, though the Colonial Office, bearing in mind the disturbances that followed the introduction of taxation in Sierra Leone, opposed it.

Lugard's first experiment in indirect rule in the South was a success, but the circumstances were rather special. Since the exile of Ovenramwen, after the 1897 massacre, Benin had been without a ruler. When, in 1914, Ovenramwen died in Calabar, his son was installed oba under the name of Eweka II. Lugard took the opportunity of instituting a native authority for Benin with Oba at its head. Direct taxation was introduced and accepted by the people. This success is hardly surprising when one remembers how complete the British subjection of Benin had been, and that for over fifteen years they had been without their ruler, the repository of tribal customs.

This early success was not repeated in 1916 when Lugard introduced his native authority for Oyo, with the Alafin at its head. As Miss Perham points out, there were particular difficulties in making an emir of the Alafin. In the first place, despite his immense spiritual, political and judicial authority, the Alafin was in no easy position to head a native authority. His decisions were always voiced through an intermediary. He never appeared except behind a veil of beads, and only emerged from his palace three times a year. Thus he was virtually *incommunicado* to his people and yet had to run a system of local government that needed his intimate daily attention to every detail of their life. Secondly, though the great city of Ibadan acknowledged the authority of the Alafin, in fact this was more an act of respect than acceptance of political subordination. The city's inclusion in the native authority of the Alafin marked the beginning of many years of tension, ended only in 1934 when Ibadan was made independent.

The first open opposition to the new régime came from the Oyo town of Iseyin, where in October 1916 two representatives of the Oyo N.A., a district head and a native court judge, were murdered. The riots surrounding these incidents were put down with great speed which avoided their repetition in other parts of Yorubaland.

Much more serious was the opposition to Lugard's new policy in Abeokuta, where the native administration system proved particularly irksome. Until 1914 Abeokuta had been a semi-independent state, guaranteed by the treaty of 1893. The Egba United Government, under its Secretary Edun, aided by a British commissioner and missionaries, had developed an administration roughly modelled on the British Colonial system. When Lugard became Governor in 1912 he viewed this anomaly with the administrator's distaste. But it was difficult to find an occasion for bringing Abeokuta into line with the other Yoruba states. In 1914 the opportunity came when one of Secretary Edun's opponents, Ponlade, was arrested and died in prison. This led to demonstrations against the Egba United Government, which were sufficiently serious for the Alake and the British Commissioner, P. V. Young, to call on Lagos for troops.

As a result tension was increased to such an extent that the troops were ordered to fire on the demonstrators, an incident remembered as the Ijemo massacre. This gave Lugard the excuse to suggest that the Egba United Government's independence could hardly be called a reality if they depended on the Lagos government for support. With the agreement of the Alake he therefore abrogated the treaty and brought Abeokuta into the Protectorate under the same conditions as the other Yoruba states.

The legacy of bitterness from the Ijemo massacre came to a head with the extension of Lugard's system of indirect rule to Egbaland. In June 1918 the Egba tore up the railway line and looted stations and trains. A number of people were killed, including a chief and one European. The Alake narrowly escaped with his life; 1,000 troops were rushed in and in the ensuing battle over 500 rebels were killed. Indeed, if Nigerian troops had not just returned from the East Africa campaign, the situation might have become extremely serious. The riots were essentially a protest against the introduction of a system of government quite alien to the traditional form. There was bitter resentment against the powers of the district heads, the levying of taxes and the elevation of the Alake to a position of supreme authority where in the past he had merely been *primus inter pares* of the four quarter chiefs of Abeokuta. When the people showed their anger at these innovations they were threatened with troops, a flashback, it seemed, to the Ijemo massacre. A Commission of Inquiry, with one member, a Nigerian barrister, Eric Moore, investigated the riots and laid the blame on the new policy and its unwise application. This was a severe blow to Lugard.

If Lugard had difficulties in applying indirect rule to the West, he found it almost impossible to introduce it in the East. Except for the Delta states there were no chiefs of consequence in the Eastern region. A system that depended intimately on a fulcrum of authority, obviously had no application in so loosely organized a society as that of the Ibo and Ibibio. In the Delta earlier administrators had attempted to use the trading house as a vehicle for administrative edicts, but this meant that they had to acknowledge the existence of slavery, and in effect give support to it, since the houses were based on domestic slavery. Indeed runaway members of houses, under the House Rule Ordinance, might be arrested and restored, and none could employ a member of a house without the consent of the Head of the House. Lugard was immediately antipathetic to anything that smacked of slavery, and abolished House rule, a system which anyway had lost much of its economic and political *raison d'être*. It is, however, significant that in the Delta there was no difficulty in collecting taxes, for before the British administration the House Chiefs had imposed tax on their members. The other parts of the East were ruled through courts, which dispensed not only justice but administrative orders. In certain cases individuals with some apparent authority were raised to the status of warrant chiefs, a class that was to incur great unpopularity. Lugard was quite unable to devise any alternative system for the East. This is not surprising when one remembers that all the time he was occupied with the war and the many other problems of administration. Furthermore, the East was still not entirely pacified and in the years from 1912 to 1918 it was still necessary for the government to despatch punitive expeditions against certain groups.

All these reforms were undertaken during the First World War, in which Nigeria, because of her common frontier with the German Cameroons, played no small part. Until the outbreak of war, Germany had occupied a significant place in Nigeria's external trade. She took 44 per cent of Nigeria's exports and accounted for 14 per cent of her imports. War cut off Nigeria from this important source of trade and the situation was made more serious by shortage of shipping. This, however, was only a temporary phase, for provisions-starved Britain soon found that she needed as much of Nigeria's palm oil as she could get, and trade revived, though towards the end of the war submarine activities off the west coast made export and import increasingly difficult.

Surprisingly the war was not taken by and large by the Nigerian peoples as an occasion to throw off the colonial yoke. In the Moslem North the emirs made deep protestations of loyalty and did not waver when Turkey, the leading Moslem power, came into the war on the side of Germany. They were not even affected by the disturbed state of French Niger immediately to the north when, in 1916, the Ouilliminden tribe revolted and besieged Filingué, or when the Touraeg chief Kaossen, in league with Senussi chiefs from Tripolitania, besieged Zinder. The Senussi had apparently been goaded into preaching Holy War in Niger and Northern Nigeria by Germans based in Tripolitania and Fezzan so as to embarrass the Anglo-French war effort. Nigerian troops were sent across the border to help the French relieve Zinder.

The only disturbances that could be construed as an attempt to take advantage of the war were the revolt of the Kwale Ibo in modern Asaba division, which was said to have been aggravated by Germans, and a revivalist movement in the Delta, where the Christian 'breakaway' prophet who called himself Elijah II secured a huge following by taking advantage of rumours that Britain was leaving Nigeria because of the war. He claimed to be helping the Germans and promised the Delta peoples independence. This promise had an appeal in the Delta that it might not have held elsewhere because of the temporary collapse, immediately after war broke out, of the palm-oil trade on which most of the people of the Eastern Delta were dependent. The local European traders and administrators were blamed for this collapse. As soon as the palm-oil trade revived the movement faded away.

Nigerian troops played an important role in the war. On the 27th August 1914 a detachment of the Nigeria Regiment was sent to help the Gold Coast Regiment and French troops in German Togo, but arrived after the Germans had been defeated. On the 29th of the same month the Mounted Infantry detachment of the Nigeria Regiment occupied the German post of Tepe in the Cameroons and attacked the important river port of Garua on the Benue. They were defeated the next day in a German counter-attack. In the south of the Cameroons Nigerian forces suffered similar setbacks, a hundred soldiers being killed in an engagement at Nsanakang. It was clear that larger forces were needed to fight in the extremely difficult country of the Cameroons, with its mountains and thick forests.

A combined army was drawn up, consisting of two battalions of the Nigeria Regiment, French Senegalese troops, the Gambia Company, the Sierra Leone Battalion and the Gold Coast Regiment. They invaded the Cameroons after the successful naval bombardment of Duala on 27th September 1914. By Christmas they had driven the Germans back to Yaounde, and the important town of Edea had been taken together with the capital, Buea. The northern campaign lasted throughout 1915. In June Garua and N'gaoundere were taken, but attempts to capture Mora were unsuccessful. It was not finally until February 1916, after most of the German forces had retreated from Yaounde to the Spanish territory of the Rio Muni, that it fell to the British.

This long and difficult campaign earned high praise for Nigerian troops from many quarters, but their achievement was perhaps best summed up by one of their officers, Colonel Cunliffe: 'They have been called upon to take part in a great struggle, the rights and wrongs of which they can scarcely have been expected dimly to perceive. They have been through the, to them, extremely novel experience of facing an enemy with modern weapons and led by highly trained officers. Their rations have been scanty, their barefoot marches long and trying, and their fighting at times extremely arduous, yet they have not been found wanting either in discipline, devotion to their officers, or personal courage.'

There was to be no rest for these troops, for almost immediately four battalions were sent off to East Africa together with a large auxiliary carrier corps. No one was more pleased with their performance than the veteran campaigner in Africa, Sir Frederick Lugard. Nevertheless, he wrote to his wife of the Nigerian soldier: 'He also knows how to kill white men, around whom he has been taught to weave a web of sanctity of life. He also knows how to handle bombs and Lewis guns and Maxims —and he has seen white men budge when he stood fast. And altogether he has acquired much knowledge which might be put to uncomfortable use some day.' In fact Lugard's forebodings would have been more appropriate as a commentary on the impact of the Second World War on Nigerians. Fortunately, in the later war, it was not knowledge of weapons that impressed them so much as the realization that they and the white men were fundamentally the same and equal and that they too were quite capable of running their own affairs.

CHAPTER XIV

The Rise of Nigerian Nationalism

The years that followed on Lugard's governorship are superficially some of the dullest in Nigerian history. Yet they mark the emergence of a new class of Africans who began to think of themselves as Nigerians rather than Ibo, Hausa and Yoruba. And it was to be this group, initially confined almost exclusively to Lagos, that wrested control of affairs from the British government and attained independence for Nigeria in 1960. So, though there are no dramatic upheavals to record during the period between the world wars, though there are few administrative changes to describe, there was the slow, but all-important development of national consciousness amongst peoples of widely varying religious and cultural backgrounds.

When Lugard finally amalgamated the Northern and Southern Protectorates of Nigeria, it might have seemed, as it often did to him, that he was merely lumping together under the same administration groups of mutually incompatible peoples. Certainly his decision to keep the administration of the North and South separate was guided by such thinking. But the British had created a new political unit, and whether they or the peoples under their administration liked it or not, it was inevitable that a certain number of Africans should begin to identify themselves not with their old tribal allegiances, but with the new political entity known as Nigeria. Thus, whilst Lugard's system of indirect rule tended to preserve tribal consciousness, the needs of the new administration were to produce a new class of Africans—clerks, teachers, traders, parsons, doctors and lawyers who could no longer think in purely tribal terms. By and large they were excluded from office in the native administrations, so that they tended to look towards the central administration for an outlet for their natural desire to have some say in their own affairs. Even if they had been assimilated into the running of local government, it is unlikely that their horizons would have remained for long restricted to the administration of the village or the town.

At first Nigerian nationalism was largely promoted by non-Nigerians, and its focus was on Africa as a whole, rather than on the seemingly artificial units drawn up by the European colonial powers. Men like Edward Blyden from the West Indies, who sought the cultural emancipation of the negro, or J. P. Jackson, a Liberian, who edited the *Lagos Weekly Record* and constantly attacked the British administration, were at the spearhead of nationalist activity until the twenties. Even Herbert Macaulay, revered today by many as 'the father of all Nigerian Nationalism', was a member of the family of that most famous of all freed slaves, Bishop Crowther, a family which had ties all along the West Coast. Indeed Macaulay was agitating against the government in Lagos even before Lugard became Governor General, organizing effective mass protests against the levy of the Lagos water rate which he said was designed to benefit Europeans at the expense of the Lagosians' purse.

But while outbursts like this were of a parish pump character, these early nationalists had a wider aim. As Dr. Dike had put it:[1] 'After amalgamation in 1914, what the nationalists fought was the exclusiveness and racial basis of the Crown Colony system of Government. At the beginning, the fight was not so much for self-government, but for a measure of participation in the existing government.'

To this end the National Congress of British West Africa was founded in 1920 in order that peoples of African descent should participate in the government of their own country, an aim in part inspired not only by the writings of American negroes like W. E. DuBois but by the declaration of the American President himself on the right of all peoples to self-determination. After its inaugural conference at Accra, led by Casely-Hayford, a well-known Gold Coast lawyer, and attended by representatives of the four British West African colonies, it was decided

[1] K. Onwuka Dike, *A Hundred Years of British Rule in Nigeria, 1857–1957*. Lagos, 1957.

The Rise of Nigerian Nationalism

to send a delegation to the Secretary of State for the Colonies to demand, amongst other things:

1. A legislative council for each territory, with half the members elected Africans.
2. Control of taxation by African members of the Legislative Council.
3. Appointment of and deposition of chiefs by their own people.
4. Abolition of racial discrimination in the Civil Service.
5. Establishment of a university in West Africa.

The delegation was treated peremptorily by the Colonial Secretary, Lord Milner, and after encountering certain financial difficulties returned to Africa, so to speak, empty-handed. This hardly put the Nigerians in a bargaining position *vis-à-vis* Sir Hugh Clifford, the new Governor, who roundly denounced them in the Nigerian Council on 29th December 1920, in terms that showed how little sympathy the British official had towards the aspirations of the new African *élite*.

'It can only be described as farcical to suppose that . . . continental Nigeria can be represented by a handful of gentlemen drawn from a half-dozen coast towns—men born and bred in British-administered towns situated on the seashore who, in the safety of British protection, have peacefully pursued their studies under British teachers, in British schools, in order to enable them to become ministers of the Christian religion or learned in the laws of England, whose eyes are fixed, not upon African native history or tradition or policy, nor upon their own tribal obligations and duties to their Natural Rulers which immemorial custom should impose on them, but upon political theories evolved by Europeans to fit a wholly different set of circumstances, arising out of a wholly different environment, for the government of peoples who have arrived at a wholly different stage of civilization. . . .' He was equally critical of the concept of West African unity: 'That there is or can be in the visible future such a thing as a "West African Nation" is a manifest an absurdity as that there is, or can be, an "European Nation", at all events until the Millennium.'

But perhaps the most significant attack was on the idea that there could really be a Nigerian nation: 'Assuming . . . that the impossible were feasible—that this collection of self-contained

227

and mutuall yindependent Native States, separated from one another, as many of them are, by great distances, by differences of history and traditions, and by ethnological, racial, tribal, political, social and religious barriers, were indeed capable of being welded into a single homogeneous nation—a deadly blow would thereby be struck at the very root of national self-government in Nigeria, which secures to each separate people the right to maintain its identity, its individuality, its own chosen form of government, and the peculiar political and social institutions which have been evolved for it by the wisdom and by the accumulated experience of generations of its forebears.'

The author of this violent attack on early African claims to participation in the determination of their own affairs, was also the author of the 1922 constitution, which for the first time in British Africa provided for elected African members on a Legislative Council.

As we shall see, this was to be one of the main stimuli to the growth of Nigerian nationalism in the inter-war period.

It has been suggested that Sir Hugh Clifford's apparent change of heart was the result of the activities of the National Congress of British West Africa. But this seems unlikely both from the attitude Sir Hugh himself manifested towards it and its failure to evoke any substantial support when it sent its delegation to England. Anyway, the principle of election had already been introduced for the Lagos Town Council in 1920, before the Congress had produced its Accra resolutions.

Sir Hugh's constitution provided for a new Legislative Council, which would consist of forty-six members, twenty-seven of them officials, and nineteen of the unofficials. Of these unofficials, three members were to be elected by all adult males in Lagos with a residential qualification of twelve months and a gross income of £100 per annum, and one in Calabar. He even went as far as to say that the introduction of the elective principle was but the first step towards eventual self-government and the extension of elections to the backward parts of the Protectorate. Clifford himself declared that he had abolished the old Nigerian council and introduced this more liberal constitution because he liked 'a thing to be real and effective or not to have it at all'.

The first thing the new constitution did was to provide an

official outlet for the ideas of those coastal gentlemen Clifford
had so violently attacked. With the prospect of three seats on the
Legislative Council, several parties were formed in Lagos, and
newspapers were produced to champion their respective causes.
In the subsequent election of 1923, Herbert Macaulay's party,
the National Democratic Party, took all three seats, as it did
again in 1928 and 1933. But the limited application of the new
elective principle inevitably restricted nationalist activity to
Lagos, since there was little scope for political activity in towns
which had no seats on the Legislative Council.

Thus most of the issues that concerned Macaulay in the
twenties were essentially Lagos issues. Indeed he devoted almost
all his energies in the twenties to what was known as the Eleko
question. In 1915 the Eleko, or hereditary ruler of Lagos, was
asked by the government to persuade the local people to pay
the water rate, a commission he refused to undertake since,
though paid a salary by the government in recognition of his
special position, he was in fact denied all political power.
Piqued, Lugard deprived both him and his white-cap chiefs of
their salaries. In 1919, official recognition of the Eleko was
withdrawn because he took sides with a Lagos faction that
opposed payment of the water rate. Finally in 1920 recognition
was withdrawn altogether from Eshugbayi as Eleko, and he was
later deported. The 1920 Annual Report records: 'Political in-
trigues in Lagos resulted in the withdrawal of all official recognition of Eleko, the titular "Prince" of Lagos, who had allowed
his position to be exploited by political adventurers.' The foremost amongst these so-called adventurers was Macaulay, who
conducted an almost fanatical campaign on Eshugbayi's behalf
that seemed at times to monopolize all his political thought.

Nevertheless, he sometimes turned his attentions to larger
issues, and the ceaseless attacks on the colonial government in
the *Lagos Daily News* did much to inspire others with nationalist
zeal. Officially his party did have a national programme, and
on occasion he castigated the administration for alleged errors
far from the confines of the coastal capital.

The British administration was certainly not greatly worried
by Macaulay's activities, especially as they did really only touch
on events in Lagos. As far as they were concerned, their main
problems lay outside the restricted arena of Lagos politics,

particularly in South-eastern Nigeria where indirect rule was not proving a success.

In the North Lugard's policy, as we have seen, worked smoothly, though not along the lines he had envisaged. Indeed in the North the path indirect rule followed can only be described as retrograde. The emirates were treated more like the Native States of India than as the administrative conveniences they had been for Lugard. Officials emphasized more and more the differences between the North and South, and sought whenever possible to dispense with the services of southern clerks. This drift did not go unchallenged. In 1924, an article in the *National Review* by a Captain Fitzpatrick, a former political officer in Northern Nigeria, received considerable publicity for the stinging attacks it made on the administration of indirect rule.

'Before the British took over the country, an Emir was an Emir just so long as his hands could guard his head. The system was one of autocracy tempered by assassination. The Emirs today are maintained by British bayonets, so that there are men holding these positions at this time who would not last one week if the bayonets were to cease. . . .' He accused the emirs of corruption and extortion, describing the native authorities as instruments of oppression that were hated by the people. He feared they would be 'fruitful soil for pernicious, seditious, underground propaganda from Egypt'.

One critic of Fitzpatrick asked why he himself had not done anything about the situation. The answer to this—one does not know if Fitzpatrick gave it—demonstrates clearly the character of native administration at that time: official policy, particularly under Sir Graeme Thomson, Governor of Nigeria from 1925 to 1931, was that political officers should interfere as little as possible in Nigeria's 'Indian states'. Nevertheless, Thomson's predecessor, Clifford, had taken measures to tighten up control of administrative policy. The Lieutenant-Governors of both Northern and Southern Nigeria were placed under the Chief Secretary, who was given overall responsibility for the machinery of administration. However, it was not until the appointment of Sir Donald Cameron as Governor in 1931 that any attempt was made to check the growing separatism of the Northern administration and the ever-increasing autonomy of the emirs.

The Rise of Nigerian Nationalism

The system of indirect rule, however, had shown much greater defects in Eastern Nigeria and the Ibo, Ijo and Itsekiri areas of modern Western Nigeria. Lugard, as we have seen, had been quite unable to devise a satisfactory version of indirect rule for the small societies of Eastern Nigeria. When Clifford became Governor in 1919, one of the first things he did was to order his Secretary for Native Affairs to investigate the situation in the East. In 1922 the Secretary for Native Affairs issued his report strongly criticizing administration there. Indirect rule had been an almost total failure. Despite superficial trappings, the area was in effect administered directly. The warrant chiefs were exceedingly unpopular with the people and were backed up by little, if any, traditional authority. They were generally corrupt. Worse still, the native courts, the main agencies for British administration, were deeply resented. The court clerks and court messengers abused their positions of power so blatantly that they were described in the report as 'licensed libertines'. Despite this early interest in the problem of administration in Eastern Nigeria and the constant references in annual reports to the difficulties it represented, for the rest of Clifford's governorship no action was taken to change it. However, in 1926, after long discussions, it was decided that those people who did not pay taxes, mainly in the Eastern region and parts of the West, should be forced to pay tax in the form of a poll tax based on a $2\frac{1}{2}$ per cent assessment of their rough annual income. This, however, was to be levied on adult males only.

In 1927 assessment was begun, and sparked off disturbances in the Warri and Kwale areas of the Western region which were said to have had the connivance of certain Lagos leaders. Patrols of up to 300 men were needed to quell them and at one time the police had to fire above the heads of the crowd to disperse the rioters. Elsewhere assessment and collection provoked no open trouble.

However, late in 1929, a certain warrant chief Okugo, whilst reassessing the taxable wealth of the inhabitants of a village called Oloko, near Aba in Eastern Nigeria, began counting women, children and animals. Rumour quickly spread that this heralded the introduction of taxation of women, for the original poll tax had been preceded by a census, whose purpose had not at the time been divulged to the people. In this densely populated area of Eastern Nigeria, rumour spread quickly and soon the women of Aba and Owerri divisions were up in arms against the administration. Stores were sacked, native courts burnt down and unpopular warrant chiefs attacked. The riots spread to Calabar and Opobo, where, on the 17th December 1929, a riot of such ferocity took place that the police opened fire on the crowd and killed 32 people, wounding a further 31.

The greatest significance of these riots was that they were almost exclusively the acts of women who were able through their age-grade societies to organize themselves far more effectively than any of the local administrators, who were largely ignorant of the structure of indigenous societies, could have imagined. Furthermore, these women were spurred on by the low prices for their farm products because the depression in Europe was already having its effect in Africa.

An official Commission of Inquiry was immediately held on the riots to apportion responsibility for loss of life. It gave speedy exoneration to the officials concerned, but this seemed a vastly unsatisfactory verdict when the scope of the riots was considered. A new commission, with wider membership, was therefore set up to investigate the causes of the riots. Two of its members were African barristers—Sir Kitoyi Ajasa and Mr. Eric Moore. The Commission was asked to discover 'the origin and causes of, and responsibility for the disturbances—and measures taken to restore order, and to make such recommendations as may seem fit'.

As Miss Margery Perham has written in her detailed study of *Native Administration in Nigeria*, 'whatever view is taken of the findings of this Commission, its activities probably helped to prevent a wedge of bitterness and distrust being driven between the government and the people'. Most remarkable of all was the spectacle of European officials justifying their actions to a commission on which sat two Africans, a situation not a few of them bitterly resented.

The report of the commission was in sum a condemnation of the system of indirect rule as applied to Eastern Nigeria. More especially it condemned the way the administration had concealed the purpose of the census of 1926 which had preceded the introduction of taxation. For this reason, the commission maintained that it was barely surprising that women should have associated the actions of Warrant Chief Okugo with the introduction of tax on themselves, especially at a time of economic hardship. They also reiterated a number of the criticisms made by the Secretary for Native Affairs against native courts and warrant chiefs. The commission made it clear that there was considerable need for the reorganization of native administration in those areas.

The government started to tackle the problem of the East by trying to find out a little more about the people it was trying to govern. Anthropological reports were commissioned for most areas to ensure that any future reorganization would take into full account the natural social organization of the people.

Just after the report of the Commission of Inquiry was published Sir Donald Cameron became Governor of Nigeria, and having been responsible for the introduction of indirect rule in Tanganyika, began to examine closely the whole working of native administration in Nigeria. He was extremely shocked, not so much by developments in the East, as by the character of native administration in the North. This had been taken a step farther on the road towards the creation of 'Indian States'. Legislation had been mooted whereby *all* inhabitants of an emirate would be brought under the jurisdiction of the native authority courts, meaning in fact that Christian Southerners, expatriate Europeans and Lebanese would be tried before local Alkali courts instead of under British law. In a speech to the Legislative Council on 6th March 1933, the new Governor suggested that the administration in the North had departed from Lord Lugard's conception of native authority and that they had made feudal monarchy 'the be all and end all' of indirect rule. He attacked the administration for sheltering their Moslem rulers from contact with the outside world:

'I doubt sometimes whether we have done a great deal to impress on the minds of the Native Authorities concerned that the amelioration of the social and economic conditions of a people is one of the primary duties of an administration and that the inspiration to improvement must come from within, from the Native Administration itself.'

Later, Cameron enunciated his own policy for the reform of the native authorities of the North. Nigerian emirs should be encouraged to travel not only abroad but in other regions of Nigeria. The pagan areas of the North should be developed along their own lines and not as pseudo-emirates. He also abolished certain practices in the native authority prisons such as chaining.

Cameron did not restrict his attention to the North. In the West he made Ibadan independent of Oyo, and suggested that the native authority should have a mixed council in which the educated elements could play their part. As we have seen, the exclusion of the educated Nigerian from participation in both central and local government was one of the main stimuli to early nationalist activity. In 1932, on the installation of the new Oba of Benin, Cameron stressed the fact that the duty of political officers was to train chiefs for the increasing burdens of local administration and to that end he insisted that the Resident sit in on the council and advise on day-to-day conduct of affairs. In the East it was no time for dramatic changes, but for slow and thoughtful reorganization of a system that had been a blatant failure. For the first few years after the Aba riots, the administration spent most of its time collecting information about the people they had been trying to govern, in some parts for nearly thirty years. The 1932 Annual Report admitted: 'It has moreover been emphasized that in the case of primitive communities with European influences, it is necessary that the process of reorganization should be with comparatively small units.' By the end of 1934 no less than 199 reports on local groups had been submitted, and in the light of these and subsequent reports, the native authorities were reorganized to correspond with what were described as live units of government, which were often merely small collections of hamlets and villages.

Cameron's major reform was the abolition of Lugard's system of administrative justice. Cameron was particularly critical of a system of law exercised by the administration. 'Change the system of law, if you will, and punish the people by administrative officers exercising a kind of parental correction because the people are primitive; but remember always, pray, if you do so you will thereby be depriving the natives of any judicial court and any judicial system of law. Lugard himself had justified the administration of British law by political officers on the grounds that they knew the natives better than British-trained lawyers could. Cameron's decision to abolish the provincial courts and limit the powers of the native courts was particularly popular amongst the educated elements. In place of the provincial courts he substituted a High Court for the whole of the Protectorate, under which operated magistrates' courts where lawyers could practise. The introduction of the High Court returned once again to the well-established British principle of the separation of judiciary and executive, though Cameron did envisage that administrative officers with legal experience would act as magistrates. Finally, to emphasize the unity of Nigeria, he abolished the post of Lieutenant-Governor in Northern and Southern Nigeria.

Economically, the period between the wars was a dull one, for the effects of the severe and prolonged depression in Europe made themselves felt on most primary producing countries like Nigeria. A comparison between the export and import figures for 1921, just after the post-war boom had slackened, and those for 1938, just before the demands of a Europe at war made themselves felt in Africa, shows that relatively little economic development had taken place.

	Imports	Exports	Total Trade
1921	10,237,000	8,258,000	18,495,000
1929	13,219,000	17,075,000	30,294,000
1935	7,804,000	11,615,000	19,419,000
1938	8,632,000	9,702,000	18,334,000

On the other hand cotton, which had been grown for local use before the advent of the British and was to be of immense importance to Northern Nigeria in later years, together with groundnuts and cocoa, became increasingly valuable. General wants increased as lists of imports during these years show: they ranged from disinfectant to glassware, ammunition, drugs, china, enamelware, fancy goods, furniture, jewellery, leather goods, rubber goods, textiles, tobacco, cars, soaps, oil, etc.

Perhaps the greatest economic achievement of the administration in the inter-war period was a negative one. In many African countries, notably the Belgian Congo and the German Cameroons, part of which had been attached to Nigeria after the

First World War, large banana and oil-palm plantations had been set up, proving themselves economically far more efficient than the rather haphazard farming of bananas and palm trees in Nigeria. However, in Nigeria it had been a principle never to alienate native land, and the establishment of palm plantations in days when government interference in economic affairs was marginal, necessarily involved alienation of land to foreign companies. In the Belgian Congo the firm of Lever Brothers had extensive and profitable plantations, and their chairman, Lord Leverhulme, had his eyes on Southern Nigeria for the establishment of similar plantations. In 1924 Lord Leverhulme, at a dinner held by the Liverpool Chamber of Commerce for the Governor of Nigeria, Sir Hugh Clifford, pressed him to permit his company to acquire land and declared:

'I am certain that the West African races have to be treated very much as one would treat children when they are immature and underdeveloped. We have excellent materials. I don't know better materials anywhere for labour in the tropics than the natives of West Africa, but they are not organized. . . . Now the organizing ability is the particular trait and characteristic of the white man. . . . I say this with my little experience, that the African native will be happier, produce the best, and live under the larger conditions of prosperity when his labour is directed and organized by his white brother who has all these million years' start ahead of him!'

Fortunately for Nigeria, Clifford resisted all such attempts to impose Congo paternalist economic theories on Nigeria. But the pressures on Leverhulme's behalf were considerable. Nevertheless, both the Governor and the Chief Secretary assured the people that Lord Leverhulme's views were diametrically opposed to the declared policy of the government. The criticism made by Captain Fitzpatrick of the system of indirect rule in the North was vaunted by the plantation owners as proof that the present system of government had little to recommend it.

The threat to Nigeria seemed greater when, in 1925, Sumatra emerged as a producer of the superior palm oil by plantation methods. Clifford's successor, Sir Graeme Thomson, looked on Leverhulme's policies with a gentler eye. But at the same time the British Government sent out to West Africa Ormsby-Gore, the Parliamentary Under-Secretary for the Colonies, who had backed Clifford partly on the grounds that the introduction of the Congo system would involve government in finding compulsory labour for capitalist profit. In 1926 the matter was effectively closed when the House of Commons gave its support to the system of indirect rule as practised in Nigeria, though educated Nigerians remained fearful of the possibilities of the introduction of a foreign-dominated plantation economy for some time to come.

The nationalist energy generated by Herbert Macaulay for the 1923 elections dissipated in a tangle of Lagos politics from which it was not rescued until the late thirties, when a new generation of Nigerians who looked beyond the narrow political horizons of the capital took over control of the nationalist movement. They were to be the first Pan-Nigerian nationalists, and the outbreak of war in 1939 was to give immense stimulus to their movement for self-government and eventual freedom.

Until the 1930's, most educated Nigerians came from Creole families or from Yoruba families that had been in long contact with Europeans. It was only by the thirties that a wider selection of Nigeria's varied peoples emerged sufficiently educated to compete intellectually with this closed aristocracy.

Appropriately enough, therefore, student organizations were the main instrument in arousing the new spirit of nationalism. Foremost amongst the student organizations abroad was the West African Students' Union, founded in 1925, with the object not only of providing a centre for West African students in London, but also of promoting the understanding of African culture. The founder, a Nigerian called Ladipo Solanke, is often neglected in the annals of Nigerian nationalism. But by providing such a centre, and by his own uncompromising spirit of nationalism he added a new fire to the movement for colonial emancipation that kept it alive in Nigeria until the return of Dr. Azikiwe from America in 1937. He was an ardent critic of the conduct of administrators in Nigeria, a champion of the glory of the negro past, a constant writer of letters to the press on subjects concerning West Africa. He made extensive tours of Nigeria and other West African territories to obtain funds for the union, seeking the co-operation of traditional rulers such as the Alake of Abeokuta, who was the patron of W.A.S.U., and the Emir of Kano, who was patron of the Kano branch. By providing this focus for African activity in London, 'from a historical standpoint', as James Coleman has written in *Nigeria: Background to Nationalism*, 'Solanke was an outstanding figure in the nationalist awakening in Nigeria.'

But it was in Lagos that the next concrete development in nationalist organization took place. In 1936 the Nigerian Youth Movement was formed with Samuel Akinsanya, H. O. Davies, Ernest Ikoli and Dr. J. C. Vaughn at its head. It had grown out of the Lagos Youth Movement, organized to protest against the alleged inferior status of the new Yaba Higher College, which they felt should have been of university standard. At first the Nigerian Youth Movement was restricted in its outlook, but on the return of Dr. Nnamdi Azikiwe from America in 1937, it was geared up into a genuine national movement with a broad representation that justified its title 'Nigerian'. Dr. Azikiwe, or 'Zik' as he had always been known to both followers and enemies, was an Ibo who had been educated in America, having collected there an impressive array of degrees, which made him one of the first of his people who could seriously compete with the entrenched Yoruba aristocracy of Lagos. He had proved himself a dynamic personality, running a successful paper in Accra with I. T. A. Wallace-Johnson, and narrowly escaping imprisonment on a charge of sedition. When he arrived in Lagos he founded a paper called the *West African Pilot* which was to be the main outlet for his nationalist activities for the next twenty years. As an active politician he brought something new to Lagos politics, the interest and participation of the immigrant Ibo and Ibibio people. With Zik's support the Nigerian Youth Movement could genuinely be regarded as representing more than a mere Lagos faction.

Another important spur to this new outburst of nationalist activity was the Italian invasion of Ethiopia, a country which naturally symbolized African independence for all African nationalists. In 1935 a mass meeting was held in Lagos to protest against the Italian action and the Abyssinian Association was formed. Unfortunately, apart from its successful attack on the Cocoa Pool, a monopolistic buying agreement arranged by the major European commercial houses, the Nigerian Youth Movement achieved little that could be called concrete, being rent by internal quarrels. But this was in a way counterbalanced by the outbreak of war in Europe in 1939, which acted as an immense stimulus to nationalist activity. Until the 1939–45 war most Nigerians had been entirely cut off from the outside world. Only the small *élite* of students who travelled abroad for their studies had any effective contact with the current of ideas of the Western world, or indeed the Communist world. For most Nigerians, the European remained a special kind of being, destined to command, surrounded by apparent wealth in the form of large houses and numerous servants. Few Africans ever attained these heights, and then it was observed they rarely if ever entered into the exclusive domains of the white reservations and were rarely employed in the higher posts of the administration.

Possibly the greatest effect of Nigeria's participation in the world war was the sudden realization by a large number of ordinary Nigerians as distinct from the educated *élite*, that there were Europeans who were different from the privileged colonial administration, who were farmers and private soldiers, traders and shopkeepers, bootblacks and servants like themselves. Nigerian soldiers served alongside white soldiers of their own rank. Allied troops came to Nigeria with no more privileges than Nigerians themselves had. Many Nigerians have testified to the immense impact made by this contact between white and black of similar class. The World War projected Nigerians out of a colonial backwater into a modern world in which, because of the exigencies of war, Nigeria became suddenly important— important as a strategic link in allied defences, as a producer of primary goods essential to feed the starved allied nations, and also as a provider of indispensable troops for the Burma campaigns. Indeed the distinguished anthropologist Meyer Fortes, writing about 'The Impact of the War on British West Africa' in *International Affairs*, said: 'It may well be that the war will prove to have been the outstanding instrument of social progress in West Africa for fifty years.'

Abroad, attitudes towards colonial problems were changing rapidly. The right to empire was being challenged, and within British government circles themselves there was a certain concern about the administration of the colonies. In 1938 riots in the West Indies had prompted the British government to set up a Royal Commission to investigate conditions there. One of the main causes of unrest proved to be the very backward economic state of the islands. As a result the British government established a fund for the West Indies as well as a more general Colonial Development and Welfare Act for her other colonies. Under it, £5 million a year was set aside for colonial development projects together with £500,000 for research.

On the other hand the British Government, headed by Mr. Winston Churchill, seemed impervious to American criticisms of colonialism. The third clause of the Atlantic Charter assured 'the right of all peoples to choose the form of government under which they live . . .'. This was not unnaturally taken by African nationalists to mean that Nigeria would have eventual self-government. But Churchill and his Colonial Secretary, Colonel Oliver Stanley, denied that this clause applied to African dependencies, Churchill declaring that he had no intention of presiding over the break-up of the colonial empire. But American criticisms of colonialism were strong and were supported within the wartime coalition government in Britain by Labour members, whose Fabian Colonial Bureau kept them up to date on colonial affairs and, in particular, on nationalist aspirations. It was to such organizations as this that West African students in Britain directed their attentions.

Despite early intransigence on the part of the Colonial Secretary, Labour pressure was able to elicit from the government the promise that British policy in the colonies could be directed towards their political, social and economic development, though no indication was given of a time-table for constitutional advance.

In Nigeria, however, the Nigeria Youth Movement was unable to concentrate the various anti-colonial pressures because of the internal dissensions. Rivalry between Ernest Ikoli and Dr. Azikiwe in 1941 over who should stand for the vacant Legislative Council seat led to the effective demise of the party. Partially this was the result of press rivalry, for Ikoli edited the *Daily Service* which rivalled Zik's *West African Pilot*; partially it was the result of the character of Zik himself who had never been a man to play second fiddle in a political organization. The occasion for the break-up came when Ikoli was put forward for the seat by the party, and Zik counter-proposed Samuel Akinsanya, an Ijebu. Unfortunately for the future of Nigerian nationalism this introduced an element of tribalism that had been largely subdued till then. Ijebu Yoruba were on the whole disliked by other Yoruba, and Zik said that this was the reason why Akinsanya's candidature had not been accepted. Since Zik had all the Ibo solidly behind him this led to a tribal rift in the party, and despite efforts by Obafemi Awolowo, an Ijebu cocoa trader, to revive the party between 1941 and 1944, it never again rose above petty quarrels. On the other hand, the climate created by the World War and the current of ideas in Lagos was opportune for the creation of a nationalist movement and, on 26th August 1944, Dr. Nnamdi Azikiwe founded the National Council of Nigeria and the Cameroons with himself as Secretary and Herbert Macaulay as President. The N.C.N.C. was not a party in the ordinary sense, but a confederation of trade unions, smaller parties, tribal unions and literary groups. In January 1945 it held its first constitutional convention in which it declared amongst its aims that it intended: 'To afford the members of the advantages of a medium of expression in order to secure political freedom, economic security, social equality and religious toleration in Nigeria and the Cameroons under British Mandate as a Member of the British Common-wealth of Free Nations.' When a few months later the new Governor of Nigeria, Sir Arthur Richards, presented his con-stitutional proposals for the country, it was the newly founded N.C.N.C. that led the criticism of its various inadequacies.

CHAPTER XV

Three Constitutions

The constitutional proposals of Sir Arthur Richards in March 1945, though they were attacked on almost every side by Nigerian nationalists, mark the real turning-point in Nigeria's progress towards independence. The constitution, which came into effect on 1st January 1947, had, according to the Governor, three objects: 'to promote the unity of Nigeria, to provide adequately within that unity for the diverse elements which make up the country and to secure greater participation by Africans in the discussion of their own affairs'. The new Legislative Council was enlarged to forty-four members with a majority of unofficials, twenty-eight as against sixteen officials. Of these twenty-eight, however, only four were elected, the rest being nominated or indirectly elected. The most important feature of the new constitution was the inclusion of the North in the central legislature, a move that in itself could do nothing but further the unity of the country. However, at the same time regional councils were created for the North, East and West. Though they were mainly confined to discussion, their creation has subsequently been severely criticized as being the foundation of tribalism in Nigerian politics. Dr. Kenneth Dike, in *100 Years of British Rule in Nigeria*, has written: 'Undoubtedly the Richards Constitution is a dividing line in Nigerian Constitutional development. Before it the keynote in Nigerian politics was unification towards a centralized state and the realization of a common nationality. . . . But with the Richards Constitution this tendency towards unification was on the whole arrested. . . .' Sir Arthur Richards might have agreed with these sentiments as far as the two southern provinces were concerned, but he would have argued that the inclusion in the central legislature of the North, so long excluded from participation in national politics, necessitated some degree of regionalization to allow for its very obvious differences from the South. On the other hand, it has been argued that if Sir Arthur really wanted to contain regional and ethnic differences he would have been wiser to have followed the earlier divisions proposed by Morel and Temple, and later advocated by Zik, which would have allowed for regional differences but would also have permitted the creation of a strong central legislature. As it was, he established the basis of a very unwieldy federation with one region twice the size in area and population of the other two.

Sir Arthur obviously conceived of the constitution as allowing for the maximum participation of all sections in the national legislature. In theory there was a link between the smallest native authority and the national representative, since the native authority sent delegates to the regional assembly which, in turn, selected from among its members a delegation to the central Legislative Council.

The constitution was attacked both for its content and for the way in which it was introduced. The newly formed N.C.N.C. regretted 'the unilateral way the whole proposals were prepared without consulting the people and natural rulers of the country. . . . We respectfully suggest that a more democratic approach could have been made to avoid any possible misunderstanding. . . .' Sir Arthur Richards's predecessor, Sir Bernard Bourdillon, himself criticized the peremptory way in which the constitution was introduced, for he had promised Nigerians that they would have a full opportunity to discuss any new constitution, though it must be noted the concept of regional councils was originally his. The particular criticisms, which might not have been so vehement if consultation had taken place, were diverse. The unofficial majorities in central and regional assemblies were attacked as false since many of the so-called unofficials were nominated or quasi-officials like chiefs and native authority members. There was no change in the composition of the Executive Council which remained wholly European. The principle of election, far from being extended, had only been maintained for Lagos and Calabar on the direct intervention of the Colonial Secretary. Curiously enough, in the light of its later policy, attacks were made by the N.C.N.C. on the lack of power delegated to the regional assemblies.

Three Constitutions

These criticisms which were supported, only less ardently, by the N.Y.M., were accompanied by an effective demonstration of popular discontent. The year of the publication of the new constitution was also the year of the general strike in which Zik played an influential role. The wartime expansion of the economy, following on the increased demand for Nigeria's primary goods, led to a rapid growth of labour unions. In 1940 there were only twelve unions with 4,337 members, by 1944 there were eighty-five with some 30,000. British policy during the war had been to encourage the unions, and in 1942 the Nigerian Trade Union Congress was given official recognition. However, the steep rise in prices during the war led to real economic hardship for wage-earners, many of whom belonged to unions. After complaining bitterly about the regular adjustments of European salaries to the rising cost of living, the Railway, Ports and Telecommunication workers all went on strike, effectively paralysing many of the country's essential services. Though the new constitution was in no way responsible for the strike, the two became associated since Zik, the most ardent critic of the constitution, also backed the strikers through his two papers the *Pilot* and the *Comet*. In certain quarters it was even maintained that he engineered the strike. On July 8th his papers were banned, and shortly afterwards Zik declared that there was an officially backed plot to assassinate him. This was received contemptuously in government circles, but in the country it was widely believed and had the effect of making him a martyr. When, in fact, at the end of the strike a Commission of Inquiry recommended an increase in the cost of living allowance to workers, Zik naturally emerged in the eyes of the public as the champion of a successful strike. He was thus in a strong position to make an all-out attack on the new constitution and the so-called obnoxious ordinances that had been introduced with it. These vested mineral rights and publicly purchased lands in the Crown, and gave the government powers to depose and appoint chiefs. Since land rights and the appointment of chiefs were close to the structure of almost every Nigerian society, Zik could add fuel to his campaign against the constitution, which was little understood by the ordinary people, by warning them that their land and their chiefs were threatened by the government.

During a triumphal tour of the country Zik and his party

collected the considerable sum of £13,000, though the tour was marked by tragedy when one member of the entourage, the veteran nationalist, Herbert Macaulay, fell mortally ill. Nevertheless, when the party returned to Lagos it was to a massive reception, and with the money it had collected the N.C.N.C. was able to send to London a delegation led by Zik and composed of men from every part of Nigeria. The Labour Colonial Secretary, Arthur Creech Jones, paid little attention to the delegation, merely advising them to give the constitution a try. Unfortunately there followed financial squabbles, and when the delegation returned home with no definite achievement and a backlog of disputes over money, the N.C.N.C. suffered a real though, as it proved, only a temporary setback.

Meanwhile the Richards's constitution had come into effect at the beginning of 1947 and it was envisaged that it would last for nine years with revision after six. It was accompanied by the introduction of an ambitious £55,000,000 ten-year development plan for Nigeria, subsidized from the Colonial Development and Welfare Fund to the tune of £23,000,000. This provided for the extension of rural and urban water supplies, education, communications, town planning, hospitals and agricultural and veterinary research. Under it a department of commerce and industry was set up. At first the application of the plan suffered from lack of qualified staff for the Nigerian administrative service had been very much depleted as a result of the war.

Though Sir Arthur Richards had envisaged that his constitution would last for nine years, the new Governor, Sir John Macpherson, appointed in April 1948 said, after only a few months in the country, that progress had been so good that it was time for a change. He did not make the mistake of his predecessor in foisting a new constitution on the country without consulting the people; if anything he went to the opposite extreme by indulging the country in two years of protracted negotiations on the form the new constitution should take. Macpherson, a young Governor, together with Hugh Foot, his young Chief Secretary, proved very much a new broom in Nigeria. He was responsible for the democratization of local government in the East, and in 1948 appointed a commission to make recommendations about the recruitment and training of Nigerians for the government Senior Service. Eight Nigerians, including Dr. Azikiwe, sat on the commission which recommended that no expatriate should be recruited where a suitable Nigerian was available. Macpherson also appointed four Africans to his Executive Council, and with the appointment of Dr. S. L. Manuwa as first Nigerian Director of Medical Services, this made five.

The people were consulted on their new constitution at every level; a concession, no doubt, strongly influenced by events in the Gold Coast, where riots in February 1948 had forced government into studying constitutional reform for that country. In Nigeria village councils sent delegates to divisional councils, then to provincial and regional councils, and finally to a general conference at Ibadan.

The decisions made at the Ibadan conference must be seen in the context of the great increase in tribal feeling that had followed the introduction of the Richards's constitution. Today the origin of this tribal feeling is the source of much bitterness and recrimination by Nigerian political parties, and it may be long before it can be seen in true perspective.

Fundamentally, as we have seen, there were very considerable differences in the history of the various groups of Nigeria, as well as more points of contact than have generally been supposed. There were latent differences and antagonisms that could be called up by anyone so inclined. The argument over tribalism has been between those who believe that these differences were fixed, and that anyway Nigeria was an arbitrary colonial creation, so that any political settlement should take these factors into account by devolving government on the tribal groups, and those who believe that politics should be worked out in terms of Nigerians rather than Ibo, Hausa and Yoruba, and that this could be achieved if no one resorted to tribal politics.

In fact, originally, the increase in tribal feeling, as Dr. Kalu Ezera shows in *Constitutional Developments in Nigeria*, was caused by circumstances rather than design, and only later was it seized upon by politicians. When the British occupied Nigeria they had almost no contact with the large Ibo and Ibibio population of the East, whilst already many Yoruba had received English education and provided a small intellectual *élite* in Lagos. Population pressures and land hunger in the East forced many Ibo and Ibibio to migrate to the cities of the West and North, where they proved remarkably successful as clerks, railway workers and storekeepers. Nearly always they settled in discrete communities, realizing that the key to success under the new administration was Western education, and seeing how far behind the Yoruba they were in this respect, they formed mutual benefit associations in order to give some of their number the advantages of higher education. This tendency to group together was intensified by the close family ties that exist in most African societies and by the fact that in Northern towns Southerners were forced to live outside the walls, in Sabon Garis, or strangers' quarters. Soon these unions began to federate. In 1944, following on the Ibibio State Union, the Pan-Ibo Federal Union was formed. In 1948 Dr. Azikiwe, who had already protested against the Yoruba domination of Lagos politics, became President of this Union. Naturally his opponents retaliated by accusing him of being a tribal politician. Later he even made statements that seemed to confirm this view: 'It would appear that the God of Africa has created the Ibo nation to lead the children of Africa from the bondage of ages. . . .'

Tribal feeling had first come to the fore in the quarrel between Zik and the older members of the Nigerian Youth Movement over the candidature of Samuel Akinsanya for a seat on the Legislative Council. This quarrel resulted in Zik leaving the N.Y.M. with all his Eastern followers, so that the party became effectively a Yoruba-controlled organization.

It was not surprising, therefore, that these tribal unions also interested themselves in political affairs and the Pan-Ibo Union itself was one of the founding members of the N.C.N.C. In 1945 some Yoruba students in London formed the Egbe Omo Oduduwa, or Society of the Descendants of Oduduwa, a cultural organization which soon took on the character of a political party. In 1948 the inaugural Conference of Egbe Omo Oduduwa was held at Ile Ife, when the Oni of Ife declared that the 'Yoruba will not be relegated to the background in the future'. Among its objectives was to 'create and actively foster the idea of a single nationalism throughout Yorubaland' and to 'cooperate with existing ethnical and regional associations and such as may exist hereafter, in matters of common interest to all

Nigerians, so as thereby to attain to Unity in federation'. The N.C.N.C., at least in theory, always looked to a unitary Nigeria, partly because the fact of Ibo migration to other parts of the country would be served by a unitary constitution, and partly because its leaders wished to minimize the differences between the various ethnic groups. But the party's policy has never been very fixed on this matter.

In 1948, the intense feelings between Yoruba and Ibo, particularly in Lagos where there was severe danger of communal disorders from July to September, furthered the cause of those elements in the N.C.N.C. who wanted a federal form of government in Nigeria based on small states, and the Ibo State Union was founded as the basis of one of these states.

Until the Richards's constitution the North was largely isolated from the South, and since its traditional form of government had largely been preserved there was little opportunity for Western-style politics. However, a few Northerners had received Western education and in 1943 a group of them, including Mallam Abubakar Tafawa Balewa, future Prime Minister of Nigeria, Sa'ad Zungur, the first Northerner to go to Yaba Higher College, and Aminu Kano, present leader of the radical opposition in the North, formed the Bauchi Improvement Association. In 1949, Aminu Kano and Abubakar were among the founders of the Northern People's Congress, a cultural Congress which, like the Egbe Omo Oduduwa, was converted into a political organization to meet the requirements of the new Macpherson constitution.

The three years during which the new constitution was negotiated were dominated by tribal nationalism with the N.P.C. taking the part of the North, the Egbe Omo Oduduwa, which with elements of the old Nigerian Youth Movement became the Action Group, taking the part of the West, and the N.C.N.C., whilst it outwardly preserved its pan-Nigerian aims, taking the part of the East.

At this time, possibly only the extremist Zikist movement could legitimately call itself a pan-Nigerian party. Comprising members from all parts of Nigeria, it was violently anti-colonial, calling on workers to strike and to refuse to pay taxes. In February 1949 ten of its leaders were tried and imprisoned on charges of sedition, and the movement went to earth and might even have petered out but for the notorious Enugu shootings. The miners of the Enugu colliery had staged a go-slow strike in the erroneous belief encouraged by the Zikists that arrears of pay had been withheld from them. The government sent in a detachment of police to collect the dynamite stored in the mine fearful that either the miners would use it or that it might find its way into Zikist hands. The miners in turn feared that the police had been sent to break up the strike and rioted. The European in charge of the detachment ordered his police to fire on the strikers and twenty-one were killed. The news of the massacre was received with great horror all over Nigeria, and the Zikists, whom the government strongly suspected of engineering the strike, seized the opportunity and provoked riots in Aba, Calabar, Onitsha and Port Harcourt.

In the ensuing Commission of Inquiry the police officer responsible for the shooting was adjudged to have acted in all honesty, but to have 'made an error of judgment which fell short of that standard that might be expected from one of his rank and seniority'. To nationalists this seemed too small a penalty for him to pay, and in the Legislative Council Zik demanded unsuccessfully that he be brought back from England to stand trial. The Zikist movement reached a dramatic end when, on 18th February 1950, a Zikist attempted to assassinate Mr. Hugh Foot, the Chief Secretary. Zikists were rounded up and in April 1950 the movement was proscribed.

Meanwhile all over Nigeria discussion of the new constitution was taking place. From March to September 1949 the divisional provincial and regional conferences had been considering the future constitution, and between October 10th and 21st the drafting committee prepared a preliminary constitution for discussion by the general conference which was convened at Ibadan with all but three of its fifty-three members Nigerians. The drafting committee proposed a federal system of government with a fairly strong central legislature and executive, though considerable powers were to be delegated to the regions. The central executive or council of state would have six *ex officio* and twelve unofficial members who would be ministers. The composition of the house should be twenty-two from the East and West respectively and thirty from the North by virtue of its larger population. The North, however, insisted on representation equal to that of both the Southern regions since its population was greater than that of both combined. It also asked that distribution of grants from the central government be made on a *per capita* basis. It wanted no change in the regional boundaries though the drafting committee had recommended that these should be re-examined.

Four minority reports were presented to the general conference. All of them were very important for they contained the seeds of some of the major political disputes of subsequent years. The first minority report, signed by Professor Eyo Ita, Vice-President of the N.C.N.C., and Mazi Mbonu Ojike, attacked the regional basis of government, suggesting that Nigeria should be divided into a larger number of ethnic states. They opposed the creation of Houses of Chiefs, as well as the electoral college system, advocating in a second report that this be replaced by universal adult suffrage. A third minority report opposed the denial of franchise to Southerners resident in the North, whilst a fourth, signed mainly by Western region members, attacked the proposal that Lagos should be separated from the Western region.

When the conference's recommendations were sent to the Colonial Secretary, he gave them his general approval and referred the outstanding issues back to the Legislative Council for final solution. A select committee of the Legislature decided that the North should have equal representation with the South, but made no concessions on the major issues raised by the minority reports. In January 1952 the new constitution came into effect, with a central legislature of 148 members, half of them from the North and an executive council of eighteen members, comprising six officials and twelve ministers, four nominated by each regional assembly. In the regions the assemblies were enlarged and given legislative and financial powers. Each had its own executive council with a majority of African over official members. But neither in any region nor in the central government was provision made for the post of premier or prime minister. Revenues were to be distributed to the regions on the principle of need rather than derivation.

In the dry season of 1951–2, Nigeria's first general election was fought by the three major parties: the N.C.N.C. whose dominant policy was the achievement of a unitary Nigeria; the

Action Group, which at first was mainly intent on securing Western region interests and only later took on a national character; and the N.P.C., which was transformed half-way through the election from a cultural organization into a political party, determined to secure the North for Northerners. The N.C.N.C. won the East with a large majority; the Action Group won the West with 49 out of 80 seats (a number of the A.G. members had stood as N.C.N.C. candidates but subsequently crossed the carpet); and the N.P.C. swept the North.

Dr. Azikiwe was elected to the Western House as one of the five members for Lagos, but because of lack of party discipline he was not elected as a member of the Central House. Since the other N.C.N.C. members for Lagos refused to stand down for Zik, this left the Action-Group-dominated Western House in the position of selecting which two of the five N.C.N.C. Lagos members they would elect as representatives to the Central House. Naturally they did not choose Zik, since they were only too pleased to be able to exclude the national leader of the N.C.N.C.

The Macpherson constitution, though much more liberal in its outlook than its predecessor, and much more in keeping with the desires of Nigerians themselves, was destined for a short life. Partly this was because of its own deficiencies, partly because of the political situation at the time. From the party point of view there was a fundamental difference between the N.C.N.C. on the one hand, in which important elements wanted a constitution that would give greater powers to the central government, and the Action Group and N.P.C. on the other, both of whom wanted to retain as much power in the regions as possible. This was particularly true of the N.P.C. where long administrative separation from the South and relative political backwardness made their leaders genuinely afraid of Southern domination.

In effect, the Macpherson constitution was a compromise between these two positions and apportioned power effectively neither to centre nor to region. And since, on its promulgation, it was stated to be only a step towards further constitutional development, the various parties, despite an initial willingness to make it work, all the time had their eye on future change. Its particular defect was the position of the ministers. There was no real ministerial responsibility under the constitution since ministers were not directly responsible for their departments, but merely acted as spokesmen on departmental affairs in the Legislature and Council of Ministers, where they were charged 'when a decision had been taken . . . (with) . . . ensuring in association with the appropriate official that effect is given to the decision'. They had no responsibility for the formulation of policy in their own department. Furthermore, ministers were held collectively responsible for all decisions made in the Council of Ministers. In an ordinary party or coalition government this would be a reasonable proviso; but in a council where ministers were elected not by the national legislature but from the regional houses, and where four African ministers from one region together with the six European officials could outvote the eight ministers from the other two regions, there was definite possibility of political deadlock.

The actual breakdown resulted largely from party antagonisms. The N.C.N.C. from the outset was disappointed with the constitution, especially since its own leader had been excluded from the national legislature. In the party there was sharp disagreement between the members holding ministerial office in the Eastern and central houses, who wanted to make the constitution work, and those who were disillusioned by Zik's exclusion from the central house and wanted to withdraw their support. At an N.C.N.C. convention in Jos in December 1952, three N.C.N.C. central ministers were expelled from the party (Dr. Endeley, the Cameroons representative,[1] was not) and when it became apparent that most of the Eastern ministers sympathized with their colleagues at the centre a meeting of the Eastern parliamentary committee of the party asked for the resignation of all nine ministers so that a cabinet reshuffle could take place. The ministers duly signed resignations, but when six of them learnt they were not to be included in the new cabinet they withdrew their resignations. The Legal Secretary accepted their right of withdrawal and so they were able to remain in office only to have every Bill they introduced, including the annual Appropriation Bill, defeated by large majorities. To pass the latter the Lieutenant-Governor, Sir Clem Pleass, was forced to use his reserve powers. The East thus had a minority

[1] Included in the four ministers elected from the east.

government, led by the National Independence Party, formed by the dissident Eastern region ministers and the expelled central ministers.

As far as the N.C.N.C. was concerned the position was intolerable, yet it was the Action Group that precipitated the final breakdown of the constitution. On April 1st an Action Group backbencher, Anthony Enahoro, introduced a private member's Bill demanding self-government in 1956. It was clear that the Northern members would not support this motion, as they did not feel themselves ready for self-government, and in the Council of Ministers the four Northern ministers, together with the six European officials, voted that no minister should participate in the debate. This was opposed by the four Action Group members who felt that they could hardly disassociate themselves from so important a motion by a member of their own party. The N.I.P. ministers abstained. However, according to the doctrine of collective responsibility the Council had to present a united front in the house, so the Action Group ministers resigned. The North tried to push a milder motion asking for self-government as soon as practicable, but both Action Group and N.C.N.C. walked out of the house. The Northern members were booed by the Lagos crowds and many of them returned to their homes resolved never again to involve themselves in Southern politics. The position deteriorated when the Action Group, whose leader Awolowo had called the Northern leaders despots and British stooges, announced a tour of Kano, heart of Northern Nigeria. Though the Resident banned it at the last minute, the publicity in its favour had been sufficient to excite deep resentment by local people against the South, though in fact the Northern opposition party, the Northern Elements Progressive Union, welcomed the tour which many have criticized as being an extremely tactless undertaking in the circumstances. The situation was particularly tense in Kano because of the large Southern minority in the Sabon Gari, or strangers' quarter, and from 15th to 19th May there were serious communal riots with an official death roll of 36 killed and 241 wounded, though it is almost certain that the numbers were much larger. Tribal and regional separatism came to a vicious head in those unhappy days and it seemed that Nigeria would split in two. The long separation of North from South seemed to have left too deep an impression for their recent political marriage to succeed. The immediate result of the riots was the realization by the Colonial Secretary, Mr. Oliver Lyttelton, that his earlier complacent statement that what Nigeria 'needs is a period of reflection to let the dust die down' was far from the truth, and almost at once he announced that the Nigerian constitution would be 'redrawn to provide for greater regional autonomy and for removal of powers of intervention by the centre in matters which could, without detriment to other regions, be placed entirely within regional competence'.

The various parties sent delegations to the conference in London with many misgivings and with provisos that made its success seem almost impossible. The N.P.C. led by the Sardauna of Sokoto, had just passed a series of resolutions in the Northern House that amounted to a statement that the only conditions under which they would participate in a federation would be if all powers were delegated to the regions save defence, external affairs, customs and research. The Action Group and N.C.N.C. in temporary alliance at first refused to go if the N.I.P. attended, and stipulated that if the North were intransigent about the question of self-government they would ask for the creation of a southern federation which would take self-government in 1956, come what may. Both, however, were agreed on the delegation of residual powers to the regional governments, and as allies they remained tactfully reticent about the question of the status of Lagos. The N.I.P. however opposed self-government in 1956, but advocated the creation of a strong central legislature and the breakdown of the regions into states.

Against this unpromising background it is remarkable how much agreement was in fact reached by the delegates to the London conference. The three major parties agreed to a federal constitution in which residual powers would be transferred to the regions as distinct from the centre as had been the case under the old constitution. Nevertheless, much wider powers were given to the centre than had been envisaged by the Northern delegation. The all-important question of self-government in 1956 was cleverly side-stepped by offering self-government to those regions that wanted it in 1956, but not to the federation as a whole, thus leaving it open for the North to decide for itself when it was ready for self-government. At the time few had believed that the British government would make this important concession on a fixed date for self-government.

The most bitter issue of the conference, which broke up the N.C.N.C.-Action Group alliance, was whether Lagos should remain part of the Western region or become federal territory. The N.P.C. pressed for the latter solution, since it was anxious to ensure that the main outlet for its goods should not be under the control of any other part of the federation. The N.C.N.C., which had many members in Lagos, also felt that a federation should have a true federal capital. The Action Group, however, argued that Lagos was a Yoruba city, and did most of its trade with the Western region, and as far as the North's fears were concerned both the railways and the ports were under federal control. In the end the three parties agreed to arbitration of the issue by the Colonial Secretary, who decided that Lagos should become federal territory. Despite its agreement to his arbitration, the Action Group bitterly attacked his decision, and for a while it seemed that the resumed constitutional conference in Lagos proposed for January 1954, at which the fiscal arrangements of the federation and the position of the judiciary and civil service were to be decided, would founder over the future of Lagos. However, when the conference opened the Action Group did not raise the Lagos issue but demanded instead that the right to secession be included in the constitution. This was again rejected by the Colonial Secretary, and the Action Group acquiesced in his decision.

Once again a conference about which most people had been very pessimistic was a striking success. The rules for the actual functioning of the federation were settled by the delegates, in particular the delicate problem of distribution of funds between the centre and the regions. At the 1953 conference Sir Louis Chick had been commissioned to devise a system of revenue allocation based on 'the need, on the one hand, to provide the Federal government and Regional governments with an adequate measure of fiscal autonomy within their own sphere of government, and, on the other, the importance of ensuring that the total revenues available to Nigeria are allocated in such a way that the principle of derivation is followed to the fullest degree compatible with the reasonable needs of the Federal government and the Regional governments'. The conference accepted his basic proposals: that all import, excise and export duties should be federal matters; that all import duties on motor spirits and half the import duty and excise on tobacco should go to the regional governments on the basis of consumption; that half the net proceeds of all other import duties should be distributed to the regional governments on the basis of 40 per cent to the West and 30 per cent each to the East and North; that mining taxes should be collected federally and distributed to the regions on the basis of derivation; that income tax should also be collected federally and distributed on the basis of derivation. As *West Africa* wrote in its editorial at the time: 'Endorsement of the Chick report means economically as well as politically there will be three Nigerias.' In addition the marketing boards were regionalized, and their combined reserves of £74 million were distributed on a basis of £34 million to the West, £24 million to the North and £15 million to the East. The tendency towards the creation of three Nigerias was consolidated by the regionalization of the civil service and the judiciary, though provision was made for appeals to a Federal Supreme Court. The latter move was bitterly opposed by the Lagos Bar, whilst the former was necessitated by the increase in government responsibility devolved on the regions.

The constitution agreed on by these two conferences is essentially the constitution under which Nigeria is governed today. Nigeria became a full federation of three regions, a federal capital, and the quasi-federal territory of the Southern Cameroons, which by agreement of the conferences had been allowed to break away from the Eastern region. A national legislature of 184 members, half of them representing the North, was to be elected every five years. However, the elections were to take place region by region, and the system of election varied from one to the other. The appointment of ministers to the central executive council was not now made by the regional assemblies, but by the leader of the party which gained the majority of seats in each regional federal election. Each region had the right to three seats on the council. The principle of full ministerial responsibility for departmental affairs was settled though no provision was made for the post of leader of government business. However, in the regions provision was made for the post of Premier and an all-African Executive Council with the exception of the Governor who remained President. Residual powers were now transferred to the regions. It was finally promised that the new constitution would be reviewed before August 1956. But the 1954 constitution, despite subsequent changes, had laid down the basic pattern of government for a self-governing Nigeria.

CHAPTER XVI

Independence Achieved

The 1954 constitution marks the end of the nationalist struggle with Britain; for the next six years, until the achievement of independence on 1st October 1960, Nigerian leaders were preoccupied not so much with wresting power from the colonial government as dealing with the day-to-day administration and development of their country as well as settling the basis on which they would co-operate with each other. It was hardly surprising therefore that the year after the new constitution came into effect was a quiet one with ministers taking over departments and learning the basic mechanics of the services for which they were now fully responsible. In the regions their responsibility was even greater for with the exception of the North there was only one expatriate official in the Regional Executive Council—the Governor. In the federal elections that followed the introduction of the new constitution, the N.P.C. won 79 of the 92 Northern seats. The biggest surprise came in the West where the N.C.N.C., triumphant in the East, won 22 seats to the Action Group's 19, showing that Nigerian politics were not entirely dominated by tribal factors, though it must be pointed out that the N.C.N.C. gained much of its support in the minority area of the West. In Yoruba areas it gained support because of the unpopularity of the Action Group's taxation policy. However, as the N.C.N.C.'s close ally, the Northern Elements Progressive Union, won no seats in the North, there was still no party with truly national support. The curious situation arose that whilst the N.C.N.C. had the right to choose six federal ministers, having won both the East and West, the N.P.C. had the largest number of seats in the Federal House. This fact curbed the N.P.C. from its original intention of going it alone in the Federal House, for the presence of six N.C.N.C.

ministers made coalition inevitable. The Action Group, supported by N.I.P. (now U.N.I.P.), formed a small but active opposition.

The agreement of the N.P.C. and the N.C.N.C., whose political views were diametrically opposed on many issues, to work together in the Federal government was perhaps the most signicant development in post-war Nigerian politics since it has proved to be the basis of co-operation in the independent federation. It has made national unity possible, even if it has meant that both parties have had to compromise their political views.

In 1955 Sir John Macpherson, who had been ultimately responsible for Nigeria during its period of greatest political upheaval and progress, retired. Though the constitution named after him had proved a failure, he left praised by even the most extreme nationalist elements who recognized that Nigeria's accelerated constitutional progress was in no small measure due to his enthusiasm and understanding of the young federation's needs. His successor, Sir James Robertson, turned out to be the ideal man to represent Britain during the final phase of self-government, and happily the improved relations between Nigeria and Britain were crystallized the following year by the royal tour of Queen Elizabeth and the Duke of Edinburgh.

The visit of the Queen seemed somehow to symbolize the unity for which Nigeria was striving. Indeed, as the editorial in *West Africa* remarked at the time, 'the enthusiasm and devotion that the visit has aroused have gone beyond expectation'. The three main leaders called a political truce for the visit, and a bond of goodwill was created not only between Nigerians but between Nigeria and Britain, a bond that seemed far away from the months of 1953 when the N.C.N.C. banned the Coronation ceremonies.

Whilst Nigerian leaders were absorbed in the mechanics of government they also had one eye on the review of the constitution scheduled to take place in September 1956, when it was assumed that both the West and the East would take up the British promise of self-government in 1956. Indeed the Action Group had published in December 1955 a White Paper, which was approved by the Western House of Assembly, outlining the form self-government would take. However, because of events in the Eastern House of Assembly, the conference had to be postponed.

The N.C.N.C. had long been dogged by instability in the second ranks of its leadership. On 30th April 1956 Mr. E. O. Eyo, the chief whip of the Eastern region government, tabled a motion in the house accusing Dr. Azikiwe of gross abuse of public office in that he allowed £2 million of public money to be invested in the African Continental Bank in which he had substantial personal interest and which at the time was running at a loss. The debate was refused by the Speaker since the matter was *sub judice* because of a libel action brought by Dr. Azikiwe against Mr. Eyo. Since the Premier would not accede to the Governor of the region's suggestion that the matter be referred to an independent tribunal, the Colonial Secretary appointed a Commission of Inquiry under the Federal Chief Justice, Sir Stafford Foster-Sutton, which had the effect of delaying the resumed negotiations over the constitution.

Tales of corruption in public life were common in Nigeria at the time and concern over this was obviously one of Mr. Lennox-Boyd's main reasons for ordering the Commission in such delicate circumstances. As far as Dr. Azikiwe's supporters were concerned he was innocent even before he appeared before the tribunal, and the rather mild condemnation of the Commission that his conduct had 'fallen short of the expectations of honest reasonable people' seemed to confirm their view, especially since it was also conceded that Zik's primary motive 'was to make available an indigenous bank with the object of liberalizing credit for the people'. This was not due merely to blind personal following, but to the fact that whatever the rather cold attitude of the British might have been towards the affair, it was felt that Dr. Azikiwe had acted genuinely in the African interest by depositing government money in the African Continental Bank, especially as it was in danger of foundering. For them the bank represented an African achievement, and an attempt to rival the primacy of the British banks, one of which it was observed handled all government accounts. As Dr. Kalu Ezera points out in his *Constitutional Developments in Nigeria*, 'Zik's supporters generally believed that the whole affair was conspiracy by the Colonial Office to discredit and "dethrone" him and to perpetuate British banking monopoly in the country.'

West Africa wrote at the time very perceptively: 'The idea that a man who, like Dr. Azikiwe, has built up a bank and a group of companies, however shaky their finances, should relinquish all control of them when he becomes a Minister, is not universally accepted in Nigeria, where the joint stock company finds unfertile soil.' On the other hand the Commission of Inquiry had the salutary effect of regularizing the affairs of the bank, which, with the National Bank of Nigeria, supported mainly by the Western region, represents a very considerable entrepreneurial achievement.

Immediately after the Commission's report, delivered on 16th January 1957, Dr. Azikiwe transferred his interest to the Eastern Region Government, and went to the country as a trial of strength. He won the election by a comfortable margin of 66 seats to 18 (U.N.I.P. 5, Action Group 13) and was thus in a strong position as chief representative of the N.C.N.C. and the Eastern Region government at the London Conference scheduled for May 1957. Likewise the Action Group had gone to the country in May 1956 so that in the words of Chief Awolowo it 'could go to the next Constitutional Conference fully armed with a mandate of the people in respect of all major issues which will be raised at the conference'.

On 26th March 1957, the Federal House of Representatives, prior to the London conference and just after Ghana had achieved independence, passed a motion asking for independence in 1959. Once again it seemed at first that this might precipitate crisis, for the leader of the opposition, Chief Akintola, moving the motion, had originally asked for independence in 1957, although the North had already made it clear that she would not be hurried into regional self-government. However, the greatly improved relations between the parties were demonstrated clearly when Mr. Jaja Wachuku of the N.C.N.C. asked Chief Akintola whether he would agree to change the date to 1959, which he did, whereupon the house voted it unanimously.

The 1957 conference itself was mainly concerned with the revision of the constitution of 1954 both in the light of experience in running it and in accordance with foreseen constitutional advance. It was agreed that both the West and the East should have self-government as soon as they wanted it. The Federal House was enlarged to 320 members, who were to be elected directly on the same basis nationally with the exception that suffrage would not be extended to women in the North, in accordance with that region's Moslem susceptibilities. It was also agreed that there would be appointed a federal Prime Minister with a cabinet drawn from the House of Representatives or the proposed new Senate. The lack of a federal leader of government had hitherto been a major weakness of the constitution, but on the other hand until then it had been difficult to see how the various parties could agree on a Prime Minister, since the three national leaders were in the regional houses, and no one party commanded an overall majority. However, experience of working together and recognition of each other's talents made it possible for not only the N.C.N.C., which had been working in coalition with the N.P.C., but also the Action Group to form a national government under Alhaji Abubakar Tafawa Balewa, the former Minister of Transport and Deputy President of the N.P.C. This retiring, but extremely astute Northerner, had already impressed his colleagues as a minister, and in the house his great debating ability had gained him the respect of all legislators. Though in his early days as a national legislator he had talked in terms of Northern separatism, by 1957 he had become as convinced as anyone else of the necessity of national co-operation in the sense that he was not associated with any of the major tribal groups of Nigeria—unlike most of the Northern leaders he did not come from the Hausa Fulani aristocracy—and as a member of a small tribe, he could in a way, symbolize Nigeria as a whole and not one faction of it.

It might have seemed in 1957 that Nigeria was nearly ready for independence. The North had however refused to be rushed into self-government, on the grounds that Northern cadres were not ready to take over the region's administration. With eighteen million people to govern and only a handful of university graduates, and probably no more than 2,000 holders of school certificate, the formation of a Northern administration would be dependent on expatriates or Southerners. Moreover, the Regional Premier, the Sardauna of Sokoto, scion of the royal house of Sokoto, fully realized that the tensions existing in the region between the old forces of aristocracy as represented by the emirs and their native authorities and the new forces of democracy as represented by the government in Kaduna must on no account clash. The uncertain marriage between the two had to be handled with great care, and the N.P.C. seemed the only organization that could bridge the gap between them. The two southern regions had a head start as a result of their greater education, whilst the North, in which early agreements had excluded missionaries who had provided most of the schools in the South, had only just embarked on a large-scale education programme. Thus, before the 1957 conference, it seemed that the Northern reluctance for self-government might well hold up independence for the country as a whole, and it was with considerable relief that delegates heard the Sardauna of Sokoto announce that his region would in fact become self-governing in 1959.

By far the most complex problem confronting the delegates was that of Nigeria's minority groups, and the demand for the creation of new states that had grown up amongst them. One of the main results of the accentuation of tribal politics in the years of the Macpherson constitution was the increase in the minority reaction against the major tribal groups dominating the political life of the regions. This minority movement, always potentially existent because of historical and ethnic factors, took the form of political associations seeking the separation of so-called minority areas and the creation of new states. In the Northern region some people in the predominantly non-Moslem and non-Hausa Middle Belt formed the United Middle Belt Congress. This new party demanded the creation of a separate state for the Middle Belt so that the people could escape from what its leaders alleged was the domination of the Fulani and Hausa. This had certain roots in history for the areas claimed by this party were predominantly those which the cavalry of Usman dan Fodio had never conquered. In the Western region, as a reaction against the alleged Yoruba-dominated Action Group, was started the Mid-West State movement, supported largely by non-Yoruba-speaking peoples and in particular the people of the old Benin Empire. The N.C.N.C. also supported this movement on the grounds that the only way to create a truly united Nigeria would be to create more states, none of which would be large enough to dominate any of the others. Curiously enough the Action Group itself gave its blessing to this movement, partly because it was beginning to find the

Mid-West an electoral and economic liability and partly because it realized that if it were to champion the creation of new states in the Eastern and Northern regions it could hardly object to the creation of one in the Western region itself.

In the East the Ibo form a solid core of five million, and are surrounded by three provinces in which other groups predominate: Calabar, Ogoja and Rivers. The movement for the creation of a separate state in the East has been more complex. The main movement has been for the creation of the C.O.R. State or Calabar-Ogoja-Rivers state, but there have been subsidiary movements for the creation of an Ogoja state and a Rivers state including Ijo from both Western and Eastern Nigeria. But in all cases the movements were inspired by fear of the dominant group, and by ethnic chauvinism.

The 1957 Conference referred this knotty matter to a special commission headed by Sir Henry Willinck. Its tour of the country was naturally the time for the most vocal outcry of minority groups, and in a sense the whole problem became for a time wildly exaggerated, because of the implicit opportunity the Commission gave to the voicing of all sorts of grievances.

However the Minorities Commission came out very strongly against the creation of new states, because it felt that the fears and problems of minority groups could be better solved within the existing political framework. In each case the Commission found that the cores of the minority movements were too small compared with the area which they claimed for their new state. For instance, they argued that in the West, while most Bini wanted a Mid-West State, by no means all Itsekiri and Ijo felt happy at the prospect of its creation.

Yet the Commission admitted that minority fears of ethnic domination and discrimination in development were real, and proposed that minority areas be set up for both Calabar and the mid-West. These areas would have special councils, which could keep a watch on regional government activities and could also exercise delegated executive authority. For the Ijo areas of the Niger Delta the Commission recommended the establishment of a special development board on which the regional goverments concerned and the Federal goverment would be represented. However whilst the Commission gave no truck to the creation of a Middle Belt state in the North, it did recommend that a plebiscite be held there to determine whether Ilorin and Kabba wished to remain in the North or join up with the Western region.

Otherwise the Commission felt that minority fears could be assuaged by the entrenchment of fundamental human rights in the constitution, and by making any amendment to the constitution impossible without the virtual consent of the whole country and in particular the people most intimately affected. Finally, it insisted that the police should remain national rather than be regionalized as the N.P.C. and Action Group had requested.

At the 1958 conference the parties agreed with some reluctance to the acceptance of the minorities report. The Action Group was particularly anxious about the inclusion of the Ilorin and Kabba in the Western region, and therefore the implementation of the plebiscite recommended by the Commission, but the North, which had agreed to take self-government on 15th March 1959, made it clear that it might be at the price of independence that this point be insisted upon. On the other hand both the Action Group and the N.P.C. had to compromise over the subject of the police. Both had wanted the regionalization of the police, but the N.C.N.C. and the British government, agreeing for once, saw in the regionalization of the police a danger to political independence, particularly of minorities.

The agreement over the minorities report was, of course, largely influenced by the fact that none of the parties cared to stand out on the issue for fear of being branded as the one that held up independence. The problem still remained and will colour Nigerian politics for some years to come. In retrospect it might seem that the Commission dodged the issue, especially since it was widely known that the British government would consider the creation of new states as instrumental in delaying the date for independence. But the lines on which the Commission was thinking were made clear by one of its members, Mr. Philip Mason, in a series of articles in *West Africa*. He argued that hopes of the continued unity of Nigeria and justice for individuals must rest initially on the grounds that none of the three major parties could dominate the other and that any party seeking to get such domination within the present political structure must seek support outside its regional stronghold, and

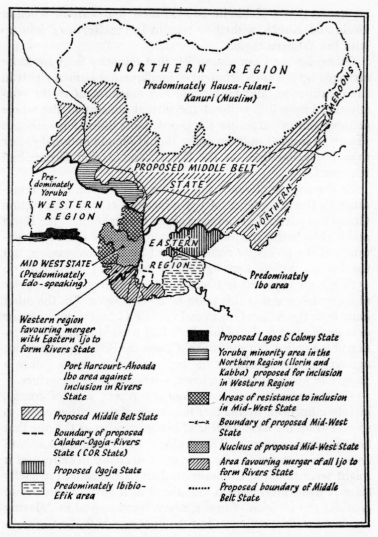

9. The various proposed political reorganizations of Nigeria, 1945–60

therefore amongst the minority groups of the other regions. This fact, together with a police force independent of any regional government, and therefore any party, would be the best guarantee of minority rights.

The outcome of the federal elections of 1959 and the campaign that preceded them showed just how dominant a factor minorities remained and how anxious all the parties, including the N.P.C. with regard to its own minority area, were to gain their confidence. A comparison of the distribution of minorities and the strongholds of opposition in each region is very illuminating (see map). However, in a surprise election just before independence the Action Group retained control of the West, having made significant gains in the mid-West as well as some losses in Yorubaland, indicating that perhaps tribal factors were receding in Nigerian politics.

The federal elections, as the table below shows, returned no party with a large enough majority to form a government by itself.

Party	North	East	West	Lagos	Total
N.P.C.	142	1	6	—	149
		(Niger Delta Congress)			
N.C.N.C./N.E.P.U. Alliance	8	58	21	2	89
Action Group	24	15	35	1	75
Independents[1]	—	—	—	—	—
	174	74	62	3	313

After a week of strenuous negotiations the N.P.C. and the N.C.N.C. agreed to form a coalition government, leaving the Action Group in opposition. During that week there had even been talk of an Action Group—N.C.N.C. alliance, which would have led to the unhappy situation of confronting South and North as Government and Opposition.

Alhaji Abubakar Tafawa Balewa, who was knighted in the New Year Honours, became Prime Minister and Dr. Azikiwe, leader of the N.C.N.C., opted for the dignified but in itself politically uninfluential post of President of the newly formed Senate which has an equal number of Senators nominated by each regional government. There was considerable speculation as to whether Dr. Azikiwe would become Nigeria's first African

[1] A number of independents were elected but declared for one or other of the major parties before the house sat.

Governor General, or whether he was waiting for the post of Foreign Minister when Nigeria, on independence, took over control of external affairs. As it turned out there were no major changes in the government on independence and Dr. Azikiwe, on 16th November 1960, became Governor General of the independent federation.

The fifteen years following the introduction of the Richards constitution had of course seen many changes in the country, particularly in the level of economic activity, all the more significant since Nigerians were now participating in development and administration. A glance at the table[1] below gives a very good indication of the rapid advance made by the country since the war:

Item	1947	1953	1958
Revenue of Governments (£thousands)	£14,193	£51,110	£81,288
Currency in circulation (£thousands)	£23,429	£51,365	£55,118
Bank deposits (£thousands)	£13,697	£31,238	£58,118
Exports (£thousands)	£44,314	£124,232	£135,690
Imports (£thousands)	£32,636	£108,290	£167,074
Railway freight tons (miles—1,000)	571,000	827,000	1,232,000
Cement imports and local manufacture (tons)	107,306	297,436	573,119

Years of careful hoarding of sterling reserves during a period of high world prices for primary products allowed the various Nigerian governments to indulge in a spate of investment spending in the five years before independence that left imports exceeding exports by £31 million in 1958, or £2 million less than the total value of imports in 1947. In the last decade imports have quadrupled in value, whilst exports have only little more than doubled and have remained almost constant in the last five years.

[1] Adapted from *West Africa.*

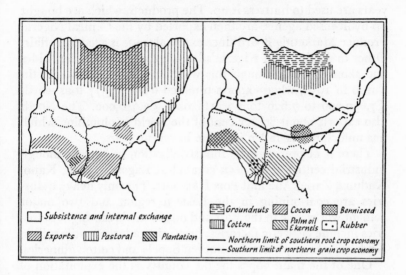

Subsistence and internal exchange

Exports Pastoral Plantation

Groundnuts Cocoa Benniseed
Cotton Palm oil E kernels Rubber
— Northern limit of southern root crop economy
--- Southern limit of northern grain crop economy

10. Nigeria's economy today

In 1956–7 national income was estimated at £800 million, and was thought to be rising at the rate of 4 per cent per annum. Population was also estimated to be rising at the rate of 2 per cent per annum, a fact that will later give cause for concern unless national income rises at a faster rate.

Agriculture is still the basis of the Nigerian economy, accounting for over 85 per cent of the country's exports. Fortunately for the country as a whole the variety of primary products is sufficiently diverse to avoid the worst effects of the vagaries of world market prices. However, the Northern and Eastern regions, which have predominantly one-crop economies, are more vulnerable than the Western region, which produces palm oil, rubber, cocoa and timber. On the average, in the last five years groundnuts coming exclusively from the North have earned about £27 million a year; palm products from the East and West, £33 million; cotton and linters from the North, £8 million; cocoa from the West, £26 million; and rubber mainly from the West but with some from the East, £7 million. All crops are bought by the regional marketing boards at a price fixed at the opening of the season. If the world price falls below this price, reserve funds accumulated in favourable years are used to buttress it up. The products, which are bought up by licensed agents, are then exported by the Central Nigeria Produce Marketing Board since external trade is a federal affair. Other major items in Nigeria's list of exports are timber, hides and skins and tin, though this was hard hit by the world tin slump in 1958, when exports tumbled from 13,577 tons worth £7,630,000 to 7,626 tons worth only £3,940,000. The North also exports about 80 per cent of the world's columbite, which has unfortunately fallen in value in recent years.

There is at present little industrialization in Nigeria though industrial centres have been created at Lagos, Ibadan, Kano, Kaduna, Zaria, Aba and Port Harcourt. The only heavy industries are coal-mining in the Eastern region and two major cement works, one in the East and one in the West. Light industries include cigarette factories, breweries, a large textile mill in Kaduna, a huge plywood factory at Sapele and cotton ginneries.

One of the main hopes for the country is the exploitation of the large oil reserves of the Niger Delta. Shell-B.P. have already spent £60 million on research and already Nigeria is exporting a small quantity each year.

The Regional and Federal governments are all aware of the necessity of increasing both external and internal trade, and their combined development programmes for the years 1955–6 to 1961–2 will account for nearly £340 million, of which some £63 million will be spent by the statutory corporations like the Electricity Corporation of Nigeria and the Railway Corporation. The national communications system has been given priority of expenditure as it is considered the key to the future economic expansion of the country. Nigeria has a road network of some 37,000 miles, but little more than 4,000 of these are at present tarred. Major highways are the responsibility of the Federal government whilst the rest are maintained by the regional governments and local authorities. In the South, where the rainfall is very heavy, and where rivers and creeks abound, road building and maintenance is an extremely costly undertaking, especially with the vast increase of motor traffic in the past ten years. However, the main artery of the communications system is still the railway, built in the early years of the century and linking the ports of Lagos and Port Harcourt with the northern cities. The total length of track is 1,780 miles, and about 2½ million tons of goods are carried on it each year. An important extension of the railway from Kuru, near Jos, to Maiduguri in north-eastern Nigeria will open up a huge new area of the North. This has been financed by a £10 million loan from the World Bank and from Nigerian sources. The total cost is expected to be £20 million. The railways and roads all link up with ports whose facilities have been greatly extended in the past decade to handle the increasing volume of exports and imports. Other important means of communication are the Niger and Benue, on which some 300,000 tons of goods are carried a year, not counting what is carried on small local craft.

Another priority in all governments' programmes has been education, for they have all felt that ultimately the progress of Nigeria must depend on the education of the people. The Western region, richer than the other governments, has even introduced free universal primary education and in November 1958 there were 6,670 primary schools in the region with over a million pupils in attendance. In both Eastern and Western regions the number of children attending school is 80 per cent of those of school age. The North, backward educationally because missions, as we have seen, were excluded, has been devoting much of its revenue towards the education of its people, both young and old, and in the ancient city of Kano a universal primary education scheme was started just before independence. The Federal government is responsible for the University College of Ibadan. The Eastern region, on the occasion of Nigeria's independence, opened a new university at Nsukka and the Ashby Commission on Higher Education has recommended expansion of the country's higher education facilities. Three further universities are being established, one in Lagos, one in the North and one in Ife. In addition there were, in 1957–8, between four and five thousand Nigerian students studying overseas.

Health services have been considerably improved in the last decade, but there is still a great shortage of money and staff to combat the glut of tropical diseases to be found in the country. In 1957 the University College Teaching Hospital at Ibadan was opened and will soon prove an indispensable source of trained practitioners as well as an important international research centre for tropical diseases.

Independence Achieved

The administration of most of these development programmes has been the responsibility of the civil service, and before independence Nigeria had to face the grave problem of the exodus of many of her most experienced British civil servants. Whilst government policy has been the rapid Nigerianization of the civil service, on the other hand it has been realized that where no suitable Nigerian was available everything must be done to encourage expatriates to stay. In 1956 the Colonial Secretary, foreseeing the dangers of a mass exodus, proposed a scheme whereby expatriate civil servants were guaranteed their pension rights by the British government and alternative employment overseas or in the United Kingdom if they should become redundant. Alternatively they could take their earned pension and a lump-sum compensation reaching a maximum of £10,000 according to service. Unfortunately large numbers of them opted for the second, and in 1958 a new scheme was introduced whereby they could draw 90 per cent of their lump-sum compensation in advance of their retirement as long as they agreed to give one year's notice. Nevertheless, large numbers of British civil servants left the country before independence.

Not all development services are carried out by the central and regional governments. Local government, particularly in the North with its mammoth native administrations such as Kano, with an annual budget of over £1 million, plays an important part in the regulation of the affairs of the country. Since the war this has been increasingly democratized. And the local government law of 1950 in the East, in fact, instituted the same local government system as is practised in Britain, a system which has subsequently been considerably modified. County Councils have been abolished and the District Officers have been given much more control over the award of contracts and hiring of staff.

In the West the local government law of 1953, whilst it retained traditional members on the councils, introduced effective elected majorities. In the North the Native Authority Ordinance of 1952 abolished the status of sole native authority enjoyed by some emirs, and in 1954 an amendment authorized the Governor to include a certain number of elected members on the councils, though these have not yet attained very much power on the councils. The development of local government has been one of the most striking achievements of post-war Nigeria, for it has allowed a very considerable degree of participation by people in the administration of their own affairs.

The federation of Nigeria which became independent on 1st October 1960 is thus a country of great diversity and complexity. But the long negotiations over the form independence should take, whilst they may have entailed compromise and disappointment, and whilst they may have exacerbated traditional antagonisms, have meant that the foundations of independent Nigeria have been solidly built. Peoples of various groups have been brought into close contact with one another, learnt about common factors as well as differences, begun to think of themselves as Nigerians rather than Hausa, Ibo and Yoruba. Indeed Nigeria, with a greater population than West and Equatorial Africa put together, is the greatest experiment in African unity yet undertaken. On its success the future of Africa may well depend. Frustrating years of constitutional negotiation and the consequent delay of independence have had their reward in the formulation of a constitution freely negotiated by Nigerians themselves, a constitution which for all its limitations can contain the various differences and tensions in the country. And though the day is not come when real unity has been achieved, the indications are that common elements in the past of the various groups of Nigeria, and the present attitude of her political leaders, will ensure the survival of the federation and that one word *Nigeria* chosen for this great land mass only sixty years ago is beginning to mean more to the country's inhabitants than their former ethnic designations.

Select Bibliography

Alimen, H., *The Prehistory of Africa*. London, 1957.

Arnett, E. J., *The Rise of the Sokoto Fulani*. (*Paraphrase of Infaku'l Maisuri of Sultan Bello Muhammed*.) Kano, 1922.

Austin, Dennis, *West Africa and the Commonwealth*. London, 1957.

Awolowo, Obafemi, *Path to Nigerian Freedom*. London, 1947.

Azikiwe, Nnamdi, *Renascent Africa*. Lagos, 1937.

Baikie, William B., *Narrative of an exploring Voyage up the Rivers Kwo'ra and Binue (commonly known as the Niger and Tsadda) in 1854*. London, 1856.

Barth, Heinrich, *Travels and Discoveries in Northern and Central Africa*. London, 1857.

Biobaku, S. O., *The Egba and their Neighbours, 1832–1872*. London, 1957.

Biobaku, S. O., *The Origin of the Yorubas*. Lagos, 1955.

Blake, —, *Europeans in West Africa*. London, 1942.

Bohannan, Laura and Paul, *The Tiv of Central Nigeria*. London, 1953.

Bovill, E. W., *Caravans of the Old Sahara*. London, 1933.

Bovill, E. W., *The Golden Trade of the Moors*. London, 1955.

Bradbury, R. E. and Lloyd, Peter C., *The Benin Kingdom and Edo-speaking Peoples, etc., plus the Itsekiri*. London, 1959.

Buchanan, K. M. and Pugh, J. C., *Land and People in Nigeria*. London, 1955.

Buell, R. L., *The Native Problem in Africa*. 2 vols. New York, 1928.

Burdon, J. A., *Historical Notes on Certain Emirates and Tribes (Nigeria, Northern Provinces)*. London, 1909.

Burns, Sir Alan C., *History of Nigeria*. London, 1956.

Buxton, T. F., *The African Slave Trade and its Remedy*. London, 1839.

Cameron, Donald, *Principles of Native Administration and their Application*. Lagos, 1934.

Select Bibliography

Cary, Joyce, *Britain and West Africa*. London, 1940.

Church, R. J. Harrison, *West Africa*. London, 1957.

Clapperton, Hugh, *Journal of a Second Expedition into the Interior of Africa, etc.* London, 1829.

Coleman, James, *Nigeria: Background to Nationalism.* U.S.A., 1958.

Cook, Arthur N., *British Enterprise in Nigeria.* U.S.A., 1943.

Crocker, W. R., *Nigeria: A Critique of British Colonial Administration.* London, 1936.

Crowther, S. A., *Journals of an Expedition up the Niger and Tsadda Rivers, etc.* London, 1855.

Davidson, Basil, *Old Africa Rediscovered.* London, 1959.

Davies, J. G., *The Biu Book.* Nigeria, 1956.

Denham, D., Clapperton, H. and Oudney, N., *Narrative of Travels and Discoveries in Northern and Central Africa in the Years 1822, 1823 and 1824.* London, 1826.

Dike, K. Onwuka. *Trade and Politics in the Niger Delta, 1830-1855.* London 1956.

Dike, K. Onwuka, *100 Years of British Rule in Nigeria, 1851–1951.* Lagos, 1957.

Dike, K. Onwuka, *Origins of the Niger Mission 1841–1891.* Lagos, 1957.

Egharevba, J. U., *A Short History of Benin.* Lagos, 1936.

English, M. C., *An Outline of Nigerian History.* London, 1959.

Ezera, Kalu, *Constitutional Developments in Nigeria.* London, 1960.

Fage, J. D., *An Introduction to the History of West Africa.* London, 1955.

Flint, J. E., *Sir George Goldie and the Making of Nigeria.* London, 1960.

Forde, Daryll, *The Yoruba-Speaking Peoples of South-Western Nigeria.* London, 1951.

Forde, Daryll, *Efik Traders of Old Calabar.* London, 1956.

Forde, Daryll and Jones, G. L., *The Ibo and Ibibio-Speaking Peoples of South-Eastern Nigeria.* London, 1950.

Forde, Daryll and others, *Peoples of the Niger-Benue Confluence.* London, 1955.

Fortes, Meyer and Evans-Pritchard, E. E., *African Political Systems.* London, 1940.

Geary, William N. M., *Nigeria Under British Rule.* London, 1927.

Select Bibliography

Greenberg, Joseph, *Studies in African Linguistic Classification*. U.S.A., 1955.

Hailey, Lord, *Native Administration in British African Territories*, 5 vols. London, 1951.

Hailey, Lord, *An African Survey*. London, 1938.

Hailey, Lord, *An African Survey Revised*, 1956. London, 1957.

Harris, Philip, *Local Government in Southern Nigeria*. London, 1957.

Hassan and Shu'aibu (trans. F. Heath), *A Chronicle of Abuja*. Ibadan, 1952.

Hermon-Hodge, H. B., *Gazetteer of Ilorin Province*. London, 1929.

Hodgkin, Thomas, ed., *The New West Africa*. London, 1953.

Hodgkin, Thomas, *Nationalism in Colonial Africa*. London, 1956.

Hodgkin, Thomas, *Nigerian Perspectives*. London, 1960.

Hogben, S. J., *The Muhammedan Emirates of Northern Nigeria*. London, 1930.

Hopen, Edward, *The Pastoral Fulbe Family in Gwandu*. London, 1959.

Howard, C. and Plumb, J. H., *West African Explorers*. London, 1952.

Hutchinson, T. J., *Ten Years' Wandering among the Ethiopians*. London, 1861.

Ibn Battuta (trans. H. A. R. Gibb), *Travels in Asia and Africa, 1325–1354*. London, 1953.

International Bank for Reconstruction and Development, *The Economic Development of Nigeria*. U.S.A., 1955.

Johnson, Samuel, *The History of the Yorubas*. Lagos, 1937.

Kirk-Greene, *Adamawa, Past and Present*. London, 1958.

Krieger, K., *Geschichte von Zamfara*. Berlin, 1959.

Laird, Macgregor and Oldfield, R. A. K., *Narrative of an Expedition to the Interior of Africa in 1832, 1833 and 1834*. London, 1837.

Lander, Richard and John, *Journals of an Expedition to Explore the Course and Termination of the Niger, etc.* London, 1832.

Langa Langa, *Up Against it in Nigeria*. London, 1922.

Lloyd, Christopher, *The Navy and the Slave Trade*. London, 1949.

Lucas, J. Olumide, *The Religion of the Yorubas*. Lagos, 1948.

Lugard, F. D., *The Dual Mandate in British Tropical Africa*. Edinburgh, 1929.

Lugard, F. D., *Report on the Amalgamation of Northern and Southern Nigeria and Administration*. London, 1920.

Lugard, Lady, *A Tropical Dependency*. London, 1905.

Select Bibliography

Macfarlane, Donald M., *Calabar: and the Church of Scotland Mission, 1846–1946.* London, 1946.

Meek, C. K., *Northern Tribes of Nigeria.* London, 1925.

Meek, C. K., *A Sudanese Kingdom.* London, 1931.

Mockler-Ferryman, A. F., *British Nigeria.* London, 1902.

Morel, E. D., *Nigeria: Its Peoples and Problems.* London, 1912.

Nadel, S. F., *A Black Byzantium.* London, 1942.

Nigeria, *The Nigeria Handbook,* London, 1953.

Niven, C. R., *A Short History of Nigeria.* London, 1937.

Niven, C. R., *A Short History of the Yoruba Peoples.* London, 1958.

Orikpo, Akoi, *Who Are the Nigerians?* Lagos, 1958.

Orr, C. W. J., *The Making of Northern Nigeria.* London, 1911.

Palmer, H. R., *The Bornu, Sahara and Sudan.* London, 1936.

Palmer, H. R., *History of the first twelve years of the reign of Mai Idris Alooma of Bornu (1571–1583) by his Imam, Ahmed ben Fartua.* Lagos, 1926.

Park, Mungo, *Travels in the Interior Districts of Africa, in 1795, 1796 and 1797, etc.* London, 1799.

Park, Mungo, *Journal of a mission to the interior of Africa in the year 1805, etc.* London, 1815.

Parrinder, Geoffrey, *The Story of Ketu—An Ancient Yoruba Kingdom.* Ibadan, 1956.

Pedler, F. J., *West Africa.* London, 1951.

Perham, Margery, *Native Administration in Nigeria.* London, 1937.

Perham, Margery, *Lugard: The Years of Adventure, 1858–1898.* London, 1960.

Perham, Margery, *Lugard: The Years of Authority, 1899–1945.* London, 1960.

Roth, Henry L., *Great Benin: its Customs, Art and Horrors.* Halifax, 1903.

Royal Institute of International Affairs, *Nigeria: The Political and Economic Background.* London, 1960.

St. Croix, F. W. de, *The Fulani of Northern Nigeria.* Lagos, 1944.

Schoen, Jacob F., and Crowther, S. A., *Journals of an Expedition up the Niger in 1841.* London, 1842.

Schultze, A. (trans. P. A. Benton), *The Sultanate of Bornu.* London, 1913.

Smith, Mary, *Baba of Karo.* London, 1954.

Smith, M. G., *Government in Zazzau.* London, 1960.

Stenning, Derek, *Savannah Nomads.* London, 1959.

Select Bibliography

Talbot, P. Amaury, *The Peoples of Southern Nigeria, Vol.* 1 *Historical Notes.* London, 1926.

Thorp, Ellen, *Ladder of Bones.* London, 1959.

Trimingham, J. Spencer, *Islam in West Africa.* London, 1959.

Urvoy, Yves, *Histoire de l'Empire du Bornou.* Paris, 1949.

Wellesley, Dorothy, *Sir George Goldie: Founder of Nigeria.* London, 1934.

Westermann, Diedrich and Bryan, M. A., *Languages of West Africa.* London, 1952.

Wheare, Joan, *The Nigerian Legislative Council.* London, 1950.

Whitting, C. E. J. (translation of), *History of Sokoto* by Hajji Sa'id. Kano, 1949.

ARTICLES

Ajayi, J. F. Ade, 'The British Occupation of Lagos 1851-1861', *Nigeria Magazine*, No. 69, August 1961.

Beier, Ulli, 'Before Oduduwa', *Odu* 3, 1956, 25–32.

Beier, Ulli and Biobaku, S. O., 'The use and interpretation of myths', *Odu* 1, 1955, 12–25.

Biobaku, S. O., 'The problem of traditional history with special reference to Yoruba traditions', *J. Hist. Soc. Nigeria* 1, 1st December 1956, 43–7.

Bourdillon, Bernard, 'Nigeria's new constitution', *United Empire*, Vol. 36, No. 2, March–April 1946.

Burdon, John A., 'Sokoto History: tables of dates and genealogy, *J. Afr. Soc.* 6, 24th July 1907, 367–74.

Fortes, M., 'The impact of the war on British West Africa', *International Affairs*, 21st April 1945, 206–19.

Fagg, Bernard, 'A life-size terra-cotta head from Nok', *Man* 95, 1956.

Fagg, Bernard, 'The Nok culture', *West African Review*, December 1956.

Forde, Daryll, 'The cultural map of West Africa', trans. *New York Acad. Sci. Ser.* 2, 15th April 1953, 206–19.

Hambly, Wilfrid D., 'Culture areas of Nigeria', *Chicago: Field Museum of Natural History* (Anthropological Series 31, 3), 1953.

Hiskett, M., 'Material relating to the state of learning among the Fulani before their Jihad', *Bull. of the School of Oriental and African Studies* 19, 3, 1957.

278

Select Bibliography

Hodgkin, Thomas, ' 'Uthman dan Fodio', *Nigeria* 1960, Special Independence Issue of *Nigeria Magazine*, October 1960.

Horton, W. R. G., 'The Ohu system of slavery in a northern Ibo village-group', *Africa* 24, 4th October 1954, 311–36.

Kirk-Greene, A. H. M., 'Who coined the name Nigeria?', *West Africa*, 22nd December 1956.

Lloyd, Peter C., 'The traditional political system of the Yoruba', *South-Western Jour. Anthrop.* 10, 4, Winter 1954, 366–84.

Lugard, Frederick D., 'Expedition to Borgu', *Geog. Journal* 6, 1895, 205–27.

Morton-Williams, P., 'Some Yoruba kingdoms under modern conditions', *J. Afr. Admin.*, 7th October 1955, 174–9.

Palmer, H. R., 'The Bornu Girgam', *J. Afr. Soc.* 12, 45, October 1912, 71–83.

Palmer, H. R., 'An early Fulani conception of Islam', *J. Afr. Soc.* 13, 52, July 1914, 407–14, 14, 53, October 1914, 53–9, 54, January 1915, 185–92.

Palmer, H. R., 'The Kano Chronicle', *J. Roy. Anthrop. Inst.* 38, 1908. 58–98.

Palmer, H. R. 'History of Katsina', *J. Afr. Soc.* 26, 103, 1927, 216–36.

Perry, Ruth, 'New Sources for research in Nigerian history', *Africa* 25, 4th October 1955, 430–2.

Urvoy, Yves, 'Chronologie du Bornou', *J. Soc. Africanistes* 11, 1941, 21–32.

Verger, Pierre, 'Yoruba influences in Brazil', *Odu*, January 1955, 3–11.

Verger, Pierre, 'Nigeria, Brazil and Cuba', *Nigeria* 1960. Special Independence Issue of *Nigeria Magazine*, October 1960.

Index

Note. The various *Mais* are indexed under 'Mai'; *Mallams* under Mallam, and so on.

Aba (Eastern Nigeria), 231, 232; after Enugu massacre, 249; as new industrial centre, 270

Abdullahi Bongia (King of Kano city state), 36

Abdullahi, successor of Mohammed Rimfa King of Kano, 40

Abdullahi, brother of Usman dan Fodio, 84, 85, 87, 88

Abdussalami, disciple of Usman dan Fodio, 82, 85

Abdussalami, Emir of Ilorin, 92, 105

Abeokuta—background to foundation of, 102, 103, 104; Dahomey attacks, 106, 107; early nineteenth-century missionaries in, 127, 128, 129; receives Sierra Leone immigrants, 127; factories at, 128; opposed to Kosoko, 139; Yoruba mission at, 148; opposes Campbell's treaty, 149, 150; Townsend resents Lagos's intervention in, 154; Rev. J. B. Wood at, 160; 1887 French mission at, 172–3, 185; in British-French trade rivalry, 185, 186; British-Egba 1893 treaty at, 188; dispute with Lagos at climax, 1867, 156; on Lagos trade route, 158; taxation introduced to, 219; opposes Lugard, 220–21; and West African Students' Union, 237.

Aberdeen, Lord, on barracoon destruction, 115

Abiodun, Alafin (Oyo), as last ruler of united Yoruba kingdom, 100; destroys Ijaye, 101

Abipa, Alafin, son of Ajiboyede (Oyo), 53–4

Aboh, trade post, 145

Abolitionists (British), 108 seqq.; and the Sugar Act, 116

Abomey, siege of (Oyo against Dahomey, 1738), 99

Abu Abdullah Muhammad b. 'Abd al-Karim al Maghili (El Maghili), historian, 39; *Instruction in the Obligations of Princes*, 39

Abu Bekri (Nupe), 195, 196

Abubakar, *see* Balewa

Abubakar Garbai (Kanemi Shehu), 198

Abuja, 87; British 1902 expedition against, 198; terra-cottas, 29

Abuyazidu (Bayajidda)-tradition (Hausa states foundation), 37

Abyssinian Association formed, 1935, 238

Accra, 163; Jaja's trial at, 179; inaugural conference of National Congress of British West Africa at, 226–7; 'Accra Resolutions', 227–8; Dr. Azikiwe in, 238

Action Group, Nigeria, 214, 248; in Nigeria's first general election, 250–1; precipitates breakdown of Macpherson constitution, 253; in temporary alliance with

Index

Action Group—*cont.*
N.C.N.C., 254, 255; opposes federal solution for Lagos, 255; after 1954, 258 seqq.; publishes 1955 White Paper on self-government, 259; 1957 success of, 261; after 1959, 267; and the minority groups, 263–5

Adahoozu, King of Dahomey (1780s), 100

Adamawa, 23, 94; in Usman's Holy War, 86; as early nineteenth-century eastward Fulani limit, 91; Morel's proposal for, 214

Adams, Capt. John, on late eighteenth-century Benin decline, 74; on Iboland slaves, 75

Adebo, Alafin of Oyo, 102

Adele, Oba of Lagos, 139

Adelu, Alafin, 150, 158

Adimu (of Ife), 47, 48

Adola, Oba of Benin, 183

Afonja Kakanfo, Ilorin revolt of, 96; *see* also Kakanfo

African Association founded, 1788, 118–19; on Park's discovery, 120

African Continental Bank, 260, 261

Agades, 80, 88

Agaie emirate (Nupe), 91

Adhwey, France annexes, 166

Ago-Oja: in Owu wars, 104; as new capital of Oyo, 105

Ague festival (Benin), 183

Ahmed Baba, Timbuktu historian, 38; treatise on slavery by, 39

Ahmed ben Fartuq, *see* Imam

Aicha Ahmed (divine), 42

Air, Bornu and Kebbi, struggle for, 41

Ais Kili N'guirmamaramama (a Bornu ruler), 42

Ajaka, son of Oranmiyan, 51, 52

Ajasa, Sir Kitoyi, 232

Ajayi, Dr., *Christian Missions and the Making of Nigeria*, 139

Ajiboyede, successor to Egugoujo, 53

Akan, in Ghana, 27

Akassa: Court of Equity, 137; Goldie's measures against, 167; as Royal Niger Company port, 171, 174; raided by Brassmen, 1895, 181–3

Akinsanya, Samuel (N.Y.M.), 238, 240, 241, 247

Akintola, Chief, 261

Akitoye-Kosoko succession dispute in Lagos, 127, 129, 134, 139, 140, 149

Aku Creoles, in new Yoruba towns, 127

Alafins of Oyo, 47, 49, 50, 51, 52; as heads of native authorities under Lugard, 220; and Basorun, 50, 98

Alake of Abeokuta, Townsend and, 129

Alaketu of Ketu, 47

Alali, Regent of Bonny, 114, 161; and King William Pepple's exile, 142–3

Albert, Sudan and *Wilberforce*, missionary ships to Niger, 125

Albert, Prince Consort, and 1841 Niger expedition, 125; and Church Missionary Society, 129

Al-Bukhari, 95

Alburkah and *Quorra* (iron steamships) in earliest trade to Niger, 124

Alecto, gunboat in Niger affair, 181

Alexander Miller Bros. & Co. in Niger trade, 164, 178

Al-hajj Umar ibn Said (Western Sudan), 83

Aliu Baba (a successor of Bello), 95

Alkalawa, 88

Allen, Commander William, on Niger expeditions, 125

Alwassa, Usman dan Fodio's forces beaten at, 86

Amakiri (of New Calabar), King William Pepple attacks, 142

Amalgamated Association (European traders) against Jaja's monopoly, 178

Index

Amalgamation Report (Lugard's, 1919), 217–18

Amanyanabo, role of in Ijo culture, 68, 69

Amazons of Dahomey, 106–7, 128

America: and slave trade, 63, 64; achieves independence, 109, 119; outlaws slave trade, 111; criticizes British colonialism, 240

Amina, queen of Zaria, 38, 44

Amir-al-mu'minin defined, 93

Amodo, Alafin of Oyo, 105

Andoni, 162

Anglo-African (paper), 153

Anglo-French Convention of 1898, 192; and fate of Bornu, 198

Angola, slave exports from, 63

Anka, Zamfarawa new capital, 80, 85

Anna Pepple house, 161; *see* Pepple

Anti-slavery patrols, 111

Aole, Alafin of Oyo, 101; and assault of Iwere, 101; curses Yorubaland, 101

Apomu, destruction of (Owu War), 103

Apongbon, *see* McKoskry

Arabs: invasion of North Africa, 31; early societies of, 25; slave trade through Kano, Katsina, 38–9; trade with Bello (ousting British), 123; in gold trade, 58; learning of, in Nigeria, 39, 80, 81

Ardo Lerlima (Fulani leader), 88

Ardra, *see* Great Ardra

'Aremo', eldest son of Alafin, 50

Arguin, 94

Argungu, in Holy War, 87

Army described (Idris Alooma's), 43

Aro of Arochuku, as Delta ports' slave controllers, 72–3

Aro Chukwu oracle, British 1902 expedition against, 204–5

Art, of Ife, 48, 53; secular Benin carvings, 56; *see* Benin, Birnin Kudu, Idah, Ife, Jemaa, Nok, Ivory

Asaba: Lander brothers capture, 123; Goldie's measures against, 166; as Niger Company headquarters, 171; in War I, 223

Ashanti states, 96; matriarchy in, 35; Ashanti War, 195, 196; Jaja's contribution to, 177

Ashby Commission on Higher Education, 271

Askia Daud, 41

Askia Mohammed I, of Songhai, 40–1

Askia Nuh, 42

Ata of Igala, 53

Atahiru, Sultan of Sokoto, 200, 202

Atiba, son of Abiodun, chooses site of 'new' Oyo, 105; death of, 150

Atlantic Charter, 240

Atlantic slave trade, 57–78

Australia, discovery of, 119; railway development in, 165

Auyo, defeat of in Holy War, 87

d'Aveiro, João Affonso, reaches Benin (1486), 57

Awaye, Ibadan attack, 153

Awolowo, Obafemi, 241, 261; tour of Kano by, 253

Awujale of Ijebuland, *see* Ijebu

Axes, Neolithic polished, 27

Azikiwe, Dr. Nnamdi, 238; rivalry with Ikoli, 240–1; founds N.C.N.C., 241; follows Morel and Temple, 243; and general strike, 244; leads London delegation, 245; under Macpherson, 246; becomes President of Pan-Ibo Federal Union, 247; after Nigeria's first general election, 251, 252; and African Continental Bank enquiry, 260; 1957 success of, 261; becomes President of Senate, 267; becomes Governor-General of independent Federation, 268

Baba Goro b. al Haji Muhammed b. al-Hajj al-Aminu Kano, historian, 39

Index

Badagry: in slave trade, 113; British influence at, 139, 140; Clapperton's journey to, 122–3; the Lander brothers' trek from, 123; Gold Coast Methodist Mission at, 127; trading with Freetown, 127; early nineteenth-century missions in, 127, 128; factories opened in, 128; as Egba trade outlet, 149; British vice-consul stationed at, 151; Freeman annexes, 153

Baghirmi, (variously spelt as Bagarimi or Beghiomi), 90; Rabeh attacks, 197; France takes over, 1898, 198; capture of, 197, 198

Bahia (Brazil), persisting Yoruba traits in, 76

Baikie, William B. (explorer), 118, 130, 131, 145, 152; as unofficial consul at Lokoja, 146; with Laird, 1854, 130 seqq.; in *Dayspring*, 145, 146, 147

Bakuba, 24

Balewa, Mallam Abubakar Tafawa, 248, 262; knighted, 267; as Prime Minister, 267

Banana exports (Belgian Congo and Cameroons), 236

Banks, Sir Joseph, as President of African Association, 119

Bantu and semi-Bantu, 23

Banza Bokwai (seven 'bastard' Hausa states), 37, 78

Baptist missions, Yorubaland, 126

Barbari, King of Gobir, 79

Barbot, James, in slave-trading voyage to Bonny, 66, 71; *Abstract of a Voyage to New Calabar . . . 1699*, 71

Bariba, Yoruba lose, 100

Barka (Cyrenaica), 83

Baro, in railway policy, 213

Barquq (Mamluk sultan), 36

Barruwa (Lake Chad), 173

Barth, Heinrich (explorer), 118, 131, 146, 148; account of mid-nineteenth-century Kano, 94

'Basorun' defined, 50, 98; seizes power in Oyo (Basorun Gaha),

96; plots against Alafin, 106

Batu tribe, 23

Bauchi, 20, 21, 27, 198; Yakubu's foundation of, 90; Morel's proposal for, 214; the Bauchi Improvement Association, 248

Bawa, successor to Barbari, 79

Bawo, son of Bayajidda, in Hausa tradition, 37

Bayajidda, *see* Abuyazidu

Beecroft, John (British consul for the Bights), 107, 137, 138, 139, 140, 141; deposes Kosoko, 139; jurisdiction of confined to Biafra, 1853, 142; death of, 143

Beeswax as trade commodity, 113, 136

'Beit-el-Mal' (native treasuries), 208, 218

Belgian Congo, exports from, 236; Belgian Congo Association (King Leopold), 167

Bell, Sir Hesketh, succeeds Lugard, 208

Bello, Sultan of Sokoto, 37, 84, 85, 86, 88, 193, 194, 197; Fulani Empire under, 93–5; Clapperton received by, 122, 123; Hajji Sa'id quoted on, 93

Belloc, Hilaire, quoted, 200

Benin: old kingdom of, 19, 25; matriarchy in, 35; bronzes of, 53; established as centralized kingdom, 46, 47, 48, 49; becomes independent, 49, 50; first Europeans in, 57; contacts with Oyo (through Ife), 54, 56, 57; early peppers trade of, 59; Ife dynasty in, 54 seqq.; fifteenth- and sixteenth-centuries' apogee of, 55; *see* Oba of Benin; in Portuguese trade, 59 seqq.; Christian Church in, 60, 61; as important slave market, 63, 73; eastward migrations from, 73; seventeenth- and eighteenth-centuries' decline of, 74; renamed Edo, 55; on Lagos

Index

Benin—*cont.*

trade route, 158; exclusiveness of, 183; fall of, as landmark in British occupation of Southern Nigeria, 183–4; Lugard in, 219; taxation introduced in, 219–20

Benin, Bight of (*see also* Beecroft), 20, 59, 112, 115, 137; as Niger outlet, 120, 121

Benin River, 144; Beecroft explores, 1840, 138; in oil trade, 180; Benin River Court of Equity, 137

Beni-Sef (nomadic group), 33, 44

Benue, 23; under Lugard, 197, 199; Morel's proposal for, 213–14

Benue River, 21, 43, 122, 123, 167, 168, 180, 223; freight on, 271

Berbers, 26

'Bere' festival, 53

Beri-Beri, Yakubu checks Buba Yero at, 90

Berlin Conference and Treaty (on spheres of influence in Africa), 1885, 167, 169, 170, 177, 178, 195

Biafra, Bight of, 20, 59, 112, 115, 137, *and see* Beecroft; heavy British commitments in, 163

'Bible and Plough' policy, 125, 129

Bida: Nupe Etsus' rule from, 91; Baikie at, 146; under Lugard, 197; C.M.S. school in, 212

Bights Division slavery patrol, 111

Biobaku, Dr. *The Egba and their Neighbours, 1831–1872*, 156, 158

Biram (a Hausa state), 37

Biri, Bikorum, Moslem rulers (Kanem), 35

Birnin Kebbi, 87

Birnin Kudu rock paintings, 27

Birnin Zamfara, 79

Bismarck, and Niger trade agreements, 167

Bivar, Dr. A. B. H., 34 n.

Blackhall's Governorship-in-Chief (Sierra Leone), 156

'Blood Men', *see* Qua River

Blyden, Edward, 226

Bojador, Cape, 57, 58

Bonny: monarchical system of, 69; as slaving state, 63, 66, 68, 70, 112, 113, 114, 116; political authority in, 69, 70; in palm-oil trade, 113, 135, 136, 142; blocking of river to, 138; Church of Scotland and, 148; standing of, in 1865, 161–2; worship of monitor lizards in, 164; French gunboat at, 166; King Pepple persecutes traders at, 138; Court of Equity at, 137, 142; and King William Pepple's exile, *see* Pepple. For trade war, *see* Jaja

Borgu: as province of Mali, 38; Moors attack, 42; as Ife's rival, 48; Ofonran expels Nupe from, 53; allied with Oyo, 105; aids Ibadan against Ijaye, 152; in British-French rivalry, 173—6; under British, 195; Lugard and, 197; Morel's proposal for, 214

Bornu: old kingdom of, 19, 25; historians of, 32, 33, 35; Kanem expansion into, 35–7; occupation of, completed, 36; trades with Kano, 39; sixteenth-century Islamic influence in, 39; defeated at Nguru, 41; provincial slave governors of, 65; in sixteenth century, 40–1; growing authority of Kebbi, 41; Kanta defeats, 41; reconstituted Empire of, as influence in Hausaland, 40 seqq.; under Mai Idris Alooma, 42; and Jukun, 44; late seventeenth-century power of, 45; the Mandara defeat, 78; in 1850s, 79 seqq.; inaccessible to Fulani, 83, 88–9; new emirates in, after Nguru, 89; El Kanemi as saviour of, 89, 90, 91; (and Nupe) 'shadow rulers' in Holy War, 92; Denham and Clapperton in, 121; British consul in, 122, 123; Royal Niger Company's failures with, 195; Britain takes over, 198, 199; Rabeh invades, 197; after Anglo-

Index

Bornu—*cont.*
French Convention of 1898, 198;
Morel's proposal for, 214; *see also*
El Kanemi, Sahara

Bosman, William, on Dahomey's army (1698), 98–9

Bourdillon, Sir Bernard, Governor of Nigeria, 243

Bowen's Baptist Mission, Abeokuta, 128; his *Grammar and Vocabulary of the Yoruba Language*, 148

Bower, Captain, in Yorubaland, 189

Brand's consulship, Lagos, 151

Brandenburgers in slave trade, 64

Brass (Nembe) in Delta slave trade, 68, 70, 114, 138; attacks New Calabar, 161; in palm-oil trade, 136, 164; Goldie's measures against, 166: the Lander brothers reach, 123; Court of Equity, 137; 1895–6 disturbances at, 171, 181–3, 191; political authority in, 69

Brass-castings for records, 55

Brazil: Dutch in, 64; slaves in, 64, 67, 76; slaves in after 'abolition', 113, 114, 116; miscegenation, 76

Brettonet massacre by Rabeh, 197

Bristol, England, in slave trade, 64, 109, 110

Britain: intervenes in Dahomey-Abeokuta affair, 107, 108; trade expansion, 119, 134 seqq.; political interference by, 138 seqq.; *and see* Beecroft, Missions, etc.; consolidates interests, 155–68; and Lagos annexation, 152; three areas of Nigerian interests of, 155; 1885 Protectorate of, 155 seqq.; in Yoruba affairs, 161; after Jaja affair, 162 seqq.; British firms' trade rivalry, 164; trade protection regulations, 163, 164; foreign competition threatens, 165 seqq.; Goldie's work for, 165–8; Protectorate, and Royal Niger Company territories, 167, 170 seqq.; first footholds of in Fulani and Yoruba territory, 186,

194; Protectorate over Egba, 1893, 188; crisis with France, 1894, *see* Lugard, Nikki; extends control north of Benue and Niger, 195 seqq.; and recent constitutional changes, 242 seqq. *See also* named governors, politicians, Slave Trade

Brohemie as Nana's headquarters, 181

Bronzes: Ife, 48; *see* Benin; Tada (Nupe), 53

Buba Yero (of Gombe, Bornu), 89, 90

Bulala people, Kanem, 36, 40; defeats of, at Garni Kujala, Lada, 40

Bulrush millet, 21

Burdon, Major, 193–4, 202, 203

Burmi, 201

Burton, Sir Richard, consul at Fernando Po, 183

Bussa people, 53, 102; Bussa invaded by Askia Mohammed, Askia Daud, 40, 41; Mungo Park murdered at Bussa Rapids, 121, 123; King of ('Lord of all Borgu') and Lugard's race to Nikki, 174; in Goldie's troubles with French, 174, 176; French occupy in 1897, 191–2

Buxton, Sir Thomas Fowell, 125, 127; *The African Slave Trade and its Remedy*, 124

Cairo, 35

Calabar: slave exports from Old and New, 63; *see* Owome; in palm-oil trade, 112, 113; Church of Scotland mission in, 126, 129, 143, 144; Mary Slessor's missionary work in (Cross River), 209–10; missions' standing in, by 1880, 164–5; politically, after 1855, 143, 144; 1929 poll-tax riots in, 232; riots in, after Enugu incident, 249; as 1957 minority group, 264;

Index

Calabar—*cont.*
proposal for C.O.R. (Calabar-Ogoja–Rivers) state, 264. *See also* New Calabar, Old Calabar

Cameron, Sir D., reforms of in North and West, 230, 233–5

Cameroons: republic of, 20, 23; slaves from, 63; concludes abolition treaty with Great Britain, 138; Germany's 1884 Protectorate, 167; in War I, 223; Southern, as quasi-federal territory, 256

Campbell, Benjamin, first British consul at Lagos, 1853, 148–9; and French 'free labour', 150; and Madam Tinubu's middleman activities, 150

Cannibalism, 182

Carnot, Théodore, French slave trader, 110

Carter, Sir Gilbert: defeats Ijebu, 188; ends Ibadan-Ilorin war, 189, 190; 1893 Yorubaland trek of, 188–9

Caseley-Hayford, Mr., Gold Coast lawyer, 226

Castile-Portugal rivalry, W. African coast, 59

Central African Trading Co., in Niger trade, 164

Central Nigerian Produce Marketing Board, 270

Chad, Lake, 21; basin, towns of, 31 seqq.; and Kanem's beginnings, 33; in Niger exploration, 121, 173

Chamba people, 91

Chamberlain, the Rt. Hon. Joseph, 176, 177

Chari river, 198

Chick, Sir Louis, and 'Chick Report', 255–6

Christianity, *see* Missions; after 1906, 206; dangers of 'total conversion' policy of, 210 seqq.

Chukwu, *see* 'Long Juju'

Churchill, Winston, view of, on African independence, 240

Church Missionary Society, 124, 125, 126, 128, 129, 147, 187, 212; political influence of, 129; and 1863 Dahomey-Egba war, 153; differences with consul (Campbell), 149–50; moves headquarters to Lagos Island, 157. *See Dayspring*

Church of Scotland Mission, 126, 129, 130, 148

Civil Service, today, 272

Clapperton, Hugh (Niger explorer), 118, 121, 122, 146; in quest for Rakah, 122; quoted, on Bornu, 1821, 90

Clarkson, Thomas (English abolitionist), 109; and African Association, 119

Clifford, Sir Hugh, 230, 231, 235, 236; denounces National Congress, 227–9

Cocoa, growing importance of, 235, 269

Cocoa Pool, N.Y.M. attacks, 238

Coleman, James, *Nigeria: Background to Nationalism*, 211, 238

Colonial Development and Welfare Act, 240, 245

Colonial expansion, 19th-century, a classic example, 134

Columbite, export of, 270

Columbus, Christopher, 59

Comet, The (newspaper), 244

Commerell, Commodore, T. E., and Jaja-Opobo settlement, 162

Compagnie du Sénégal et de la Côte Occidentale d'Afrique, 166

Compagnie Française de l'Afrique Equatoriale, 166

Company of African Merchants (1865), 146

'Congo System', 236–7

Conferences, pre-1954 constitution, 249–57; of 1957, 262 seqq.; of 1958, 265

287

Index

Constitution: 1949 discussions, 249 seqq.; of 1954, as end of Nationalist struggle with Britain, 258

Consuls, 169–90

Cook, Captain, South Pacific voyages of, 119

Cook, E. L., *British Enterprise in Nigeria*, 181

Cotonou, France annexes, 166

Cotton, 20, 21, 26, 235, 269

Courts of Equity, 163, 179

Cowries as currency, 66, 186, 194, 207; Laird replaces by coins, 145

Creech Jones, Arthur, 245

Creek Town (Old Calabar), 69, 130, 144

Crockett, Davy, 128

Crops, subsistence and specialized, of early days, 21, 27, 29; *see also* named crops (groundnuts, cocoa, millet, rubber, yams, etc.)

Cross River, 23, 129, *and see* Ikotana; and slave trade, 68, 71; Beecroft and, 138; Church of Scotland missions at, 148; 1893 troubles (Akuna-Ibo attacks), 180. *See also* Slessor, Mary

Crow, Capt. Hugh, in slave trade, 66, 112

'Crown Colony' system, 226

Crowther, the Rev. Samuel (later Bishop), 125, 126, 127, 129, 131, 148; becomes bishop, 147; Townsend and, 147–8; activities of, 163, 164, 211, 226; *Grammar and Vocabulary of the Nupe Language*, 148

Cuba, slaves in, 76, 113, 114, 115

Culture and religion, 132

Cunliffe, Col., on Nigerian regiments in War I, 224

Dahomey, 20, 24, 54, 59, 96, 98, 99; various attacks by, 99, 106, 107; *see* Amazons; raids Abeokuta, 1851, 128; in 1850s wars, 150, 151, 153; attacks Ibadan, 159; as French base, in 1890s, 172, 173, 174, 184, 185; *see* Slavery

Daily Service (Ikoli's paper), 240

Dalzell qu., on Dahomey, etc., 99, 100

Dan Makafo (in Satiru rising), 202

Dan Yahaya, Battle of, 87–8

Dapper, *Description de l'Afrique*, 74

Darfur, 23

Dar Kuti, Rabeh conquers, 197

Daura (one of 'Seven Hausa States'), 37, 38, 44

Daura, Queen, in Hausa tradition, 37

Davies, H. O. (N.Y.M.), 238

Dayspring, wreck of the, 1857, 145, 146, 147

Decoeur, in race for Nikki, 174, 175

Degel (Gobir), 81, 82

Denham, D., on Bornu in 1820s, 90; on Clapperton–Oudney Niger expedition, 121, 122

Denman's barracoon-destroying policy, 115

Delta, *see* Niger Delta

Denmark, and slave trade, 64, 111

Denton's Ijebu troubles, 187

Dike, Dr. K. O., qu., 112, 137, 145; *A Hundred Years of British Rule in Nigeria*, 226, 242; *Trade and Politics in the Niger Delta*, 142

Dikwa, 197; given to Germany, 198

Docemo, 136, 149, 150, 151; cedes Lagos to British, 152

Dougou (Beni-Sef leader), 33

Dounama (Kanem Moslem ruler), 35

Duala, 1914 naval bombardment of, 223

Du Bois, W. E., 226

Duke Town (Old Calabar), 69, 130, 144; slave rebellion in, 141

Dutch in slave trade, 64; abolition by, 111

Dutsin Wake, Battle of, 80

'Eastern Route' (Lagos to interior), 158

Index

Ebute Metta, 156
Ede, 52; in Ogbomosho-Ikoyi war, 102
Eden, Richard, qu. on 1553 Benin voyage, 62
Edinburgh, Duke of, in Nigeria, 1956, 259
Edinburgh Review qu., 126
Edo, Edoni, 55
Education: and status, 132–3; backward, in North, 263, 271; missionaries and, 148, *and see* Missionaries; introduction of 'Western', 211–12
Edun, Yoruba, general, 105
Edun, Secretary of Egba United Government, 220–1
Edward IV of England, 59
Effon, in Ekiti Confederation against Ibadan), 159
Efik people, 23, 70, 71, 76; language of, 148; treatment of slaves by, 129, 141; *see* Old Calabar *and* Egbo
Egba, 49, 141; declare independence from Oyo (1780s), 100; in Yoruba inter-tribal wars, 103–4, 107, 113; and missions, 127; and Lagos, 149; in trade, 149, 150, 157; resumes war with Dahomey in 1850s, 150, 151, 152; and British, 152, 153, 188; wars and brief peaces, after 1863, 153–8; blocks Ibadan-Lagos road, 155–6, 158; United Board of Management of, 156; as middlemen, 160; and French, 186; oppose Lugard, 220, 221; Egba-Alake, 104
Egba-Oke-Ona, 104
Egbado (Oyo-controlled), 49
Egbe Omo Odudukwa, founded 1945, 247, 248
Egbo Society, Old Calabar, 70; recreated in Cuba by Efik and Ibibio slaves, 76
Egharevba, Jacob, *Short History of Benin*, 47
Egugonjo, 53

Egypt, early influences from, 26, 27
'Ekeji Orisa', 50
Ekiti people, 49, 106, 158; *see also* Ijesha; Ekiti-Parabo (confederation against Ibadan), 159, 160, 184
Ekpe, and human sacrifice, 130
Election principle, 228, 229
Electricity Corporation of Nigeria, 270
Eleko question (Lagos), 229
El Eldrissi, *History of Africa and Spain*, 34
Elijah II, Delta prophet, 223
Elizabeth II, 1956 tour of Nigeria, 259
El Kanemi (Bornu), 84, 89, 90, 92, 121
El Maghili, *see* Abu Abdullah
Emirates, after 1899–1900, 191–203
Enahoro, Anthony (Action Group), 253
Endeley, Dr. (Cameroons, on N.C.N.C.), 252
'Enogie' defined, 54
Enugu: in railway scheme, 213; shootings, in 1949, 249
Epe: Kosoko in, 149; Freeman destroys, 153
Equipment Treaty, 113–14
Eshugbayi (Eleko), 229
Esilogun-Adele dispute, Lagos 1911, 140
Eso (Oyo officials), 50
Ethiopia, 26; Italy invades, 238
Eunuchs as provincial governors, 65
Evian (Bini leader), 47
Ewedo (Ife dynasty ruler in Benin), 54, 55
Eweka I, first Ife ruler in Benin), 54
Eweka II of Benin, 219
Ewuare, *see* Ogun
Ewuare the Great, of Benin, 55, 57
Explorers, role of, 117, 118–33; *see also* Gomes, Niger, *and* named explorers
Eyamba V, Duke Town king of Calabar, 130

Index

Eyo, Mr. E. O., 260

Eyo Honesty, King (Creek Town, Calabar, 130, 143, 144

Ezera, Dr. Kalu, *Constitutional Developments in Nigeria*, 246, 260

Fabian Colonial Bureau, 240

Fad-el-Allah, claims Bornu, 198

Fagg, Bernard, on Nok culture, 28–9

Falconbridge qu., on Slaver conditions, 109

Federal solution, 254–5, 261–2; *see* Nigeria

Fernando Po, 62, 137, 140, 152, 183; Palmerston's interest in, 115; Beecroft at, 1827, 137, 140; consulate transferred from, to Old Calabar, 1872, 163

Ferry, Jules (P.M. of France), annexations under, 166, 172

Fezzan, 23, 31, 35, 36; in War I, 223

Fiadoor, in Benin slave-trading, 73

Fiji, early 'indirect rule' in, 196

Filingué, 223

First War, Nigeria and, 222–3

Fitri, Lake, 34

Fitzpatrick, Captain, attacks 'indirect rule', 230, 236

Flegel, Herr, forestalled by Goldie, 157

Fon, *see* Nago

Foot, Hugh, 245, 249

Foote's consulship at Lagos, 151

Forde, Professor Daryll, 29

Forde, *Culture Map of West Africa*, 29

Forest kingdoms, 46–56

Fortes, Meyer, on War II and West Africa, 239

Fortified villages, ancient, 27

Foster-Sutton, Sir Stafford, 260

'Four provinces' proposal, 214–15

Fourah Bay Institute, Freetown, 130

Fox, Charles James, 109; in African Association, 1788, 119

France: in slave-trading, 64; takes Dahomey, 173; extends hold in West Africa, 175–6; Lugard against, 176 seqq.; as Trade rival

in Delta, 161, 165–6, 172, 173, 177, 185, 186; *see* Decoeur, Ferry, Mizon, Nikki; position of, by 1898, 198; in Bussa, 191–2

'Free labour', 1857 French scheme, 150

Free trade after 1906, 206–7

Freeman, Thomas B. (missionary), 127

Freeman, Governor (Lagos), 152–3

Freetown as freed slaves' settlement, 111, 112, 127

French Revolution, 109

Fulani Empire, 19; language of, 21, 23; overthrows Habe dynasty, *see* Usman dan Fodio; early history of, 80; old and new, 86–8; cattle-owning and town-elements, 78–95 *passim*; position of, by 1830, 91–3; under Bello, 93–5; decadence of, 93; trade under 'Fulani Pax', 93; Fulani Jihad literary revolution, 95; Fulani Empire after Berlin Conference, 1885, 168; and Lugard, 193 seqq., 200

Gaha, Basorun (Oyo), 99–100, 102

Gaiser, G. L., purchases Mahin Beach, Lagos, 166

'Gaisuwa' defined, 82

Galadima people, 35, 89

Galvão, Antonio, 57

Galway, Vice-consul (Benin River), 183

Gambaron (Katsina), 78

Gambia Company, 223

Gambia River, 119, 120

Gamergum, Idris Alooma takes, 42

Gao (port of Niger), 41

Garin Gabbas, in Holy War, 87

Garmi Kujala, 40

Garua, in War I, 223

Gatarwa, in Holy War, 87

Gbagura towns, in Owu wars, 103–4

Gbebe mission station, 147

Gbogun, 102; Fulani capture, 104–5

Gboho, 106

'Gbonka' defined, 52

Index

Gentil, French officer in Baghiomi, 197, 198

George IV of England, El Kanemi and, 121

Germany: as trade rival in Delta, 165–7, 172, 177; Cameroons as Protectorate of 1884, 167; 1898 acquisitions by, 198; in export trade, 222, 235–6; Cameroons in War I, 223–4

Gézo, King of Dahomey, 102, 107, 127–8, 139

Ghana, 23, 35; achieves independence, 261

Ghat, 94, 95

Gimbana, Yunfa attacks, 82

Ginuwa, founder of Warri, 74

Gironard, Sir Percy (N. Nigeria), 208, 213

Glover, Lieut., later Sir J. H. (admin. in Lagos): routs Egba, 152–4; expands British interests, 155–8; arranges 1871 Conference of Rulers (against Egba and Ijebu), 158; chastises Porto Novo, 154; with Baikie, opens direct trade route to Lagos, 146, 153; on Jaja affair, 161

Gobir (Hausa state), 37, 38, 45, 78; rivals Kano, 1731–43, 78, 79, 80; holds out against Fulani, 93

Gold, 58, 59

Gold Coast, see Ashanti War; regiment, in War I, 223, 224; 1948 riots in, 246

Goldie, Sir George, 165, 192; studies of Efik language by, 148; treaties made with local chiefs by, 166, 167; general policy of, 165–9; charters refused to, 166; on Tonkin affair, 172; and German Cameroons, 173; and Frances Dahomey Protectorate, 174; sends Lugard to Nikki, 174; moves into Nupe, 176; view of 'indirect rule' of, 196

Gollmer, Herr, German missionary, 127

Gombe (Bornu) emirate founded, 89, 90

Gomes, Fernão, Portuguese explorer, 59

Goshawk, H.M.S., in Jaga deportation, 179

Gosling, Sergt., reports on Satiru incident, 202, 203

'Goumsa' (senior wife), 35

Granville, Lord (Foreign Secretary), and Jaja trade troubles, 161, 178

Granville Sharp, see Sharp

Great Ardra, 98

Greenberg, Joseph H., Studies in African Linguistic Classification, 22, 23

Groundnuts, 20, 21, 206, 235, 269

Guangara, 41

Gudu, Usman dan Fodio's flight to ('Hijira'), 82

Guinea Coast, 23, 27, 64

Gujba (British Bornu), French raid, 198

Gwandu (twin Fulani capital with Sokoto), 86, 88, 167, 194, 195; and Britain, 199, 200, 202, 203; loses power over Emirs, 208

Gwari (Hausa 'bastard' state), 37

Gwato, port of Benin, 183; in slave-trading, 60, 73

Gwoni Muktar, Fulani leader, 89

Habe kingdoms, 80, 81, 82 seqq., 93, 98; role of women in, 95; of Zaria, 198

Hadeija: Fulani defeat, 87; becomes emirate, 90; hostile to British, 202, 203

Haiti, origin of Voodoo in, 76

Hajji S'id, History of Sokoto, 93, 95

Hanno the Carthaginian, 57

Harding, the Rev. T. (C.M.S.), 187–8

Hausa, Hausaland, 21–30, 37–40, 42, 53; and Bornu, Songhai, 40, 41; ancient trade of, with Yoruba, 52; and Brazil slave revolt of 1807–13, 76–7; and European

Index

Hausa—*cont.*
coast trade, 78; seven 'bastard' states of, 37, 38; Islam in, 38, 39, 40; 16th-and 17th-century involvements, *see* Birnu, Songhai; 18th-century changes, 45, 78 seqq.; rise of Fulani in, 80 seqq.; rule through slaves in, 65; slave markets of, 56; Baikie's hopes of trade with, 146; Lugard's hopes, 1902, 199, 200; new economy of, post-1906, 207; and 1960 independence, 273; language of, 21, 22, 23; 'Bakwai', 37

Havana, slaves in, 67

Health services, modern, 271

Hearn & Cuthbertson (trading in Calabar), 144

Henry the Navigator, Prince of Portugal, 58

Henshaw (Calabar), 130

Herodotus, on Phoenician contacts, 57

Hewitt's consulship, Jaja and, 177

Hides, skins, as modern exports, 270

Higgins, Henry (Acting Colonial-Sec.), 184–5

Hinderer, Mr. and Mrs. (C.M.S.), 128

Hiskett, M., translator of *Kitab-al-Farq*, 81, 82

Hodgkins. Thomas, *Nigerian Perspectives*, 75 n.; on Usman, 83

Hoenigsberg affair (Nupe), 172

Holt, Mr., Liverpool trader, 178

Holy War, *see* Usman dan Fodio

Hong Kong, Lugard as Governor of, 203

Hope Waddell's Calabar mission, 128; Efik Vocabulary, 148

Houghton, Major (Niger explorer), 119–20

House rule, *see* Niger Delta

Human sacrifice, 74, 130, 132, 141, 143, 183, 184, 187, 188, 189

Hutchinson, T. J. (consul), 144; *Ten Years' Wandering among the Ethiopians*, 143

Hutton, Thomas & Son, at Abeokuta and Badagry (factories), 128

Hutt's Select Committee, 116

Ibadan: background history, 102–6; defeats Ilorin at Oshogbo, *c.* 1840, 106; at war with Ijaye, 1844 and 1858, 106, 150–3; after Lagos annexation, 152, 155 seqq.; and Egba, 150 seqq.; withdraws from Ilesha, 156; expels missionaries 157; slave raids on Eketi from, 158; motives of, 159; on Lagos trade route, 158; in 1870, 158–9; in 1877, 159; 1882 wars of, 160; achieves independence from Oyo, 184, 220, 234; British treaty with (Sir G. Carter), 189; Ibadan-Lagos railway, 191; 1948 conference at, 246; industry in, 270; University College of, 271. *See also* Ife, Igbajo, Ijebu, Ijesha

Ibami mission, 165

Ibi, Ibibio, 23, 43, 76, 168; resist unification, 204, 205, 221–2; Ibibio State Union, 1944, 247, 248

Ibn Batuta (historian), 38

Ibn-al-Sabbagh (historian of Katsina), 39

Ibo, Iboland, 19, 23, 75; Aro subsection of, 72; as slave source for Delta, 68, 75, 77; over-population, 75; groups in Br. West Indies, 75; and Lander brothers' capture, 123; slaves from re-settled in Calabar, 1848, 130; asks for missions, 147; 'indirect rule' fails, 231; and 1960 events, 273; and 'Zik', 238, 247, 264; comparison with Yoruba, 246–7

Ibrahim Nagwamatse, Emir of Kontagora, 193

Ibuno (Ibeno), 178

Idah, 56, 126, 192, 204; bronze castings, 53

Idirisu, son of Jumada, 91

Idris Alooma, King of Bornu, 42–3

Index

Ife (*see* Oduduwa), 20, 29; role of, in Yorubaland, 50, 98; as ancient home of Yoruba, 46, 47; as Benin-Oyo link, 49, 54; bronzes and terracottas of 48, 53; in Owu war, 103, 105; and Ibadan, in 1879, 159; destroyed by Modakeke and Ibadan, 160, 184; Ife-Ijebu slave trade, 103

'Ifole' defined, 157; and Lagos, 70

Igala, 53

Igbajo war (Ibadan against Ilesha, 1867), 156

Igbessa, on Lagos trade route, 158

Igbira, 94

Igbo, 94

Ijaw, *see* Western Ijaw

Ijaye: Abiodun destroys, 101; role of, in New Oyo, 106; in wars against Ibadan, Oyo, 106, 150–3

Ijebu, 49, 103, 104; resist missions, 128; as middlemen and opponents of free trade, 159, 160, 185, 186; 1858 allies of, 150; 1882 peace with Ibadan, 160; Sir Gilbert Carter quells, 1892, 188; and N.Y.M. break-up, 240

Ijebu-Ode trade route, 158, 187, 188

Ijebu-Remo, 150, 157; Egba attack, 153

Ijemo massacre, 221

Ijesha, 52, 105, 106; as middlemen, 160; join Egba, Ekiti and Ilorin against Ibadan, 159

Ijo: groups, language, 23, 67–8; and imported slaves, 68–9, 141; on Lagos trade route, 158; failure of 'indirect' rule among, 231; in 1957 264; Willinck Commission proposal for, 265

Ikirun, 185

Ikoli, Ernest (N.Y.M.), 238, 240–1

Ikorodu, 150; on Lagos trade route, 158; Egba besiege, 1865, 153–4; Glover defeats Egba at, 154, 157

Ikotana mission (Cross River), 165

Ikoyi, 102, 103, 104; Ilorin captures, 104

'Ilari', 50, 98

Ilaro (Egba capital); Yoruba mission at, 148; on Lagos trade route, 158; Maloney's British garrison at, 186

Ile-Ibinnu, 55

Ile Ife as 'origin of life', 46; Bini Seek ruler from, 47, 54–5

Ile Ife conference (E.O.O.), 247

Ilesha, 50; in 1858 alliance, 150; in 1867 war, 156; Ilesha-Oyo agreement, at end of civil wars, 184

Ilo, 40, 176

Ilorin, 20, 49; first Fulani Emir of, 92; in 1858 alliance, 150 (*see also* Ijesha); at height of wars, 102–6; in 1882 trade with Ibadan, 160; and Royal Niger Co., 176, 190, 195; at end of wars, 184, 188; and hostile Emirs, 196; under Lugard, 197; absorbed in Protectorate of Northern Nigeria, 204; Morel's proposal for, 214; Willinck Commission decision on, 265

Iluku, 106

Iman Ahmed-ben-Fartua (chronicler), 42, 43

Independence of Nigeria, 1960, 225, 258 seqq.

India as trade outlet, 58, 119; early 'indirect rule' in, 196

Indians (Mexico and Peru) under Spanish, 63

Indirect rule, 132; as Lugard's aim, 195 seqq., 208, 217–18, 225; in East, 221–2; in North, 230; in South, 219–20; in West, 221; reasons for failures in, 230, 231, 232–3

Indonesia, ancient East Coast trade with, 27

Inna Gharka, mother of Bello (learned woman), 95

Interesting Narrative of the Life of Olaudah Eguiano or Gustave Vassa, the African, written by himself, 75 n.

Investigation, H.M.S., 163

Index

Iperu, Egba capture, 153
Iron in early cultures, 29, 37
Isaaco, Mungo Park's servant, 121
Isago, Yoruba mission at, 148
Iseyin murders (opposing Lugard's Oyo policy), 220
Isiaga, 107
Islam (for Islamic kings, *see* Mai kings): reaches Hausa, 38, 42; and slavery, 39; zenith of, in Kano, 39; early failure of, in Benin, Oyo, 56; early foothold gained by, 53; comparative success of, among Fulani, 80; and Hausaland's indigenous religion, 81; in 18th and 19th centuries, 83; and break-up of Oyo Empire, 100; and N. Nigeria missionary ventures, 131; Lugard's agreements concerning, 209, 212. *See also* Moslem missions
Ita, Professor Eyo, 250
Itsekiri, 68, 74, 231; mid-West state project, 264
Ivory, 66, 74, 113, 121, 136; carvings (Benin), 55, 56
Iwe-Irohin (Yoruba mission newspaper), 148, 153
Iwre, 101
Iwo, Maku's unsuccessful war against, 102
Iyase, 55

Jackson, J. P., 226
Jaja (king of Opobo): role of, in Bonny, 1865, 161, 162; in trade war against British, 177–80
Jamaica, slaves in, 67
Jamaicans, in Church of Scotland Calabar mission, 129
James Pinnock & Co., in Niger trade, 164
Jameson, Robert, *An Appeal against the Proposed Niger Expedition*, 125
Jebba, 173; Lugard at, 174, 175; in railway development, 213
Jemaa terracotta, 28
Jengi, 91

Jews (Portuguese) of São Thomé, 60
Jibrelli (of Gombe) resists British in Bornu, 198
Jihad, *see* Holy War
Joao II of Portugal, 60; as 'Lord of Guinea', 59
Johnson, Mr. (Secretary, Egba United Board of Management), 156
Johnson, Samuel, *History of the Yorubas*, 46, 49, 50, 51, 52, 100; as delegate, 184, 186, 187, 188, 189
Johnston, H., consul during Jaja troubles, 178, 179, 180
Jones, G. I., on Egbo, 70
Jos, plateau of, 20, 21, 27, 28; Jos N.C.N.C. Convention of 1952. 252
José, Domingo, in Akitoye-Kosoko struggle, 139
Judar Pasha, invades Timbuktu, 42
Juju rock, Jebba (*Dayspring* wrecked on), 145, 146, 147
Jukun kingdom of Kororofa, 43–4, 45; people of, 27; matriarchy in, 35; Fulani and, 80, 90, 91; Buba Yero attacks, 90; Emir of Muri's inroads into, 19th century, 91
Jumada (of Nupe), in civil wars, 91
Justice, judiciary, major changes in, 234–5

Kabba province, 195; under Lugard, 197; after Willinck Commission, 265
Kaduna, 262; as industrial centre, 270
Kagara, 28
Kaiama, 174; Lugard at, 1892, 175; French take over, 176
'Kakanfo', Oyo army leader, 50, 101; K. Afonja, Governor of Zlorin, 92, 100; K. Oyabi, and Gaha, 100
Kalabari people, 23
Kamerun, 197
Kanajeji, King of Kano, 38

Index

Kanem: ancient, 20 seqq.; Zaghawa Kingdom precursor of, 31; historians of, 32; establishment of, 32 seqq.; Moslem infiltration, 34; in decline, 35-6; becomes kingdom of Bornu, 36 seqq.; and Idris Alooma, 42, 43; El Kanemi reinstates, 90; France takes over, 1898, 198; Kanemi dynasty, 198. *See also* El Kanemi

Kanembu, of old Kanem, defeat Fulani, 89

Kano (Hausa state), 21, 37, 38, 87; apogee of, 39; agriculture of, 39-40; Leo Africanus, in, 41; decline of, 41; Askia Daud invades, 41; in Trans-Saharan trade, 41-3; Katsina replaces as chief Hausa city, 45; Jukun, Zamfara and Fulani attacks on, 44, 78, 79, 87-8; in mid-19th century, 94-5; Clapperton visits, 122; Baikie visits, 146; way of life in, 193; shelters Magaji of Keffi, 199; railway reaches, 1911, 206, 213; British government school near, 212; Morel's proposal for, 214; supports W.A.S.U., 237; Awolowo's tour of, 253; 1952 riots, 253-4; industry in, 270; education in, 271; today's budget, 272

Kano, Aminu (radical leader), 248

Kano chronicle, 38, 44

Kanta, governor of Kebbi, 41, 87

Kanuri-Jukun affinity, 43-4

Kanuri language, people, 23, 35, 36

Kaossen, Touraeg chief, 223

Karari, first Kebbi king of Argungu, 87

Katagum (Bornu Emirate), 89, 90

Katsina, 37; enthronement ritual in, 40; early wars of, 38, 40; Leo Africanus in, 41; in trans-Saharan trade, 41-2; growing stature of, by late 17th century, 45; Zamfara rivals by early 18th century, 78-9; Fulani defeat, 1807, 87, 88; separated from Maradi, 88; under

Lugard, 200; Morel's proposal for, 214

Katsina chronicle, 38, 51

Katsina Ala, 28

Katsina Laka (? Guangara), 41

'Katunga', 49, 105

Kazaure, 87

Kebbi (Hausa 'bastard' state), 37, 41; in Holy War, 86, 87; opposed to Fulani, 92

Keffi, Magaji of, 198-9; death of, 201

Ke Ghamma (army leader under Mai), 35

Ketu, Yoruba kingdom, Dahomey, 24, 47, 158

Kiawa (Katsina town), 79, 80

Kihisi, 106; Lugard's 1892 treaty with, 175; France takes over, 176

'Kingmakers' (Benin), 54, 55

Kingsley, Mary, *West African Studies*, 171

Kirk, Sir John, in Brass disturbances, 171, 191

Kisoki (Hausa king), 40

Kisra, 25

Kitab-al-Farq, attrib. to Usman dan Fodio, 82, 93

Koelle, the Rev. S. W. (C.M.S.), *Grammar of the Bornu or Kanauri Language*, 148

Kontagora, 192, 193, 195, 196; under Lugard, 197; Morel's proposal for, 214

Kori, Alafin, 52

Kororofa, 37, 38, 43, 44

Kosoko: *see* Akitoye; Britain deposes, 129, 148; Campbell's treaty with, 149; missionaries oppose, 149-50

Kru language, 23

Kuka (Bornu), 122

'Kulabu' defined, 94

Kuru-Maiduguru railway, 271

Kurumi Kakanfo (General), 106, 153

Kwa sub-family, 23; Kwa Ibo, 177-9

295

Index

Kwale Ibo, poll-tax revolts by, 231; in War I revolt, 223

Kwang, shelling of by Mizon, 173

Labis, Alafin (Oyo), 99–100

Lada, 40

Lafiagi Emirate (Nupe), 91

Lagos (*see also* Akitoye, Esilogun, Mahin), 20, 55, 63, 77; in slave trade after 'abolition', 113, 116, 135; missionaries and, 129; Beecroft invades, 140; Campbell proposes protectorate for, 151; Britain annexes, 1861, 151–2; importance of, to Britain, 148–55; five main routes to interior from (in Glover's time), 158; in 1885, 160, 161; detached from Gold Coast by French annexations, 166; French 1887 threat to, 172–3; as 1888 palm-oil trade centre, 184; Nana tried in, 181; French railway project affecting, 185; 1886 Yorubaland peace treaty at, 184; 1886 status changes, 184; takes in most of Yorubaland, 204; 1899–1900 conditions, 192, 204; merged with S. Nigeria Protectorate, 1906, 205; remains British colony, 215; new-type Africans of, 225–6; election to Legislative Council in, 228, 229; Eleko question in, 229; new movements in, 238; Yoruba *élite* of, 237, 238, 240; Ibo rivalry, 248; future of, in Federation, 255; industry in, 270

Lagos Daily News, 229

Lagos Weekly Record, 226

Laird Macgregor Co., in Niger trading, 124, 125, 145, 146; steamer contracts of, 141, 145, 152

Lakanle (Oyo leader), 104

Lake, Thomas (with Lander brothers), 123

Lambert, Nicholas, in early pepper trade, 62

Lander, Richard *and* John (explorers), 118

Lawrence, Professor A. W., on Ife art, 48

Lecky, on 'abolition', 110–11

Lekki, Freeman annexes (from Kosoko), 153

Leo X, Pope, 41

Leo Africanus, 40, 41, 119

Leopold, King of the Belgians, in Congo, 167

Lever Bros., in Belgian Congo, 236

Leverhulme, Lord, as 'paternalist', 236–7

Levine, Lieut. (West African Naval Squadron), 112

Linguistic divisions, 21–2

Lisbon, in slave trade, 60

Liverpool: in slave trade, 64, 66, 77, 109, 110; in legitimate trade, 134, 136, 141–7; resent Royal Niger Co. in Delta, 171

Livingstone, Col., opposes Jaja, 162

Local government, 272–3

Lodder, Lieut. (mission to Ibadan and Ijaye), 151

Lokoja, 131, 145 seqq., 167, 176, 195; British consulate at, 163

'Long Juju' (Aro oracle), 'Chukwa', 72, 73, 75

Lugard, F. D. (Sir Frederick), 19; in 'race to Nikki', *see* Nikki; as High Commissioner, Northern Nigeria, 192 seqq.; 'indirect rule' as aim of, 195 seqq.; and Fad-el-Allah's claim, 198; conquest of Sokoto, Kano, 200, 201; Satiru setback to advance of, 202–3; as Governor-General, Hong Kong, 203; merges N. and S. Protectorates, 1912, 206–13; as Governor-General of Nigeria, 212 seqq.; rejects 'provinces proposals', 214–15; sets up Nigerian Council, 215; remodels judiciary, 216–17; develops native administration, 217 seqq.; on War I Nigerian forces, 224; and Eleko question, 229; and small societies of Eastern Nigeria, 231

Lynslager, Consul, 143, 144
Lyttelton, Oliver, 254

Macaulay, Herbert, 226, 229, 230, 237, 241, 245
McClintock, Major, 198
Macdonald, Sir Claude, Governor of Benin River, 180, 182, 209
McKoskry, Vice-Consul (Lagos), 151, 152
Macleod, J. M. (Consul at Lokoja), 163
Macpherson, Sir John, Governor of Nigeria, 245, 251, 252, 259; *see* National Council
M'Queen's Niger theory, 121
Maghreb negroes, origin of, 39
Maguira (Queen Mother), 35
Mahdi, *see*
Mahin Beach, Germany acquires, 166
Mai rulers, 34, 35–6, 78; Mai: Abu Amr Uthman B. Idris, 36; Ahmed, 88, 89; Ali, 43, 44; Ali Gazi, 36; Dala, 42; Dunama, 42, 89, 90; Dunama Dibbalemi, 36; Humé, 34, 35; Ibrahim Zaki, 89, 90; Idris, 34; Idris Alooma, 42, 43, 44; Idris Katakarmabe, 40; Kuchim Biri, 35; Omar, 36; Selma, 34; Umarmi, 44
Maiduguri, 198; railway to Kuru, 271
Majia, Etsu of Nupe, 91
Maku, Alafin of Oyo, 92, 102
Malaria, in early Niger expeditions, 124, 126, 131, 134
Mali, Empire of, 35, 38, 39, 80
'Mallam' defined, 39; Mallams: Alimi, ally of Kakanfo Afonja, 92; Dendo, in Nupe wars, 91; Isa, in Satiru rising, 202–3; Jibril, famous teacher, 80; Musa, of Zaria, 87
Maloney's missions, to Ilorin, etc., 184, 186, 199; Johnson criticizes, 187

Manchester goods, as anti-slavery factor, 110
Mandara people, 42; defeat Bornu, 78
Mansfield, Lord Chief Justice, in Slavery judgment, 108–9
Manuel, King of Portugal (1516), 61
Manuwa, Dr. S. L., first Nigerian Director of Medical Services, 246
Mao (Kanem), 33
Maradi, 88
Marata (Gobir), 80
Marghi, 42
Marroki, King of Zamfara, 79
Martinique, *see* Ouidah
Masaba, King of Nupe, 146, 153, 156, 166; trade policy of, 163
Mason, Philip, on minorities, 265–6
Matriarchy and Koranic requirements, 35
Maye, Chief (Ibadan), 104
Meek, C. K., 26
Meroë, 27
Methodist missions, 126, 149
Middle Belt: tribes, 23; minority groups, 263
Middle Passage (in slave trade), 65, 77, 108
Millet as subsistence crop, 31
Milner, Lord, and National Congress of British West Africa, 227
Mina, 59, 60, 61, 213
Minorities, 1957, 263–7; minority reports before 1952 decisions, 250; Minorities Commission, *see* Willinck
Miriam (learned woman), 95
Missau, detached from Bornu, 90
Missionaries, missions, 117, 118–33; role of, in building modern Nigeria, 124 seqq.; three principal groups, 126; aid Abeokuta against Dahomey, 1851, 128; as educators, 148, 263, 271; 1850–65 expansion, Southern Nigeria, 148; racial bitterness in (Townsend-Crowther), 148; press war among

Index

Missionaries—*cont.*
    at time of Ibadan-Ijaye war, 153,
    157 (*see* Hinderer, Townsend);
    Moslem, 211, 212; 19th-century
    challenges, 209–10; 'total con-
    version' attitude of, 209–12
Mizon, Lieut., in French trade war,
    173
Modakeke, 105, 159, 160; makes
    peace with Ife, 184; in final peace
    settlement, 184–5
Moddibo, Alama (Fulani leader), 91
Mohammed Korau, King of Kat-
    sina, 38
Mohammed Kukuna (Kano), 44
Mohammed Rimfa (Kano), 39, 40,
    41
Mohammed Zaki (Kano), 44
Monitor lizards, worship of, 164
'Monopoly clause', in 1886 Royal
    Niger Company Charter, 169;
Monopoly in action, 170 seqq.
Moor, General, 181
Moore, Eric, Nigerian barrister,
    221, 232
Mora, in War I, 224
Morel, E. D., editor of *African Mail*,
    213, 214, 243
Morland, Colonel: expedition of
    against Yola, 197; against Kano,
    200
Morocco, 123; *see* Maghreb
Morton-Williams, Peter, 48, 52
Moslem missions, 211, 212; Moslems
    repatriated from Brazil, 76–7
Muhallabi, Arab historian, 31
Muhammad Ammad ibn Abdullah
    (Mahdi), 83
Muhammadu, Etsu (of Nupe), 91
Muhammedu Fodi (Kebbi), 87
Muhammed ibn Ali-al-Sanuoi (Cy-
    renaica), 83
Muhammed ibn Abd-al-Wahbab
    (Saudi Arabia), 83
Muhammed ibn Masaneh (his-
    torian, Katsina), 39
Mudcock, G. P., *Africa: Its Peoples
    and their Culture History*, 26

Muri, Buba Yero controls, 90; as
    Emirate, 91; under Lugard, 197;
    Mizon at, 173
Murzuk, 94

Na Alhaji, Fulani leader, 88
Nadel, Dr. S. F., *A Black Byzantium*,
    52
Nafata, King of Gobir, 81
Nago and Fon revolts, 1826, 35, 77
Nagwamatse, 196
Nana, Governor of Benue River,
    180, 181
Napoleonic Wars, 119, 121
Napoleon II, and Regis Aine plan-
    tations. 150
Nassawara under Lugard, 197
National African Company, 160
National Congress of British West
    Africa, 1920, 226, 227
National Council for Nigeria and
    the Cameroons (N.C.N.C.), Azi-
    kiwe founds, 1944, 241; attitude
    of, to Richards's proposals, 243;
    Pan-Ibo Union as founder-mem-
    bers, 247; favours unification,
    248, 250, 251; after 1954, 258
    seqq.; in Nigeria's first general
    election, 251; and breakdown of
    Macpherson constitution, 251
    seqq.; instability in, 260; after
    1959, 267
National Democratic Party (H.
    Macaulay), 229
National Independence Party, 252,
    253, 254; becomes United N.I.P.,
    259
National Review, 230
Nationalism, West African, 225–41
Native Authority Ordinance, 1952,
    272
Native Court Ordinance (Lugard),
    216
Naturalism in Ife art, 48
Navy treaties with coastal chiefs, 115
Nelson steamer, 163
Nembe, Nembe Creek, 23, 182–3
Netherlands, *see* Dutch

Index

New Calabar, 69, 70, 71, 73, 161, 162; slave treatment, 129, 138; as Bonny's palm-oil trade rival, 136, 89; Court of Equity, 137

N'gaoundere, in War I, 224

Ngazargamu, Bornu's new capital, 36, 44, 89

N'guigmi, 34

Ngurnu, 41, 88-9

Niger Coast Protectorate after 1900, 192, 204

Niger Company (Royal Niger Company), 169-90; awarded charter, 1886, 169; and consuls, 169 seqq.; bitterness against comes to head, 1895, 181-2; move into Nupe, Ilorin, 176, 194-5; and Lugard, *see* Nikki; treaties of, with Sokoto, 194; and Oil Rivers Protectorate, 180, 190; Lord Salisbury withdraws charter, 1899, 191, 192, 204

Niger Delta: old city states of, 19; slave-trade ports of, 64, 67, 68 seqq.; development of 'House Rule' in, 68-9; slaves as basis of economy of, 70; opposes Laird's new-style trading, 145-7; British consolidation in, 155 seqq.; French rivalry in, 161, 165; strife with middlemen of interior, 159; opening-up of interior changing policies of, 134, 135, 136, 145 seqq.; trade changes after 1865, 147, 155 seqq.; Jaja as power in, 161-2; British commitment in, 163; middlemen in 1870s, 164; inter-firm rivalry in, 164; Goldie re-organizes trade of, 165-8; Akassa ousting, 171; Sir Claude Macdonald's role in, 180; Lugard abolishes 'House Rule' in, 222; present-day oil reserves of, 270

Niger (river and region), 20, 21, 34, 35, 40, 53; pre-Kanem empires in, 35; Franco-British Niger—N. Nigeria boundary (1900s), 88; as 'legend' for explorers, 118, 119;

river as trade highway, 155; explorations after 1788, 118 seqq.; Mungo Park's, 120, 121; Major Peddie's, 121; Denham-Clapperton-Oudney trans-Saharan expedition to, 121; M'Queen's theory, 121; Lander brothers discover river mouth, 123; new trade possibilities, 123-4; 1841 expedition of Society for the Extinction of the Slave Trade, and for the Civilizing of Africa, 125, 126; Barth-Richardson-Overweg exploration, 131; Beecroft's 1835 expedition, 137-8; *Niger mission, see* Crowther; position of by 1880, 164; becomes predominantly African, 126-7; Dr. Baikie's 1854 expedition and, 130; mission background, 130-31, 147; drawbacks of mission's trade connections, 147; 'Niger Districts' defines by 1885 Protectorate, 167; Niger Navigation Act revision of 1884, 167; Ilo stretch of river passes to French, 177; freight carried by river, 271; local government as modern development, 272-3

Nigeria: early history, 20-38; birth of, 19-30; unification of, 204-24; rise of nationalism in, 225-41; the 'three constitutions' of, 242-57; achieves independence, 258-73. *Detail:* old kingdoms, 19 seqq.; birth of independent federation, 1914, 19; as sovereign federation, October 1960, 20; Ijo as ancient Delta dwellers, 67-8; arrival of first Europeans (to Benin), 57; roots of British 'indirect rule', in, 95; cultural exchange with Brazil, through slaves, 76-7; Barth explores North, 131; early missionary traders' profound effect on South, 131; Britain's annexations, 146; first foothold (Lagos, 1861-2), 152; role of missionaries (q.v.),

299

Index

Nigeria—*cont.*

traders, explorers, 118, 122, 124 seqq.; late 19th-century resistance to British encroachment, 177 seqq. *See also* Poll tax; British occupation of Southern, completed 1897, 183–4; name chosen, and alternatives, 192; Northern, as new Protectorate, 1899–1900, 192; slow British occupation (*see also* Lugard), 198 seqq.; Satiru crisis, 202–3; three areas of, under Colonial Office, 192; unification, 204 seqq.; native traditions respected, 209; *but see* Missionaries, total conversion; Niger Coast Protectorate absorbed, 1899-1900, 192, 204; merged with Lagos Protectorate, 1906, 205; Lugard works to complete unification, 216–17; Emirate of Ilorin absorbed, 204; Sir D. Cameron in, 233–5; 1908 and 1910 trade figures, 206; Western education in, 211–12, 271; breakdown of traditions after 1906, 205; Lugard's 1912 plans for, 206, 208, 212–13; the 1912 amalgamation, 213; railways in, 213, 270–1; 1914 proposals for, 213–15; Lugard sets up Nigerian Council, 215; regiments of, in War I, 223–4; independence achieved, 225, 258 seqq.; Northern discrimination against South, under 'indirect rule', 230, 247; interwar trade figures, 235–6; students' organizations abroad, 237–8; *Nigerian Youth Movement* founded, 1936, 238; breaks up, 240–4, 247; in War II, 239; background to 1954 constitution, 242 seqq.; *Nigerian Trades Union Congress* officially recognized, 244; North-South rivalries in 1950s, 248 seqq.; minority groups, 1957, 250, 263–7; first general election in, 250–1; as federation of three regions, 256–7; 1945–60 proposals, 266 seqq.; outcome of 1959 federal elections, 267; national income, 1956–7, 269; summary of post-war economy, 268–71; present population of, 269; agriculture today, 269, 270; industrialization, education, health services, 270, 271; local government, 272–3; civil service, 272; independent federation as vital experiment, 273

Nikki, Lugard's race to ('Nikki steeplechase'), 173–6; old alliance of, with Oluewu, 105; France takes over, 177

Njimi, first Kanem capital, 33–4, 34 n.

Nok, 28, 29

Northern Elements Progressive Union, 253; after 1959, 267

Northern People's Congress, founded 1949, 248; in first general election, 251; after 1954 constitution, 258, 259, 262 seqq.; after 1959, 267

Nsanakang, in War I, 223

Nsukka, new University at, 271

Nubia, 26

Nupe (Hausa 'bastard' state), 37; as Ife rival, 48; Ajaka opposes, 52; destroys Old Oyo, 52, 53; Tada bronzes of, 53; in Usman's wars, 91; Baikie's trade connection with, 146; Glover's trade hopes for, 153, 156; Ibadan invades in 1870s, 158; Goldie assists, 167; German trade threat at, 172; Royal Niger Co. conquers, 176, 194; Lugard and, 195; hostile Emirs of, 196. *See also* Masaba

Nupe (Nyffi) cloth, 94

Nur al-Albab (Usman dan Fodio), 95

Obas (Oba of Benin), 45, 46, 51, 54, 65, 96; in Lagos succession dispute, 1836–41, 139; Oba (Yoruba) role of, under British, 208; Lugard's view, 219

Index

Oban mission, 1879, 165
Ode, on Lagos trade route, 158
Oduduwa (conquest myth of Ife), 47, 48, 51
Offa, in civil wars, 160, 184, 185
Ofonran, successor of Onigbogi, 53
Ogbomosho, 148, 189
Ogboni, role of in Oyo, 98
Ogiamwe, son of Evian, 47, 54
Ogilby, John, 73
Ogiso (early Kings of Benin), 47
Ogoja, 205, 264; resists unification, 205
Ogun (Ewuare of Benin), 55
Ogun River, 156
Oguola, King of Benin, 48, 55
Ohen (Ife king of Benin), 55
Oil, see Palm oil; Oil Rivers after 1885, 169, 173; Oil Rivers Protectorate, 170, 171, 178, 179
Ojiji, Alafin of Oyo (1698), 98–9; 12th Alafin of, 54
Ojike, Mazi Mbonu, 250
Okba ben Nafi, conqueror of Fezzan, 31
Oke Igbo, on trade routes, 158, 159
Oko-Jumbo (ex-slave) achieves power in Bonny, 161, 162
Okoyong people, of Cross River, 209–10
Okrika people, 23, 161, 162
Okugo, Chief (in Oloku), poll-tax blunder of, 231–3
Old Calabar (Efik trading state), 68, 69, 70, 71; and slavery, 68 seqq., 116, 141; in palm oil trade, 136; Court of Equity, 137; Beecroft's intervention in (slave rebellion), 141; 1855 trade crisis in, 143; Fernando Po consulate transferred to, 163. See Lynslager
Old Oyo, collapse of (1825), 52, 101, 102, 105. See Oyo
Olinda (King Eye Honesty's oil boat for direct trade), 144
Ologobosere, messenger of Ovenramwen, 183
Olorum–Odududwa myth, 46

Olowu of Owu, 46, 51
Olubi, the Rev. D. (C.M.S.), 187
Oluewo, Alafin of Oyo, 105
Olupopo of Popo, the, 46
Oluwole, son of Adele (Lagos), 139
Omar, son of El Kalemi, 90
Ondo, on Lagos trade route, 158, 159
Oni (kings) of Ife, 48, 51
Onigbogi, king of Yorubaland, 52, 53
Onikoyi of Ikoyi, 51; in Owa war, 102, 103
Onisabe of Sabe, the, 46
Onitsha Ibo, 55, 73; Onitsha base for Niger mission, 131, 147; in trade, 145 seqq., 164; Onitsha riots, after Enugu, 249
Opele, Bale of Gbogun, 102
Opopo (see also Jaja), 137, 162, 179; 1929 poll-tax riot at, 232
Opobo, king of Bonny, 113
Oral history, 24, 25
Oranmiyan, King of Benin, 47, 48, 49, 51, 54
Ormsby-Gore's 'Congo system' investigations, 236–7
Oshogbo, Ibadan defeat of Ilorin at, 106
Otta, Dahomey attacks, 106
Oudney, N., 121, 122
Ouidah, 'free labour' exports to Martinique from, 150; Dahomey attacks, 99
Ouilliminden tribe revolts, 1916, 222
Ovenramwen, Oba (Benin), 183–4, 219
Overweg, see Barth, Richardson (explorers)
Owen, Captain, and Opobo of Bonny, 113
Owerri, 1902, resistance of, against unification, 205; poll-tax revolt of, 232
Owome (New Calabar) in slave trade, 68, 70
Owu people, 46, 50; Olowu of, 51; in first Yoruba inter-tribal war, 103

Index

Oyo, Yoruba empire of, 19; early organization of, 45–50; Alafins of, 51 seqq.; legendary kings of, 51; slaves from, 75; 'Old Oyo' destroyed by Nupe, 52, 92, 101, 102, 105; new site of, 105; outline of post-17th century history of, 54 seqq.; 18th-century authority of, 96–7; subjects Dahomey, 98–100; Yoruba mission to, 148; in 1858 civil war, 150, 151, 152; in Glover's conferences, 157; taxation in, 219, 220; Alafin of, attitude to Ibadan-Lagos strife, 159–60; French woo, 172–3; Britain's 1888 treaty of friendship with, 172–3; Dahomey attacks, 185; Sir Gilbert Carter at, 188–9; Bower quells, 189–90

Oyo Mesi (councillors), 50, 98, 100

Paine, Thomas, *The Rights of Man*, 109

Palma (port); Campbell cedes to Kosoko, 149; annexed by Freeman, 153; Jaja and, 161

Palmer, Richard (emissary of Lugard), 219

Palmer, Sir Richmond, writings of, 26, 31–2, 33

Palmerston, Lord: and oil trade, 115; receives Crowther, 129; and the Lagos succession troubles, 140

Palm oil trade, 19, 21, 66; connection of, with abolition of slave trade, 110, 113, 117; in 1830s, 112–15, 132, 135, 136, 141; 'palm-oil ruffians', 117, 136; 1856 exports from Egbaland, 150; in 1908–10, 206; Porto Novo's embargo on, 151; French threat to, 172–3; developing importance of, 184, 222, 223, 269. *See also* Belgian Congo, Sumatra

Palm wine, 62

Pan-Ibo Federal Union, 1944, 247

Park, Mungo, 118, 119; murder of, 120–1, 123

Patani, Goldie's measures against, 166; Mizon and, 173

Pategi (Nupe), 91

Peddie, Major (explorer), 121

Peel, Sir Robert, reduces sugar import duty, 115

Peppers as trade commodity, 59, 60, 61, 62, 66, 74

Pepple kings, of Bonny, 66, 71, 72, 112, 114; King William Pepple in trade, 138–9, 142–3, 161; King George Pepple, 161

Perham, Margery, *Lugard*, 175, 192, 196, 220; *Native Administration in Nigeria*, 232

Pettoford, sharpshooter, working for Egba, 153

Phillips, Rev. C., 183, 184

Philomel, H.M.S., in Nana troubles, 181

Phoebe, H.M.S., in Nana troubles, 181

Pillars of Hercules, 57

Pina (chronicler), 60

Pires, Duarte (Portugal), 61

Pitt, William, 109, 119

Pleass, Sir Clem, 252

Pleiad, trading vessel, 134

Police 'regionalization', 1958; decision, 265–6

Poll-tax, 231–2; riots, 232–3

Ponlade, 220

Popo, Great and Little, Yoruba loss of, 100; France annexes, 166

Port Harcourt: in railway scheme, 213; riots in, after Enugu incident, 249; modern industry in, 270

Porto Novo, 54, 98; British bombard, 151; Glover attacks, 154, 158; France annexes, 166, 172

Portuguese: reach Benin, 57, 58, 59; and slaving, 60–4; late 15th-century trade monopoly of, in West Africa, 59; leave Niger after 1520; 62; 1580 union with Spain, 63

Possoo, Epe ruler, 153

Index

Presbyterian mission, Calabar, *see* Slessor, Mary

Primogeniture principle, departures from, 50, 54

Puttkamer, Herr von (Lagos German consul), 172

Qua Ibo, *see* Kwa Ibo

Qua River 'Blood Men', 141

Quinine, 126, 131

Quorra, *see* Alburkah

Rabba, Nupe capital, 91

Rabeh, Sudanese adventurer, in Bornu, 197, 198

Railways, modern, 270–1; Railway Corporation of Nigeria, 270

Rainbow (steamer), 145

Rajada, in Nupe civil war, 91

Rakah, 122

Rano, Hausa state, 37, 38

'Rawani baki' defined, 94

Regional basis of government (1949 discussions), 250–4; regional assemblies (1945 proposals), 243–4, 250, 251; regional marketing boards, 256, 269, 270

Reichard, Herr (geographer, on Niger), 120

Remo route, from Lagos to interior, 158

Rennell, Major, Niger theory of, 120

Richards, Sir Arthur, Governor of Nigeria, 241, 242; 1945 proposals of, 242 seqq., 268

Richardson, James (explorer), 131

'Rigona' defined, 94

Rio del Rey, 167

Rio Muni, in War I, 224

Rivers State proposal (Calabar-Ogoja-Rivers state), 264

Robertson, Sir James, 259

Robins, Chief Willy Tom (Calabar), 143

Roth, Henry Ling, *Great Benin: its Customs, Arts and Horrors*, 184

Rowe, Governor (Lagos, 1883), 160

Royal Niger Company, *see* Niger Company

Rubber, timber, etc., of East Nigeria, 21

Russell, Lord John, and the Hutt decision, 116

Sabon Birni, 79

'Sabon Garis', 247, 253

Sabongari, Usman at, 85

Sacred kingship, 47

Sahara, 38, 40, 57, 78

Saki, 150; and New Oyo, 106; Yoruba mission at, 148

Salisbury, Lord, 191–2; opposes Chamberlain's tactics with French on Niger, 177

Sandam, 88

Sango (of Oyo), 51–2

Sansandi, 94

São Thomé, in Benin-Portugal trade, 59–62

Sarkin Zazzau, kings of Abuja, 87

Satiru massacre (crisis in North Nigeria Settlement), 202–3

Say-Barruwa line (French sphere), 173–4, 177

Schön, Rev. J. F., on 1841 Niger expedition, 125, 126; *Grammar of the Hausa Language*, 148

Secession right, Action Group claims, 255

Sef dynasty (Bornu), 90; Sefawa (Kanem), 34, 36, 37

Select Committee of 1865 (British West Coast withdrawal), 134

Self-government, 253, 254, 259–60, 261, 265

Senegal, Senegal River, 15, 23, 40, 58, 119

Senelle, Comte de, in Niger trade struggle, 166

Senussi, in War I, 223

Sequiera, Ruy de, 57

'Seven provinces', proposal for Nigeria (Temple), 214

Shagamu, in Lagos-Ibadan trade, 186

Index

Shari River, 122

Sharp, Granville, anti-slavery crusade of, 108, 109

Sharpe, Major, Resident at Kontagora, 193

Shaw, Flora, later Lady Lugard, 19

Shehu, 95

Shehu Ahmadu (Western Sudan), 83

Sierra Leone: freed slaves settled in, 124, 125, 127; Christian Africans from, in Calabar trade, 143, 144; and Lagos, 156, 157; taxation introduced in, 219

Simpson, W. H., in Masaba negotiations, 163

Slaves, slave-trading, 34, 43, 57 seqq., 66, 67, 72, 74, 75; Atlantic trade, 57 seqq.; *see* Bristol, Liverpool, Buxton, Sharp, Wilberforce; early profits from, 56, 63, 65; African attitude to, 65; privileged slaves, 65; Portuguese monopoly, 59–62; Spain in trade, 63; Dutch in trade, 64; minor powers in trade, 64; France's large-scale involvement in 64; goods exchanged, 66, 72; slaver conditions, 66–7; 'scramble sales', 67; in Delta generally, 70 seqq.; and depopulation, 75, 77; suppression of trade, 108 seqq.; economic background to abolition, 110; of Kano, 95; slave raiding after Jihad, 95; by Kontagora, 193; Fowell Buxton's suggested alternative to, 124; missionaries and, 126; surviving, *see* Kosoko; in Fulani economy, 194; and trade expansion (domestic slaves), 157; by Keffi, 198; as element in background to Yoruba civil wars, 160; late raiding by Nupe, 176; late surreptitious Benin involvement, 181; Ilorin in, 185; Lugard's attitude to, 202

Slessor, Mary (missionary), 209–10; as vice-consul for Okoyong, 209

Smith, Dr. M. G., *Government in Zazzau*, 94

So people, 36

Society for the Abolition of the Slave Trade, 109, 112

Society for the Extinction of the Slave Trade and for the Civilization of Africa, 125

Society for the Suppression of Human Sacrifices in Calabar, 130

Sodeke, of Abeokuta, 104; relations of, with missionaries, *see* Townsend

Sokoto, 21, 88, 91, 93; under Sultan Bello, 93–5; Clapperton visits, 122; in British-French-German rivalries, 167, 174; loses power over Emirs, 208; as twin Fulani capital with Gwandu, 194; hostile to Lugard, 199–201; loyal to Lugard after Satiru, 203; Morel's proposal for, 214; Sardauna of, and N.P.C., 254, 262–3

Solanke, Ladipo, in Nigerian nationalism, 237

Somersett v. *Knowles* (slave case), 108–9

Songhai Empire of Gao: as leading power in Sudan, 40–1; early invasions of, 40, 41; decline of, by late 16th century, 42; Katsina profits from decline of, 45

Sonni Ali, of Songhai, 40

Soyenbola, Oni Koyi of Ikoyi, 104

Spain: in anti-slavery agreement with Portugal, 111, 113; in 1580 union, 63

Stanley, Col. Oliver, 240

Stock, Eugene, *History of the Church Missionary Society*, 124

Students' organizations, 237–8, 240

Sudanese states, 31–45; early tribal conquests in, 32 seqq.

Sugar-slavery link, 64, 115–16; Sugar Act, 116

Suicide, prescribed, 50

Sulumannu, Emir of Kano (1807), 88

304

Index

Sumatra, palm oil of, 236
Sweden, slave trade abolished by, 111

Tabkin Kwatto, Fulani beat Gobir at, 85
Tada (Nupe) bronzes, 53
'Talakawa' defined, 84, 203
Talbot, P. A., 26
Tanbikhu 'l-ikhwan (Usman dan Fodio), 82
Tanganyika, Sir D. Cameron introduces 'indirect rule' in, 233
Tapa, lost to Yoruba, 100
Taubman, *see* Goldie
Taxation: early (Kano, Bornu), 34, 40, 43; Fulani resentment of, 82, 84; Bello reforms system of, 93; under British economy, 206, 217–18, 219, 220, 221. *See* Poll tax
Taylor, the Rev. J. C., in *Dayspring*, 147
Temple, Lieut.-Governor (North Nigeria), 214, 218, 243
Tepe, in War I, 223
Thompson, Joseph, defeats Germany's Sokoto aspirations, 167
Thomson, Sir Graeme, Governor of Nigeria, 230, 236
Tié (possible Njimi location), 33
Timber, present exports of, 269, 270
Timbuktu, 38, 42, 94; Mungo Park's journey to Bussa from, 121
Times, The, qu., on 1841 'Bible and Plough' expedition, 126
Timi (hunter) in Oyo history, 52
Tinubu, Madam, Lagos 'middleman', 150
Tiv people, 23, 25–6
Togoland, German, 174, 223
Tonkin, disaster, 172
Toronkawa clan, 80
Townsend, Henry (missionary), 127, 128; opposes Crowther's elevation to bishopric, 147, 148; and Egba-Dahomey war, 153, 154; in Lagos political scene, 149

Traders as builders of modern Nigeria, 118, 122, 132–3; and missionaries, 125; growth of legitimate, 134 seqq.; trade goods, 66, 136, 235; *see* 'Trust'
Tribal differences, and constitutions, 76, 241, 246, 247, 248, 263
Trinidad, slaves in, 76
Tripoli, Arab merchant base, 94, 95, 123
Tripolitania, in War I, 223
'Trust' or credit goods, in Delta palm-oil trade, 136, 144
Tryon, Lieut., at Bonny, 114
Tschadda River, 131
Tsetse fly, 30
Tsoedi, king of Nupe, 52, 53
Tsuntsuwa, Usman dan Fodio defeated at, 85
Tuareg (Touareg) people, 35, 38, 86; as old enemies of Fulani, 87; black litham worn by, 94
Tunis, 35
'Turkedi' defined, 94
Turkey, in War I, 222
Twi language, 23
Twin murder, in Calabar, 129
Tyrwhitt's consulship, Kuka (Bornu), 122

Ubini (or Benin), 55. *See* Benin
Udagbedo, Ife king (Benin), 55
'Umaru' as Fulani leaders, 87; Umaru Dallaji, 88; U. Dumyama, overlord of Sandam, 88
Umoru, King (Nupe), 166
United African Company (Goldie), 165–8
United Middle Belt Congress, 263
United Native African Church, 1891, 211
Urhobo tribe, 55
Urvoy, Yves, *Histoire de l'Empire de Bornou*, 32, 33–4, 43, 89
Usama, Benin capital, 54
Usman dan Fodio, leader of Jihad (Holy War), 39, 78–95; motives activating, 25, 83–5; early life of,

Index

80–1; three phases of war, 85–8; and Middle Belt, 263; Lugard on, 201; effect of, on Northern Nigeria, 192–3; writings of, *see Kitab-al-Farq, Nur al-Albab, Tanbikhu, Wathiquat*

Utrecht, Treaty of (1713), 64

Uwaifiokun, Benin usurper, 55

Uyanga mission, 165

Vansina, Dr. J., 24, 25

Vaughn, Dr. J. C. (N.Y.M.), 238

Venn, Henry (C.M.S.), 126, 147

Victoria, Queen, and the C.M.S., 129

Voodoo, 76

Wachuku, Jaja (N.C.N.C.), 261

Wadai: allied with Mai Ibrahim of Bornu, 90; Idris Alooma attacks, 42; Rabeh's conquest of, 197; Zaghawa in, 31

Wallace-Johnson, I.T.A., 238

War canoes, in Delta 'House rule', 69, 70

Warri, Itsekiri kingdom: as slave source, 68, 74; 'House rule' pattern in, 69; 1927 poll-tax revolts, 231

Warships and trade, 144

Wathiquat ahl al-Sudan (Usman dan Fodio), 83

Waziri (Vizier) of Sokoto, 194

Wedgwood, Josiah, as founder-member of African Association, 119

Welsh, James, trade-voyager to Benin, 1588, 66

West Indies: African slaves in, 64, 67; Spanish rule in, 63; Niger slaves lose identity in, 75; Britain's trade with, 109, 110; 1938 riots in, 239–40

West Africa, 256, 259, 261, 265, 268

West Africa after Berlin Conference, 168

West African Co., in Niger trade, 164

West African Frontier Force, 191, 195, 196, 202, *and see* Lugard

West African Pilot, 238, 240, 244

West African Squadron (abolition surveillance), 111, 115, 116, 140

'Western route' (Lagos to interior), 158

Widgeon, H.M.S., in Nana troubles, 181

Wilberforce, William, 109, 110; and the Hutt decision, 116; and the African Association, 119

Willcocks, Captain (under Lugard), 196

Willinck, Sir Henry (1957 Commission on Minority Groups), 264–5

Windam, Capt., qu. on Portugal's influence on Benin, 61; 1553 voyage to Benin, *see* Eden, R.

Wombai of Kano, 200

Women, learned (after Fulani Jihad), 95

Wood, Rev. J. B., at Abeokuta, 160

Wood carvings of Benin, 55, 56

Wushishi, 195

Yaba Higher College, 238, 248

Yagba, in Ekiti Confederation, 159

Yaji, King of Kano, 38; attacks Korokofa, 44

Yakuba, King of Kano, 39

Yakubu, Emir of Bauchi, 90

Yam crops, 21, 27, 75

Yamusa (Bornuese Fulani), 87

Yandaka, 88

Yaounde, in War I, 224

Yauri (Hausa 'bastard' state), 37

Yemen, as Jukun and Kanuri place of origin, 43

Yeri, 35

Yerima, provincial governors (early Kanem), 35

Yola: 1851 expedition to, 131; Baikie's 1854 expedition to, 130–1, 145; Mizon at, 173; Emirate of, 91; and Lugard, 197, 199